The Common Sense Ethics of a Blue Collar Philosopher

The Prerequisites of Morality and Beyond

S.G. Applebee

PublishAmerica
Baltimore

First printing

ISBN: 978-1-61582-777-0
PUBLISHED BY PUBLISHAMERICA, LLLP
www.publishamerica.com
Baltimore

Printed in the United States of America

In memory of Kevin

Meaning: Although we all search for it, very few will ever find it. When Kevin left us, it was then that I discovered that, although finding meaning is the key to true happiness, it's the actual *search* for meaning that's truly important. When we no longer possess the desire to search; when we no longer hold a passion for life; when we have lost all hope for the future; it is then that we die inside. And when we have died from within, it's inevitable that the cold touch of death will soon take hold of us from without. Kevin, I hope you have found in death the answers you so desperately longed for in life.

Foreword and Acknowledgments

Before I begin, I would like to say why, and how, this book came into being. In essence, I decided to write it because if I didn't, no one else would've. Now, that may sound a bit egotistical, but it's really not. I think everybody has at least one good book in them, but most people simply choose not to write it. The time and effort it takes is simply unbelievable—especially for a well researched nonfiction book like this one. It was, without a doubt, the most difficult thing I've ever done in my life. Maybe that's because of my Attention Deficit Disorder, or maybe it's because I'm just a blue collar guy at heart, but either way, I have a new found respect for anyone who even attempts such an undertaking.

Another reason I wrote this book was so people could have a simple-to-understand, commonsensical guide to living a moral life. Now, I'm not saying it's perfect, or that it's a *complete* guide to living a moral life; only that it's a good start on the road to building a good solid moral foundation. In no way does this book hold all the answers, just like no other book holds all the answers. But it does give the basic premises, prerequisites, and principles on which morality rests—and that was my main objective.

Some other reasons I wrote it was to show the average, everyday, moral productive citizen that they have the *right* to keep what they have earned; that they have no *moral* obligation to take care of those who *choose* not to take care of themselves; that they have the *right* to give to who *they* choose to give to; that the government has no right to *take* what *they* have earned and give it to those who *have not* earned it; that the 20th century American paradigm of entitlement is not only unconstitutional, but totally immoral as well; that it's this "entitlement" mentality that's destroying America from within; that no adult human being has the right to be a parasite upon another human being; that no government has the right to *force* one human being to be a host for another human parasite; that the battle has never been between the haves and the have-nots, but between the dos and the do-nots; and last but not least, I wrote it to show that, ultimately, morality comes down to the choices we make and the actions we take—or in essence: Freedom; and not un-provable religious myths, speculations, assumptions, doctrines and dogmas.

You see, I have never, not for one second of my life ever, believed in God. And I've always wondered how people could believe in something that goes against *every single* law of nature and *every single* human sense—including commonsense. I learned early in my life that religion was nothing more than taking someone's word for something, who had already taken someone else's word for something, who had already taken someone else's word for something…etc. In essence, it was based on nothing more than here say—and that simply wasn't (and still isn't) good enough for me. And all my life I grew up as though there was something wrong with me simply because I didn't *believe* what the majority in society told me to believe. There was so much societal pressure to conform that I didn't even come out of the closet totally and completely about my Atheism until my twenties. Until then, I hid in the comparatively comfortable world of agnosticism (although all my close friends always knew I was an Atheist).

Anyway, for me, there isn't (and never was) really even a real choice of whether or not to believe in God. Saying I have the choice to believe in God is like saying I have the choice to like tomatoes—I don't, I never have, and I probably never will. To believe in God goes against EVERYTHING my mind sees as truth and reality. In order to believe in God I would have to deny my very tools of survival. I would have to deny Reason, Rationality, Reality, Logic, Objectivity, Honesty, Integrity…etc (And by the way, if a God created these things would he want me to deny them? Of course not.). The only *real* choice I have would be to *fake* believing in God, or to *pretend* to believe in God (which in my opinion, is what most people do), but that wouldn't be honest would it? And wouldn't God want us to be honest? And if there's a God, he would know I'm pretending wouldn't he? So as others approached morality from a religious paradigm, I had to approach it from a commonsensical paradigm. While others based their morality on religious dogmas, doctrines and the opinions of others; I based my morality on what was verifiable and rational to my own mind. With that said, let me give you some of my background.

I come from, what I believe to be, an average American background. My mother and Father both worked full-time and did their best to do what was right for their children, but unfortunately for me (and them at the time), that simply wasn't enough. I was told that I was pissed-off from the moment I came out of my mothers womb in the smoldering mid July of 1964, and I guess I've pretty much stayed that way into the present (although now I'm much more tempered). But what I've tried to do is turn my A-type personality into a positive and not a negative. I'm still angry about many things, but now I understand and control the reasons why I'm angry. I'm angry about all the injustices in the world and I simply don't understand why we don't just put an end to them; I'm angry about all the unfairness in the world and I simply don't understand why we don't put an end to it; but most of all, I'm angry about all the injustice and unfairness now perpetrated by the American government against the American people—and I would like to help put an end to it as soon as possible. Now don't get me wrong, America is still the greatest country on earth, but I'm afraid it's not going to stay that way much longer because its people no longer value freedom, and thus, it's lost its moral base. The American people are allowing the government to destroy America from within, and another reason I wrote this book was in order to help stop it—if still possible.

Anyway, getting back to my up bringing. My mother and father both believed in God, but my family never attended church regularly. They both tried to teach me right from wrong, but I really didn't care to listen while I was growing up. I saw the world as unfair, and if it was going to be unfair to me, I was going to be unfair to it. I did alright until my teen years, but once my parents divorced, all hell broke loose. I spent those years doing anything I could possibly do *as long as* I wouldn't get caught. I was an out of control, pot smoking, street-fighting, trouble-making thief who lived life on the edge. What finally pulled me out of it was when I started listening to a Radio Talk Show host named Mark Scott who introduced me to the philosophy of Objectivism. It showed me that although the overwhelming majority of human beings are irrational when it comes to dealing with life's big issues, *I* didn't have to be. And from that moment on I have tried to live my life by a rational set of standards.

However, although I still consider myself an Objectivist, I need to point out that many Objectivists probably don't consider me an Objectivist (And that would most likely include Ayn Rand herself). This is because although I agree with her basic philosophical premises on Metaphysics, Epistemology, Ethics and Esthetics, I don't always agree with her Politics because I don't think she was always objective when it came to her politics (mostly because of her views on Libertarians). And because of this, many people say I shouldn't call myself an Objectivist. However, I don't see it that way. By using the term "Objectivism," Ayn Rand opened the door of interpretation on exactly what it *is* to be "objective" in any given case, and in regards to Libertarians, I don't think *she* was objective. Now if she would have called her philosophy "Randism" (or something like it), that would be different. In that case they would have a point. But as I have already said, since it's about being "objective" I think I have every right to disagree with her on exactly *what* is objective.

With that said, I would also like to point out that I'm forever indebted to her for her philosophy of Objectivism, and that this book would have never been possible without it. And although she would disagree with my view on Libertarians, I think she would've taken pride in the fact that her philosophy changed me from a person who would've done great damage to society, to a productive citizen who is contributing to society in a positive way.

As to other acknowledgements, I would like to begin with my wife Cheryl and my sons Nick and Tony. Their patience and understanding over the years have really helped me stay focused on this book. I'll probably regret for the rest of my life the hours upon hours I've lost spending time with them in order to write it, so I hope some good will come out of it in the end. And I also hope they'll understand why I had to write it. I can only say that my love has grown for my family over the years, and I hope that all the time and effort I put into writing it will be worth it for everyone in the long run.

Next I would like to thank my mother. Her unconditional love pulled me through the toughest times of my life, and for as long as I live, I'll never understand just how she had the patience to do so. I would also like to thank her for always allowing me the freedom to be who I wanted to be. Without it, I could've never became the man I am today.

Then there's my father. Although our relationship over the years has usually been rocky and distant, and I've never had a close relationship with him; I learned from his example the importance of common sense, practicality, and hard work. I also learned from his example that no matter where you start out in life on the economic latter, hard work and determination will inevitably improve your situation.

Next I would like to thank Kerry Roop, Kakan Garcia, Hayme Serrato and Jim Soubly. The first three put up with me while I was trying to find my way in life; and gave to me much more than I could ever possibly give back in return. And although they probably never knew it, the time and effort they put into me made a big difference in turning my life around. As to Jim Soubly, what can I say? He was the best teacher I ever had. If I only would've had a few more Mr. Soubly's in my teen years, things would've been a lot different for me growing up. It's truly a shame that Americans no longer understand the real value of great teachers.

Next I would like to thank all the people who's books and lectures I've listened too (or read) over the years—because it was their efforts that built the foundation of my knowledge and wisdom. First among them being The Ayn Rand Institute, The Atlas Society, all the professors who've done lectures for The Teaching Company, and all the libraries I've had the privilege to borrow educational resources from. Thank you all for simply doing what you do.

Last but not least, I would like to thank my editor and literary agent Robert Fenton. He did a great job and I really appreciate all his help, suggestions, and most of all, his candor. However, because of my thick-headedness, there are many things in this book he wanted me to change where I didn't take his advice. So if there are times when things seem like they should've been written differently, or not written at all, the blame is mine, not his.

I would like to end this with a few apologies. To begin with, I would like to apologize to anyone who I didn't give credit too in this book for any original ideas I may have used of theirs. My only excuse is that when you spend over a thousand hours a year listening to recorded books and lectures, it's impossible to remember exactly where you may have heard a piece of information. So to anyone who believes I may have "stolen" an original idea of yours, I'm sorry, I didn't do it on purpose. Please remember that people can, and do, come to the same conclusions all the time without ever being exposed to one another. However, if after this book gets published and someone comes forward believing I used their idea on any particular subject, I will gladly give them credit if that was actually the case.

With that said, I hope you enjoy this book and I hope it will introduce you to ideas you've never thought of before. After all, this book is truly about one thing and one thing only—Ideas! And I hope those ideas will help to expand your mental paradigms and make you a wiser, more understanding, and most of all, more *moral* human being. Yes, much of this book is extremely controversial. However, the point is not to enrage, but to inform. And although many people will probably not only detest it, but condemn it as well (mostly because of the chapter on religion), its questions and conclusions simply cannot be ignored if you are truly concerned about the subject of ethics and morality. With that said, let's begin.

Preface

No matter what religion you believe in, what philosophy you agree with, or what your opinions are on any individual moral issue, there are three prerequisites that must be met in order for something to be considered in the realm of morality: Reason, Freedom and Intent. All three play an equal part of any decision concerning morality or you're simply no longer in the realm of morality. Of course there's much more to living a moral life than Reason, Freedom and Intent, but it *must begin* with all three. I'll be returning frequently to these prerequisites throughout the course of this book because they are the premises on which it rests.

I'll also be making a crucial distinction between 'committing a moral act' and 'doing the right thing'. Most people don't make this distinction, but it must be made for a proper analysis of morality. Sometimes people can 'do the right thing' *without* 'committing a moral act'; such as doing the right thing for the wrong reason, doing the right thing without knowing it, or doing the right thing without trying to. When any of these three things happen, *they are not* moral acts. And of course the opposites also apply (such as doing the wrong thing without being immoral). Many examples will be given throughout the course of this book on the difference, so be prepared for some redundancy.

I will also be taken for granted that the reader understands *why* human beings need morality. Although exactly *what* is moral or immoral will always be in dispute, the *need* for morality is not. The very fact that you've chosen to read this book proves at least *you* understand the need.

Another thing I need to point out before I begin is that, in most cases, my definitions come from Ayn Rand, and can be found in her writings. However, the Ayn Rand Institute has chosen to only give me permission to use a couple of her definitions in this book, so if you need one that's not here, you'll have to go to her own works to find it. Or, for the sake of convenience, there's also a pamphlet entitled 'Glossary of Objectivist Definitions' by Allison Kunze and Jean Moroney that can be used to find a definition more quickly. However, when a definition cannot be found there, it's my own.

Chapter 1: Reason

Reason, rationality, intelligence, the ability to think, the ability to form concepts, volitional consciousness—or whatever you wish to call it—in order for something to be in the realm of morality, a being must have the ability to recognize that there *is* such a thing as morality. Every form of life known to man is amoral *except* man itself. Whether you're talking about Insects, fish, animals, or other mammals makes no difference. They're all *amoral* because they don't have the ability to reason through moral issues. They live by instinct or by what they have learned, on a very limited scale, through their environment. Only human beings have the ability to distinguish between the concepts of moral and immoral, and they must do it through the deliberately conscious act of thinking.

The best way to prove this fact is by asking a couple of questions: What if mankind did not exist on earth? Would morality still exist on earth? Let's imagine for a moment that a plague whipped out all mankind—would morality still exist? There would still be mammals, animals, fish, insects…etc., but would there be morality? Of course not. Nature would revert back to how it was *before* the existence of modern humans—survival of the fittest, luckiest, sneakiest, most brutal, most adaptable…etc. Without *reason* you're without morality—period!

This is why we treat and judge animals, children, and insane people differently than we treat and judges other adults. They're held to a lower moral standard because of their inability to conceptualize right from wrong, good from bad, just from the unjust…etc. *Truly* insane people will never be able to, and children simply haven't lived long enough to have a large enough base of knowledge and understanding to do so. Children *can* 'do the right thing' (that is of course according to the adults view of what the "right" thing is), but they can only commit moral acts when they can understand *for themselves* that they are committing a moral act. Like animals, children who are forced to do good deeds *are not* committing moral acts. Until they reach the age of moral consent, and I'm not really sure exactly when that is, they simply submit to an authority figure. And it's the morality of that authority figure that is followed until the child is old enough to understand *for himself* what morality means and consists of. Only then can they be moral and commit moral acts.

As an adult, whether you believe in Creationism (the belief that God created everything, including life, out of nothing) or Evolution (the theory that life came into existence by a natural process) makes no difference. If you believe in creationism, it's reason (no matter how flawed or illogical) that's guided you to that decision. One of the things that *all* religions have in common is that the believer must *freely choose* to become a member of that particular religion. The person must voluntarily agree with, and comply too, the tenets of that religion. In other words, if a religion is forced on an individual, he is *not* a true believer—no matter what the outside appearance may be.

All religions believe in freewill, and freewill can only exist if the ability to reason exists. Although some individuals belonging to various religions may not believe in freewill, the majority do. Believe it or not, there continues to be an on-going debate over whether or not freewill even exists. Many opponents of freewill accept the validity of *reason,* but not the validity of freewill. To me, the denial of freewill is one of the most absurd notions ever conceived of by man. To deny freewill is to deny both reason and reality. Freewill is the corollary of reason, you simply cannot have one without the other—period!

And for people who agree with the theory of evolution, reason must also be the beginning of morality. Morality could not have existed before the emergence of modern man because the ability to reason was not developed to a high enough degree. If the theory of evolution is correct, modern man (or his semblance) has been around for tens of thousands of years, or perhaps even a hundred thousand years—but mankind's ancestors go back millions of years. Obviously, the further back you go, the less moral humans would be. If you go back far enough in time, morality did not exist at all. As man slowly developed, his *reason* slowly developed, which slowly lead to the development of moral codes. Obviously, he could only develop moral codes *after* he became able to reason to a great enough extent.

It's only been in the last five or ten thousand years that civilization *as we define it* has existed. So sometime over the last few millennia of man's existence, human beings developed the ability to reason deeply enough to become moral beings. Obviously, the possibility to be moral could not have existed *until* mankind's reason developed to a great enough extent (I also need to point out that I'm deliberately trying not to give exact evolutionary time-tables here because they're constantly changing. For years the oldest skull of a human ancestor ever found dated back roughly 3 million years. But more recently, a skull dating back approximately 7 million years was discovered. So if you're looking for exact dates, you'll have to look elsewhere. I'm just giving a general overall observation, not a detailed timeline of evolution).

I'll prove that animals are amoral by using a few examples. I realize these examples are overly simplistic, but I think the simpler they're kept, the better they'll be understood. To some of you, it may seem ridiculous that I spend time on something that's so self-evident to most of us, but I believe at least a few examples need to be given.

When a dog protects its owner from harm, is it committing a moral act? No, because it didn't go through the process of reasoning through the moral issue involved. It did not think to Itself (in the present or the past) "I shall protect my companion from harm because it's immoral of that other person to initiate force against him. My companion is minding his own business and just wants to be left free from obstruction to pursue his own goals and objectives. In a civilized society, people must not use force against one another *except* in the case of self-defense, in which I'm applying. If people are allowed to commit random acts of violence against others, unobstructed by law, we will not have a civilized society." Is this what goes through an animals mind? Of course not. Animals simply can't think like that. Their "thinking" is more in the line of the instinctual 'helping protect the pack protects me', or 'he feeds me', 'he's my companion'…etc. Remember also that when an animal does a good deed, we're projecting our idea of the "good" onto them. What they're doing is instinctual, not intellectual. Well, I should say *mostly* instinctual. Other species besides humans do posses intelligence, but it's a limited intelligence depending on the species; and although it is limited, it's still intelligence none the less. It's just not to a high enough degree to be able to make moral choices.

Is a police dog being moral when it serves as an officer of the law? Of course not, it doesn't even know it's performing a service. It didn't choose to be a police officer, a human being made that choice for him. It's simply doing what it's been trained to do. Even though it may be doing a number of "good" deeds, it's still not committing moral acts. Remember that there *is* a difference between the two. And of course the opposite also applies. A dog that's been trained to attack humans is not being immoral. It doesn't have a high enough intelligence to choose to be moral or immoral. It follows orders—period! It survives to the best of its natural abilities—period! It does what it's being coerced to do—period! Without the intervention of humans, it wouldn't be out policing the world and doing good deeds, it would probably be out chasing cats and going through your garbage at night.

My next example on the intelligence of animals is from my own childhood. I remember watching a wildlife show on television about the migration of the wildebeest in Africa. At one point in the program, a pack of lions attacked and killed one of them and began to eat it *while the other wildebeests just ran by casually.* Well, this made no sense to me. All I kept thinking was "why don't the wildebeest just kill the lions"? I mean, come on! Here were thousands of wildebeests and only a few lions. The wildebeests could have easily trampled to death every single lion they ever met—so why weren't they doing it? I believe my father explained it to me perfectly (if not a little bluntly) when he simply said: "They're just too stupid to figure it out."

Another example from more recent memory is that of whales. While watching another nature show, the narrator was going on and on about how intelligent whales are; that when they "sing" they're imparting millions of bits of information to other whales far away. Now, this may or may not be true, I'm no expert on whales; but I have read or listened too many books on history, and on whaling, and I do know this: Men in *rowboats* used to hunt and kill these "brilliant" creatures with reckless abandon, and in some places, still do. Here you have the largest, most powerful creature on earth being killed by men in *rowboats*. It seems to me that if they're so brilliant, they would've simply capsized the boat and killed all the men on board. So why didn't they? Many whale enthusiasts might say they didn't because they're just too loving a species to hurt humans. Of course this is ridiculous, but even if it were true, they still could have easily gone underwater and maneuvered to get away. Although whales don't have gills to breathe underwater (they're mammals not fish), they still could've stayed underwater long enough to escape. And even if they are "too loving" to hurt humans, they still could've just tipped over the boat and swam away. I guarantee that if whales were remotely as intelligent as humans, they would've used a variety of strategies to escape. So why didn't they? Remember what my father said?

While we're on the topic of whales, here's another example. Every year hundreds of pilot whales wash up on beaches across the planet and die. The phenomenon goes something like this: A wounded, sick, or hurt whale washes up on shore and gets beached. As this is happening, the wounded whale keeps wailing for help (sorry, it's just that the word just fits so perfectly). The other whales hear its cries, follow it, get washed up on shore and are beached with it. And since they're unable to remove themselves from the beach, they die (not exactly a sign of high intelligence). If they're lucky, some human beings will notice this disaster and take pity. These people will spend hour after hour working to keep the whales wet, and hopefully be able to push a few of them back into the ocean (many times after these whales are pushed back into the ocean, they swim right back only to be beached again). The few that are saved may be the same whales that return in the future to go through the same ordeal. Now, I like whales as much as the next guy, but my feelings don't change the fact that, compared to humans, whales, like all other species on earth, are intellectually impotent. And because of this lack of superior intelligence, whales are not moral or immoral but amoral.

When a shark attacks a human, is it being immoral? Of course not. The shark is only doing what its nature intended for it to do. It's hungry, it attacks, it eats—period! It doesn't think about any moral ramifications of its actions. It doesn't think about a human beings "Right" to life, liberty, and the pursuit of happiness. It has absolutely no concept of rights—and never will. It's basically an eating machine; and like machines, sharks are not moral or immoral, but amoral.

How about Parrots? Are parrots being immoral when they curse or make otherwise abusive statements? I seriously hope there's nobody out there who'll even attempt to argue this point, but who knows? Of course they're not being immoral, all they're doing is mimicking whatever they were taught to mimic. They can't understand the concept of cursing—they can't even understand the concept of words. To parrots, words are simply sounds (or a crude form of communication)—no more, no less. They're experts at mimicking sounds—period! And since parrots aren't intelligent enough to understand the concept of morality, they are neither moral nor immoral, but amoral.

Now let's look at another example of a dog. In a state of nature, a dog will chase after cats or other natural prey, but with the proper training, it won't. It doesn't stop chasing cats because it believes it's morally wrong, it stops because it's either going to be punished or rewarded. Animals do not live by a conscious code of values. They live by that which is instinctual, expedient or practical, i.e., that which has worked in the past. Animals cannot think long-term, and because they cannot think long-term, they cannot make moral choices.

Human beings understand (at least some do) that the reason morality is so vital for survival is because it's the only way to plan long-term. Without some type of moral code, humans could not plan long-term, and without long-term planning, you could not have civilization. Now, I'm not saying a moral code must be *perfect* to have a civilization. No civilization that has ever existed had a perfect moral code. But it must *at the very least* have a basic set of principles such as Do not murder, Do not steal, Do not lie…etc. Can you imagine what life would be like if humans had absolutely no moral codes at all? How long would civilization last if the majority of humans didn't value honesty? Or what would happen if the majority of humans didn't value integrity? Without moral codes, we would live our lives (for as long as they lasted) as animals do in the state of nature—complete and absolute anarchy. And I don't mean anarchy in the human political sense; I mean anarchy in the state of nature sense. If the vast majority of humans were moral, then anarchy among humans might be possible because people would be tempered by their individual moral codes. But anarchy among the rest of the species on earth is simply kill or be killed, anything goes, survival of the fittest, i.e., nature *without* Mankind.

My last example from the animal world will be that of chimpanzees. Even though chimpanzees are our closest relatives, they still don't posses enough intelligence to be moral or immoral. From my understanding, they have roughly the intellectual abilities of a three year old human, and three year old humans simply cannot make moral choices. Even though different cultures place the age of moral consent at different ages, *none* believe a three year old can make choices in the realm of ethics. Chimps may be more intelligent than any other species on earth *besides* humans, but they still can't reason to a high enough degree to be moral. They may be able to communicate through sign language to a limited degree; they may be able to use tools to a limited degree; they may even be able to "think" to a limited degree; but they simply cannot reason through moral issues—period! Although chimpanzee DNA is roughly 95% to 98% identical with human DNA (I don't know if it's true, but I even heard one expert who said it's closer to human DNA than it is to gorilla DNA), they simply don't have the intellectual abilities to be moral or immoral, so they remain amoral.

I really didn't want this book to turn into a debate over how much intelligence different species possess, but to anyone who believes animals have the ability to reason through moral issues, I say: show me one. This entire book could be spent trying to convince people that human beings possess intellectual powers that no other species on earth possess, and I still wouldn't be able to convince some people. So if you're one of those people who believes other species on earth are as intelligent as humans, you may as well quit wasting your time reading this book an throw it in the garbage. Or better yet, why don't you give it to one of your animal friends to read?

Ok, now let's get away from using animals to prove the premise that morality is based on the ability to reason, to using the example of a robot. Can a robot be moral? At this point in history, the answer is no. In the future, technology may advance enough to give robots the ability to think for themselves, be self aware, have a conscience…etc., but as of this writing, they cannot. At this point in history, artificial intelligence, at its most advanced level, is roughly equal to that of insects, and insects are not moral or immoral, but amoral. A robot could only be moral if it had the ability to go beyond its programmer's perimeters and reason for itself, and I don't believe this will happen until far, far into the future—if ever.

This is also another place to make the distinction between 'committing a moral act' and 'doing the right thing'. A robot, like an animal or child, *can* do the right thing, but it *cannot* commit a moral act. Once again, in order to commit a moral act, it must know *for itself,* and by its own reason, that it's committing a moral act. It must be of a high enough intelligence to be able to distinguish between right and wrong, good and evil, just and unjust…etc., and until it can make these distinctions *on its own* and outside of its written program, it will remain amoral.

Just for a quick example, imagine that in the future a robot is designed to run into burning buildings, find people, and then carry them to safety. Is the robot being moral? Of course not, it's only doing what it was programmed to do—no more, no less. Robots are *amoral* because they only make decisions their programmer has programmed them to make—it has no *real* choice in the matter. And since it's the programmer making the choices, it can only be the programmer who is being moral or immoral.

This would also be true in the opposite. If the robot was programmed to kill people indiscriminately, it would not be evil—its programmer would, and for the same reasons mentioned already. Robots cannot be moral or immoral because at this point in history they simply don't have a high enough intelligence, and without a high enough intelligence, morality is not possible.

That's not to say that just because a being has a high enough intelligence it'll be moral. We all know that's not the case. There are many examples throughout history of humans who have had high intelligence, but were not moral. But the fact remains that in order to be moral, a being must be able to reason *for itself* on moral issues. And this does not, and I seriously doubt if it ever will, apply to robots.

Now I would like to get back to freewill for a moment before I move on. The problem with trying to prove freewill exists is that no matter what I say, opponents will simply claim it wasn't a *real* choice, but an automatic, environmental, or chemical response. So all I can do is show why *I* know freewill exists based on my own life experience. Of course *my* life experiences might not prove anything to *you* about freewill, but that's the best I can do at this point in time on this subject. So here goes.

For roughly the first two decades of my life I had absolutely no moral problem with stealing. I knew my parents and society said it was wrong, but I simply didn't care. And although I didn't steal much until my late teen years, I thought that as long as I didn't get caught, there was nothing inherently wrong with it. In other words, *not* getting caught *was* my moral standard. So I spent much of my late teens as a thief. And although I always had a job and was a good worker, I thought that the only way a guy like me would ever really get ahead in life was to steal.

Well, in my last year of High School I got a job at a small factory. It was typical monotonous factory work, but there was one great benefit—the people I worked with listened to talk radio (of course at the time I didn't see this as a benefit, and of course I would've much rather to listen to music, but sometimes we are blind to advantages, aren't we?). The knowledge I accumulated over those eleven years became the foundation of my life-long love of learning. Anyway, to make a long story short, there was a talk show host named Mark Scott who introduced me to the ideas of Ayn Rand and the philosophy of Objectivism—and it changed my life! He taught me *why* stealing was wrong; he taught me *why* honesty and integrity were not just meaningless words, but virtues to live by; he taught me that if I was ever truly going to be happy, I would have to live by a rational set of principles. In other words, he completely changed my life paradigm.

So what does this have to do with freewill? Everything! I made the *choice* to no longer live my life as a part-time thief; I made the *choice* to take responsibility for myself; I made the *choice* to live my life long-term and rationally, instead of shot-term and irrationally. Without freewill I could never had made this choice. Now don't get me wrong here, I'm still the same person. On rare occasions, I still find myself looking at something valuable that someone left outside for the night and think to myself how easy it would be to steal—I just don't act upon it. I *choose* not too.

That was over twenty years ago and I've never looked back. Freewill exists or I would still be who I was—period! I *chose* to change the way I looked at life, and the only way I could've done that was if I possessed freewill. Yes, we're all born with certain characteristics, but we *create* our own character through the choices we make and the actions we take. So in a way, freewill is also a prerequisite of morality, but I just put it under the banner of 'choice'.

Another way to prove the existence of freewill is in relation to values. Human beings are the only species on earth that can choose their own values. Of course there are some basic values we cannot choose to do without (food, water, air...etc.), but by-and-large, we have many values we *can* choose as individuals (such as whether or not to get married, whether or not to have children, our career, whether or not to be logical, whether or not to exercise, whether or not to have integrity, what types of food to eat, who to choose for our friends, how honest we're going to be...etc). In essence, we could not choose any of these things were it not for the possession of freewill.

Ok, now that I've proven the first premise (that all morality is based on the ability to reason), lets move on to the next (that Freedom is a prerequisite of morality).

Chapter 2: Freedom

The only possible way to begin this chapter is to start off by clarifying what I mean by Freedom. In essence, I define freedom as 'the absence of restraints imposed by others'. You may or may not agree with the balance of my clarifications, but we have to start somewhere, right? So here goes.

Throughout history there have been two competing viewpoints on the concept of freedom: the spiritual and the political. The spiritual viewpoint of freedom comes from thinkers such as Plato, Jesus, and Gandhi, among others. These thinkers believed that freedom is a state of mind, such as in the saying "the truth shall set you free." They believe freedom is mostly *internal* and not *external*. They believe freedom is dependant upon ones own state of mind, or intellectual paradigm. Although this can be a positive way to view life, it's none the less, a false view of freedom. What these thinkers are truly identifying is *enlightenment,* not freedom—and enlightenment has nothing to do with freedom. A man can achieve enlightenment without having freedom, but he cannot have freedom without enough men in his society achieving at least a limited degree of enlightenment. "The truth shall set you free" sounds wonderful, but "the truth" does not set you free. It may *enlighten* you, but it will not "set you free" if you're a slave. It will not "set you free" if you live in a society that does not recognize freedom as a value. It will not "set you free" if the price of that freedom is the forced extraction of half your earnings. *Enlightenment* is a state of mind, freedom is not. *Freedom* is in relation to others; it must be valued by the majority in a society or *none* will possess it. *Enlightenment* can be achieved *by anyone, at any time, and under any circumstance*—even slavery. But it must be achieved on ones own. *Freedom* is only possible if others *leave you alone*—there's a profound difference (If you're interested in a good example of enlightenment, I suggest you read 'Mans search for meaning' by Victor Frankl). I may touch upon enlightenment later in this book, but for now lets get back to the *political* viewpoint of freedom.

People who believe in the *political* viewpoint of freedom, believe freedom is *external* and not *internal.* They believe that freedom is in relation to others in a society. There are also two viewpoints on political freedom. The first comes from thinkers such as John Locke, Thomas Jefferson, John Stuart-Mill, Ayn Rand, and modern day political thinkers known as Libertarians. These people believe in freedom in the same sense most Americans of the past believed in it. They believe people have the right to do whatever they want *as long as* they don't violate the equal freedom of others to do the same. They believe everyone has the right to "Life, Liberty, and the pursuit of Happiness" and that these rights are "unalienable"; which means they cannot be taken away by anyone—including the government. These are the thinkers I agree with, and it's their view of freedom I'll be using because it's the correct one.

The second political viewpoint of freedom comes from thinkers such as Jean Jacques Rousseau, Karl Marx, Franklin Delano Roosevelt, and modern day liberals. They believe that without *economic equality* you cannot have freedom. They make the ultimate mistake of not differentiating between having the *power* to do something and having the *freedom* to do something. However, their viewpoint is undoubtedly the majority opinion around the world today, and it's most certainly the majority opinion among modern "intellectuals." And as a matter of fact, it can be argued that this viewpoint has become the majority opinion of most Americans, and judging by the politicians they put into office, it's probably true. But this opinion of freedom couldn't be more false. Thinkers who come from this position believe it's up to the government to enforce economic equality *regardless* of who becomes enslaved in the process. They believe governments should "force people to be free" (as Rousseau put it) by forcing the unwilling to submit to impractical, unrealistic, paternalistic, authoritarian, totalitarian, or egalitarian forms of government. This is quite simply the *exact opposite* of freedom.

When a government uses force against a man who has used force against no one, it's no longer a defender of freedom, but it's most dangerous enemy. The initiation of force is the *antithesis* of freedom—the two are mutually exclusive. You don't force a man to be free by taking away his freedom. You can no more force a man to be free than you can force him to be enlightened. In essence, the 'economic equality' concept of freedom couldn't be more false; and it also doesn't achieve the goal of economic equality *or* freedom, but inevitably, makes beneficiaries out of some and serfs out of others. The very fact that I have to even mention this convoluted view of freedom just proves how the concept of freedom has become completely bastardized by modern intellectuals.

I would also like to make a couple of short personal observation concerning Marx and Rousseau. To begin with, I find it very interesting that Marx didn't earn his own way in life. He spent his life mooching off Friedrich Engle and anyone else he could find to mooch off of. So in a way, it's no wonder why he believed in the economic equality version of freedom; psychologically, he couldn't admit to himself he was nothing more than a human parasite. If other people hadn't supported him, he would've had to pull his own weight; and if he had to pull his own weight, he probably would've ended up going down in historical obscurity where he belongs.

I guess it wouldn't bother me so much if his actions only affected himself and his wife, but he had children to take care of; and those children suffered miserably because he spent all his time writing and very little of his time actually working. Of course writing can be a form of work, but if you don't make enough money doing it, then you need to get another job—especially if your children are suffering! The fact that he let his children suffer instead of getting off his ass and finding a job, speaks volumes about his character in my opinion.

Wouldn't it be nice to spend your entire day doing whatever you wanted to do *and* have someone else pay for it? It might be nice, but in most cases, would it be moral? And what would happen if everybody tried to do it? Just imagine if nobody actually worked or produced anything, but everybody depended on others for their sustenance? How long would that society survive? Just look at the one society that embraced Marx's philosophy and tried to implement the economic equality version of freedom to its fullest extent, e.g., the Soviet Union. Its only real means of production was invading other nations, enslaving their populations, and stealing their economic resources. As soon as it was no longer able to do this, its economy collapsed from its own dead weight. And if you look around at the rest of the modern world today, you'll see that the overwhelming majority of it also believes in the economic equality version of freedom; and depending on the degree to which they each try to implement this egalitarian economic philosophy, the individual citizen's economic well-being is either affected in a positive, or a negative, manor. The more a government attempts to impose economic equality, the more its citizens suffer; the more a government leaves its people free to regulate their own pursuits of industry, the more they enjoy economic prosperity. It really is that simple.

As to Rousseau, what can you say about a man who dumps all his children in an orphanage? It's no wonder why he was for the 'economic equality' version of freedom. I guess to him, everyone should have the equal opportunity to take care of his children. I understand that economics and ethics are different disciplines, but sometimes, as in these examples of both Marx and Rousseau, I think it's important to show how one can affect the other.

I also need to point out that I'm talking about freedom *as applied to the individual* and not to a group or collective. The standard of freedom *must* be the individual because that's the only way freedom can be objectively applied. For example: Historically, whenever a group of people stood together to form a nation, state, city, etc., they were working toward individual freedom. They believed that their values were so closely aligned with the other individuals forming that community, as opposed to the community they were breaking away from, that together, they could achieve the ability to live the life they chose, i.e., achieve freedom for themselves. It's a fact of reality that there's strength in numbers; that as individuals, it's nearly impossible to get groups of people to respect your rights, but in large enough numbers though, we as cooperating individuals can achieve things that would not be possible for any *single* individual. It's a shame, but one of the things history has taught us is that the only thing some humans respect is power, and in numbers, there's power.

To many, if not most humans, *might* makes right (at least when it comes to politics). If humans could've achieved freedom on their own, they would have. In fact, there was a time when men could leave civilization and live free out in the wilderness on their own, but no more. Now, the only way to be *free* is to convince enough people in your society that freedom is one of the highest of values. In fact, it's no longer possible to be left alone and free *unless* you can convince others in your society you have the *right* to be left alone and free. And in order to do this, Americans must be convinced, once again, that freedom only applies to the individual and can never be applied to a group. Or look at it like this: Russia is "free." China is "free." Cuba is "free." Iran is "free." Iraq is "free." India is "free," but are their *people* free? No. All nations have fought for the right of self-determination, but *self-determination* can only apply to the *self*.

The founding fathers of The United States believed in *unalienable individual rights*, the political foundation of freedom, and explicitly stated it in the Declaration of Independence. However, somewhere along the road, our people, our intellectuals, and our government turned away from individual rights and turned toward the false notion of *collective* or *group* rights. That tragic turning point came roughly at the beginning of the 20th century under the *legal* leadership of Oliver Wendell Holmes, and under the *political* leadership of Franklin Delano Roosevelt. Both of these men believed the convoluted idea that the "social good" superseded both individual freedom and unalienable rights. Of course it can be argued into eternity exactly what "social good" actually means, and whether or not taking away individual freedom is actually a social good; but the fact remains that in late 19th century and the early 20th century there was an intellectual paradigm shift *away* from *individual* rights and toward *collective* or *group* rights. Oliver Wendell Holmes began this philosophical shift away from liberty by explicitly re-defining what liberty meant, but first we must go back even further to see what Americas founding fathers meant by liberty.

Across the board, the founding fathers defined liberty as the right to do as you please *as long as* you didn't violate another's right to do the same. They held individual freedom and private property as the highest of political values. For a few quick examples I'll quote Thomas Jefferson: "A wise and frugal government, which shall restrain men from injuring one another, which shall leave them otherwise free to regulate their own pursuits of industry and improvement, and shall not take from the mouth of labor the bread it has earned. This is the sum of good government."

And: "Rightful liberty is unobstructed action according to our will within limits drawn around us by the equal rights of others. I do not add 'within the limits of law' because law is often but the tyrants will, and always so when it violates the rights of the individual."

And: "A government big enough to supply everything you need is big enough to take everything you have. The course of history shows that as government grows, liberty declines."

And last but not least: "Not meddling in the affairs of others is a mark that society is going on in happiness. If we can prevent the government from wasting the labors of the people, under the pretext of taking care of them, they must be happy." Notice that there's absolutely no ambiguity in those quotes. So at least when it came to Jefferson we know *exactly* what he meant by liberty. And also note the key sentence in that last quote: "under the pretext of taking care of them." Throughout all history, those in power have used this rationalization to violate the freedom of the people under the guise of "taking care of them" and it being "for their own good." I think it was Benjamin Franklin who summed it up quite nicely when he said something like: "Those who would trade liberty for security deserve neither."

Now let's look at Oliver Wendell Holmes' idea of liberty: "To claim that a citizen may do as he likes so long as does not interfere with the liberty of others to do the same, which has been a shibboleth for some well known writers, is a perversion of what the constitution means by liberty" (I know, I know, what the hell does "shibboleth" mean? It's worth looking into if you don't know).

Anyway, let's go on to see how he views liberty. I think the best definition of how Holmes saw liberty was actually written by his ideological heir, Supreme Court Justice Hughes: "What the constitution means by liberty is: Liberty in a social organization which requires the protection of law against the evils which menace the health, safety, morals and welfare of the people." That's the definition of liberty? It's almost as if these two Supreme Court Justices never even read the Declaration of Independence. If you define liberty the way they do there can be no such thing as unalienable rights as defined by the Declaration of Independence. The government can take away any citizen's "Right to Life, Liberty, or the Pursuit of Happiness" any time it believes someone is being "evil" or "immoral." It can throw you in prison for "menacing" the supposed "health," "safety," "morals," or "welfare" of anyone at any time. Just about any action we take falls under one of these ridiculously generalized categories. If someone sells you cigarettes, alcohol, fattening food, a car, a pair of roller blades, or even a set of golf clubs (more people die playing golf than any other sport) aren't they potentially threatening your health and safety? And in how many different ways are our individual moral codes assaulted *every single day* when we go out into society? You usually can't go out in public without someone, in some way, assaulting your sensibilities. This is such a convoluted definition of liberty, I just can't believe Americans actually fell for it.

You see, to Holmes, an individual is like an inanimate object; or perhaps in relation to society, a finger to a body. If a finger is giving you some type of physical ailment, just cut it off. Even if the finger *isn't* giving you a physical ailment, you just *believe* it is, cut it off. In Holmes definition of liberty, human beings are just automatons serving society in any manner the majority sees fit. Basically, you're just a worker ant who's only reason for existence is to serve the Collective Borg known as "society." I challenge *anyone* to name just one of America's founding fathers who define liberty in this way. Even though Americans at the time didn't understand it (and still don't), this new convoluted way to define liberty is the main reason why our government no longer recognizes true private property or unalienable Rights. It was the beginning of the end of freedom in America.

In essence, one of the reasons why this happened was because justice's like Holmes and Hughes said that the right to private property could not be found in the Constitution, and strictly speaking, they're right, it's not in there. And, in their opinion, since the right to property wasn't explicitly stated in the constitution, then it really *wasn't* a right; and thus, it didn't have to be respected by the government. But the problem with their thinking is that they completely ignore the rights that were *already established* by the Declaration of Independence. The Declaration of Independence states "We hold these truths to be self-evident, that all men are created equal, that they are endowed by their Creator with certain unalienable Rights, that among these are Life, Liberty, and the Pursuit of Happiness—That to secure these Rights, Governments are instituted among men…etc.." It's all right there. The *very reason* the Constitution was written in the first place was to "secure these Rights"—and what were "these Rights"? "Life, Liberty, and the Pursuit of Happiness"! The very fact that our judicial system has ignored these rights since roughly the turn of the 20th century speaks volumes—especially knowing that the right to private property was considered one of the *most important* of all rights by the founders because without it, no other rights are possible. *Implicit* in the "Right to Life, Liberty, and the Pursuit of Happiness" is the right to private property—you cannot have *any* without the others. They're corollary rights that cannot be separated, no matter what the Supreme Court said and did.

Just for a quick look at Holmes contempt for individual rights, let me to give just a few examples. First I'll point to the 1927 Supreme Court decision upholding a state's "right" to forcibly sterilize "mentally retarded" Americans (the case of Terry Buck). In this case, Ms. Buck had already been forcibly sterilized by her state and the Supreme Court upheld the decision. Chief Justice Holmes wrote: "This sacrifice was appropriate for society because three generations of imbeciles is enough." And what was the proof that this woman was mentally ill? Simple, her mother and grandmother were. After the decision, it was proven that she *wasn't* mentally ill.

What did Holmes think about an individuals right of free speech? "Little as I believe in it as a theory, I hope I would die for it." What kind of twisted ethical position is that? He doesn't believe in free speech, but he hopes he would die for it? What kind of a convoluted value system is that? He goes on to say: "Of course when I say I don't agree with it as an opinion, I don't mean that I do believe in it's opposite. But on their premises, it seems to me logical for the Catholic Church to kill heretics, and the Puritans to whip Quakers, and to see nothing more wrong with it from our ultimate standard, than I do with killing Germans when we were at war." He sees nothing more wrong with it? He sees no difference between killing heretics and whipping Quakers, compared to going to war with a hostile nation? The *difference* is simple! The so-called "heretics" and Quakers were not trying to use force against anyone—they were just individuals who wanted to be left alone (By the way, Jesus, Mohammad, Moses, The Buddha, or any other originator of a religion, was defined as a heretic in their time as well). The Quakers were persecuted for simply expressing their unpopular opinions. The Germans on the other hand, were attempting to militarily dominate other nations. If Mr. Holmes couldn't see the difference between torturing and killing people for simply having a belief, or expressing an opinion, and fighting against an aggressive nation, I really don't know what to say. Except for maybe: How can any rational person consider this man one of our greatest Supreme Court Justice's?

Last but not least, what did Holmes think about natural rights? In 1916 he wrote: "All my life I have sneered at the natural rights of man." I really don't think anything else needs to be said concerning his view of individual rights and *real* freedom.

And then of course there was Franklin Delano Roosevelt. FDR was to politics what Holmes was to the legal profession—its greatest destroyer of freedom. Because of the legal precedents set by Holmes, FDR was legally able to completely destroy unalienable individual rights and replace them with *collective* or *societal* "rights" (which of course aren't truly rights at all). Before FDR, the Supreme Court consistently declared most types of government meddling in economic issues unconstitutional. Even *during* FDR's presidency the Supreme Court consistently shot down his socialist agenda. The only reason they finally gave in was because of FDR's infamous *immoral* court-packing scheme (which could easily be an entire chapter on ethics all by itself).

Anyway, things like the income tax were shot down time after time. But after the start of the 20th century, mostly because of Holmes' influence, the Supreme Court pretty much gave government permission to do just about anything it wanted in the economic realm. FDR ran with this permission for all it was worth. Under his political leadership, America essentially became a socialist nation. From this point on, the government began to take control over most aspects of economic life in America.

Of course this trend began before FDR with such things as The Federal Reserve (1913) and The Federal Trade Commission (1914), but government power grew exponentially during FDR's reign. Social Security (1935), Minimum wage (1938), and a myriad of other Statist programs began at this time ("Statism" meaning a governmental system that concentrates power in the state at the expense of individual freedom). In other words, individuals no longer had unalienable economic rights, but had to ask permission, or pay homage, *before* they could act in the economic realm. Even if two *consenting* adults *freely* agreed to something, the government now had the Supreme Court's permission to stop them from doing it. And of course this was based on some convoluted idea of the "social good." This is simply not freedom, but Statism! So from this point on, *individual* rights declined, and *collective* "rights" grew.

For another quick example, I'll briefly address the 1942 case Wicker vs. Filborn. Under the Agriculture Adjustment Act, the government only allowed people to grow a limited amount of wheat. And even though Mr. Filborn only grew wheat for his own farm animals, the government went after him for violating the Agriculture Adjustment Act by using the Interstate Commerce Clause in the Constitution. So even though he didn't sell *a single ounce* of his crop (which obviously means he didn't sell anything across state borders) the Supreme Court upheld the government's power to limit the amount of wheat Mr. Filborn was growing. So as you can see, this case is a perfect example of the end of economic freedom in America, and also the perfect example of government inserting itself were it truly never belonged. The Founding Fathers (even those such as Alexander Hamilton who wanted a more powerful federal government) would've been outraged. I could give many more examples, but I only wanted to show the paradigm shift away from freedom and toward statism.

Before I go on to *true* freedom, let me give one more example of the twisted logic used by proponents of statism (or *group* rights). I actually heard a history/economics professor explain FDR's political philosophy with the rationalization: "In order to save freedom, he had to take freedom away." As long as I live I can't imagine I'll ever hear a more ridiculous rationalization, but hey, you never know.

Now that I've covered what I mean by freedom, lets move on to show why it's the second prerequisite of morality; keeping in mind that freedom, as with the concept of rights, is *always* applied to the individual and *never* to a group or collective.

I think when people speak of freedom, liberty is implied; and when people speak of liberty, freedom is implied. Either way, both are necessary for morality to exist. I think a new word like 'Freeliberty' is needed to combine the two concepts, but for now I'll just be using the word 'choice'. "Choice" in this book will be defined as the freedom to not only choose ones own destiny, but the liberty to act upon it. Whenever I use one of these four words, all four will be implied (unless otherwise specified). However, before I go on, I would like to say that I hope the term Freeliberty catches on in the future because the term Freedom has been so watered-down that it no longer holds any meaning. Politicians spout the word as freely as they spend taxpayer dollars, but they've completely forgotten what it actually means. Just think about it. Have you ever heard a Democrat or Republican come out *against* freedom? Of course not, they're always touting the value of freedom. But how can they *both* be *for* freedom? Fact is, they can't. And fact is, *both* party's are anti-freedom. But I'll get to that in the chapter on politics. For now, let's get back to freedom and choice.

All morality is based on choice. Without the possibility of choice, there is no possibility of morality. A human being must *freely choose* to be moral. If an action was not freely chosen, it was not a moral act. This is also where the distinction between 'committing a moral act' and 'doing the right thing' is so crucial. A person cannot be forced to be moral. If you're forced or coerced into "doing the right thing" you have not committed a moral act. This is why morality cannot be legislated. You can attempt to legislate behavior; you can force people to "do the right thing" (as *you* see it, or as society sees it), but you cannot force them to be moral. Three obvious examples on the difference between the two are: doing the right thing for the wrong reason; doing the right thing without knowing it; and doing the right thing without trying too. None of these are moral acts. They'll be discussed in more detail in the next chapter on 'Intent', but for now let's continue with Freedom.

I'll begin to prove morality is based on freedom by giving an extreme, but precise example. First, imagine a man locked in a soundproof room. Then imagine he's blindfolded, gagged, and chained to a bed so he can't move. For good measure, let's say he's fed intravenously so the gag never has to be removed. He has absolutely no way of communicating with any other human being, not even the men guarding him. So, is this a moral man? Obviously, there's simply no way to know. A human being can only be moral or immoral by his speech or actions. Since he has no freedom of speech or action, there's no way of knowing his moral character. He could be the most evil man in the world, or the most moral man in the world, but he could never be judged one way or the other without the possession of his freedom.

Now let's say the gag is removed from his mouth so he can speak. Now can he be judged to be moral or immoral? Yes, but only to a very *limited* degree. Since the man now has freedom of speech, an attempt can be made to determine his moral character. But only to a certain extent because he has no freedom of action, and you don't know his intentions.

An example of this would be if the guards opened his door and he heard a child crying in another room. It would be logical for the man to assume that the child was in the same predicament he's in. If he then pleaded with his captors to set the child free, it could be considered a moral act. You still wouldn't be able to determine his *entire* moral character, because he has no freedom of action, but it would be a start. Of course I realize this scenario is highly improbable, but I used it anyway because it shows perfectly why, without freedom, morality is not possible.

A more probable example of the above type of scenario would be that of slaves, inmates, prisoners of war…etc. Can they be moral? Yes, but only to the extent that they are free. Unlike the last scenario, these people do possess some freedom. It's true that their freedom has been severely limited, but they still have the freedom to make some choices. So yes, they can commit moral acts. If a slave gives part of his food to another slave who's being punished by having his food withheld, is he being moral? Yes, it could be considered a moral act—but only because he has enough freedom to make that choice. He has *freely chosen* to help. However, if a slave is forced by other slaves to "pitch-in" part of his food to help the punished slave, he is no longer committing a moral act because the choice has been taken away from him. No choice, no morality—period! In other words, take away *all* of a human beings freedom and he cannot make *any* moral choices; take away *some* of a human beings freedom and he can only make *some* moral choices; and take away *none* of a human beings freedom and he can make *all* the moral choices he *chooses* to make. There's not a single example that anyone can give where morality *is not* based on the ability to choose, i.e., Freeliberty.

A human being can only be moral to the extent that he is free. The more freedom a human being possesses, the more moral acts he can commit; the less freedom a human being possesses, the less moral acts he can commit. But the fact remains that in order to commit a moral act, he must have the freedom to commit it. The problem with this fact is that the opposite also applies. The more freedom a human being possesses, the more *immoral* acts he can commit as well. This is why in a truly *moral* society, a man's freedom is limited to the exact same freedom possessed by others in the society—no more, no less. A man has the right, if we are going to live in a moral society, to live his life in any manner he chooses *as long as* he does not violate the exact same freedom of choice that others in his society possess.

It's also only in a completely free society that a man's true moral character can be known; because it's only in a completely free society that a man has the ability to make all of his moral choices without the threat of physical coercion. As long as men are not initiating force against others (the only way to take away another's freedom) they have the *right* to be left alone to develop their own moral character—for better or for worse.

For my next example on why morality is based on freedom, we'll again have to use our imagination. Let's say someone invents a 'morality chip'. After this computer chip is installed in a person's brain, they are mentally compelled to do the right thing. Of course this would depend on who defines "the right thing," but since I'm writing this in America, we'll use a Christian perspective on morality. When the chip is installed, the person lives their life Christ-like in every possible manner, i.e., every word or action this person takes is according to the teachings of Jesus. And since we're using our imagination, let's imagine Jesus himself programmed the chip. When installed, a person is compelled to speak and act completely in accordance with the programming of the chip—there is absolutely no choice in the matter. As long as the chip is installed, this person is a perfect Christian—period!

So, is this a moral person? Of course not. He *is* doing the right things (according to Christians), but since it's the chip making the decisions, it's only the programmer of the chip who can be judged as moral or immoral. The man cannot be judged as moral or immoral because he has no choice in the matter. If we then remove the chip, and he continues to live his life in a Christian manner, he may now be considered moral (at least according to Christians), because he is now doing it by choice. We can also replace the term *Christian* with *Muslim, Hindu, Confusion, Aristotelian, Platonist*…etc., and the idea would still hold true. If you don't agree, let's try the opposite.

Let's say an 'immorality chip' is *involuntarily* installed in a man's brain; and after the chip is installed, the man goes out and kills someone. So, did he commit murder? Absolutely not. Yes, he did *kill* someone, but he did not commit murder. If he had no choice in the matter, it couldn't be murder. However, if the man *voluntarily* chose to have the immorality chip installed, *knowing* it was an immorality chip, then yes, he would be guilty of murder. Either way, both examples show why freedom is a prerequisite of morality.

The thing about freedom is that it's much easier to describe what freedom *is not* than to describe what freedom actually *is*. Sometimes I describe freedom in the same way someone once describe pornography. I can't remember who it was, but a Supreme Court Justice once said something like "I can't define pornography, but I know it when I see it." Well, in a way, that's how I see freedom. I have a hard time trying to completely define freedom, but I sure as hell know when it's being taken away from me. In essence, freedom is lost whenever the initiation of force, or the threat of force, is used in human relations. If someone is forced to do something, their freedom has been taken away—period! And if their freedom has been taken away, they cannot make moral choices (or any other choices for that matter).

This is why the principle that it's wrong to initiate force against other human beings is so crucial. If a society allows the initiation of force, whether it's done by one citizen against another, by one group of citizens against another group of citizens, or by the government, the first casualty is *always* morality itself. However, there is an exception to this rule when it comes to certain, very limited, legal circumstances; but those are rare, and only under certain *legal* circumstances. However, even under those circumstances the government's not actually being moral, it's only, at best, 'doing the right thing'.

The most obvious examples of loss of freedom are such things such as murder, rape, theft, kidnapping, fraud…etc.; and of course these types of actions are the reasons why human beings devised the idea of government in the first place. But there are many more ways freedom can be taken away that Americans at large have forgotten. Without me going into too much detail right now, allow me to give some examples.

If the government takes a percentage of your income to give to the "needy" (yes I'm talking about welfare), and you have no choice in the matter; has your freedom been taken away? Absolutely. And if your freedom has been taken away, did *you* commit a moral act when the government forced you to do it? Absolutely not. If you do not freely give it, it cannot be a moral act. If the government asked you to give it, and you did, then it could be considered a moral act. In order for a moral act to be committed, the "committer" must do it without any physical threat or coercion from others. Only then can the deed be considered a moral act.

If the government takes 14% of what you produce and invests it into a retirement Ponzi scheme (yes, I'm talking about Social Security), and you have no choice in the matter, has your freedom been taken away? Absolutely. Did you just commit a moral act? Absolutely not. Did the government? Once again, absolutely not. Since you have no choice in the matter, it cannot be a moral act. Even if the program resulted in more people being better off in their old age (of which I couldn't disagree more), it still wouldn't be a moral act on your account. It would be the same as a thief stealing money from you to give to a starving child. It may be argued by some that the thief is committing a moral act, but it certainly cannot be argued that *you're* committing a moral act. But in actuality, is the thief (or government) committing a moral act? Absolutely not. Since choice is not involved, morality is not involved. You may argue that the thief (or government) is 'doing the right thing' (as *you* define it), but it cannot be argued that a moral act has been committed. When people are threatened with imprisonment or death if they do not do as they're told, it is no longer in the realm of free choice; and therefore, no longer in the realm of morality.

The military draft is a case of where freedom has been taken away. The Income tax is a case of where freedom has been taken away. Laws against the consumption of alcohol, drugs or tobacco are cases of where freedom has been taken away. Laws against prostitution, gay marriage, or certain kinds of sex acts, are more cases of freedom being taken away. Laws such as the minimum wage, Social Security and Welfare are even more cases of freedom being taken away…etc. I'll cover these in much more depth in my chapter of politics, but for now, I just wanted to give a few examples. And please note that I'm not saying at this point that any of these things are moral or immoral, I'm simply saying that banning such things (or forcing them on people) means the government is taking away freedom; and if it's taking away freedom, it's taking away one of the prerequisites of morality; and without its prerequisites, morality cannot exist.

Chapter 3: Intent

The third prerequisite of morality is *intent*. In order to commit a moral act, a person must *intend* to do so. This is also where the distinction between 'committing a moral act' and 'doing the right thing' is so crucial. As I stated earlier, most people don't make this distinction, but it *must* be made for a proper analysis of morality. If a person does the right thing for the wrong reason, does the right thing without knowing it, or does the right thing without trying to, they *did not* commit a moral act. Allow me to give some examples.

Let's say a man works at a large corporation and is wanting to move up the corporate ladder. One day his company decides to raise some money for a charity, and is looking for contributions. So the man thinks to himself "Hmmm, this would be a great opportunity to make myself look good. I bet if I give a few thousand dollars, I'll get noticed by upper management and it could help me improve my position with the company." This would be a case of doing the right thing for the wrong reason, and as such, could not be considered a moral act. Obviously, since his intentions have nothing to do with helping the charity, only with helping himself, he did not commit a moral act. Now let's look at another example.

Man #1 is walking down the street and the person in front of him (man # 2) accidentally drops his wallet. Man #1 bends over, picks up the wallet, and begins to put it in his pocket. He then notices that man #3 has witnessed the entire incident, so he taps man #2 on the shoulder and gives him his wallet back. So, did man #1 commit a moral act? Absolutely not. Since his *intent* was to keep the wallet, it *was not* a moral act. He did 'the right thing' by giving the wallet back, but he did not commit a moral act. If man #3 hadn't witnessed the event, man #1 would've walked away with man #2's wallet. Since man #1 did the right thing *for the wrong reason*, it cannot be considered a moral act. Once again, in order to commit a moral act, a person must *intend* to do so. On to the next example.

Man #1 points a gun at man #2 and tells him to give all of the money in his wallet to a starving child who's living on the streets. Man #2 complies. So, did man #2 commit a moral act? Absolutely not. He may have 'done the right thing' by giving his money to the starving child, but since he was *forced* to do it, it was not a moral act. If you're going to argue that it was still a moral act even though he was forced to do it, then we can never know who is *truly* moral, and who is not. If someone pointed a gun at Adolf Hitler and told him to "be nice and treat everyone justly or I'll blow your brains out" and Hitler complied, would that have make Hitler a moral man? Of course not. But if you believe there's no difference between 'doing the right thing' and 'committing a moral act', then there's no getting around the fact that, under *your* definition, he would be.

Next I'll use an example of two men going to fight in a *just* war. Man #1 voluntarily joins the military, and man #2 is drafted. So which man committed a moral act? I hope it's obvious by now that only the action taken by man #1 can be considered moral. Man #2 may have 'done the right thing', but since he was *forced* to do it, it cannot be considered a moral act. Now, what if it's an *unjust* war? Then Man #1 is no longer committing a moral act, but an immoral act. And Man #2 may or may not have committed a moral act—it would all depend on the circumstances. Throughout history moral men have been forced to fight in unjust wars, but that doesn't make them immoral. It may make them non-heroic, but it does not make them immoral. A man does not have to be a hero to be moral. It's in extreme situations where heroes show themselves to be more then just average moral men. But heroes are not only men who do great things *in* war, they're also men who have the courage to go against their government and stay out of unjust wars—unfortunately, usually to their own detriment.

So, can a man forced to fight in a just or unjust war be moral *after* the fact? Yes. Even if the original choice was not his own, he can still commit moral or immoral acts while in the service of his country. The moral freedom to make the original choice may have been taken away from him, but once he's there, he can commit moral acts *in direct proportion* to the freedom he still possesses. If he saves a life or commits other acts of heroism, they can be considered moral acts. However, if his sergeant tells him to run out in the middle of a mind field, pick up a wounded soldier and carry him to safety while being fired upon by the enemy, and that if he doesn't do it he'll be shot for insubordination; it's no longer in the realm of free choice, so it's no longer in the realm of morality. But if the soldier *volunteered* to rescue the fallen soldier, it could be considered a moral act.

Sometimes it's just a matter of luck whether or not someone 'does the right thing', but it's *never* a matter of luck whether or not someone 'commits a moral act'. I was watching the News on television when a man was asked whom he was going to vote for in the coming election. Well, he was so unsure that he decided to just flip a coin. This in itself can be considered an immoral act, but even if he got lucky and voted for the moral man (assuming the fat chance that there was one), it still couldn't be considered a moral act because he left it up to chance and not reason; or maybe better put, he left it up to *luck* and not *intent*. He did 'the right thing' without trying too, so he did not commit a moral act. Here's another example.

Man #1 has just robbed a place of business. As he's escaping through the front door, he turns to shoot the clerk (man #2) so there will be no witnesses left. As he's pulling the trigger, a customer (man #3) inadvertently pushes the door open into the robber causing him to trip and hit his head on a countertop. As the robber is laying on the floor unconscious, the clerk calls the police and they take him off to jail. So, did man #3 commit a moral act? Of course not. He may have thwarted a robbery, he may have even saved another mans life, but since he didn't do it *intentionally*, he can get no moral credit for it (although he can get credit for calling the police if he does so). He just happened to be in the right place at the right time. Since he 'did the right thing' without trying too, he *did not* commit a moral act. However, if he had seen the crime in progress and *deliberately* pushed the door into the criminal, then it would've been a moral act. And only then could he be considered a moral hero.

Or how about this example? Man #1 walks into a store to buy something. Unknown to him, the owner of the store (Man #2) is giving 10% of all profits made during this week to a charity that feeds, clothes, and educates poverty stricken children. So, did man #1 commit a moral act? No. Since man #1 didn't know man #2 was committing this charitable act, man #1 can get no moral credit for it. The right thing may have been done, but since man #1 didn't know it was being done, it cannot be considered a moral act on his account. However, if man #1 *intentionally* spent money at this store because *he knew* of the owner's charitable act, then his actions can be considered moral.

My last example distinguishing between 'committing a moral act' and 'doing the right thing' is in relation to parenting. Let's say we have two sets of parents that both take care of their children. However, one set of parents do it because they love them and know it's their responsibility to do so, while the other set of parents do it more out of a sense of obligation, and because if they don't, they may go to prison for child abuse or neglect. Obviously, the first set of parents are 'committing a moral act', while the second set of parents are simply 'doing the right thing'. And we know this because if it wasn't for the law coercing the second set of parents, they would've quit taking care of their children long ago. Thus, as always, intent is the deciding factor.

The question you may be asking yourself right now is: How can anyone ever know another's intentions? Simple, you can't—at least not perfectly. All you can do is listen to what they say and watch to see if their actions are in line with their words. Without question, the hardest part of determining another's moral character is determining their intent. However, it's fairly easy to do with people you spend a lot of time with though. You can learn pretty quickly if a person is honest and has integrity just by being with them over a decent amount of time. But one thing is for sure, in order to discover if another person is honest, you must first be honest with yourself. The beginning of wisdom is the acknowledgement of reality. If you're not honest with yourself, whether you know it or not, you cannot be honest with anyone else. Truly great men (or women of course) search for the truth in *all* aspects of life. And what is the search for truth? It's the search for reality *as it is!* And only after they know reality *as it is*, can they think about ways to improve it.

So how do you discover another's intentions if you've never met them? This is much more difficult, but it can be done to a certain extent. A good example of this is when it comes to electing public officials. How do you find out whether a politician is moral or not? First you must listen closely to what they say. Then you must look into that person's history and see if you can find contradictions or inconsistencies. Then (if possible) find out how they voted on past legislation. Once you've done these things you can basically determine their moral character. It really all comes down to one thing: Did this person vote for legislation that upheld freedom, or did this person vote for legislation that took freedom away. Morality is based on choice, and choice is based on freedom; therefore, morality is based on freedom. If a politician's votes were anti-freedom, then their votes were anti-morality—period! Yes, it really is as simple as that.

Now, how do you discover if a person is moral if you don't know much about them? Simple, you can't, but that's all right. If we spent our lives trying to discover the moral character of everyone we've ever met or heard of, we wouldn't have time for anything else. The important thing to know is the moral character of the people in our personal lives, the people in our business lives, and the people we elect to public office. In the first two cases, if you don't treat others ethically and demand they treat you ethically, you're just setting yourself up for a life of unhappiness and frustration. If you're getting into a serious relationship, whether it's personal or business, you must take the time to identify for them *your* most important values and virtues. You must also make sure they know that you're not going to put up with any immoral nonsense or unethical behavior. And most importantly, you must speak and act according to those virtues and values, i.e. you must have integrity.

When it comes to the people you elect to public office—good luck! These people can affect your happiness almost as much as your personal or business acquaintances, but you won't be able to do much about it if they're immoral. As long as government officials don't have too much power over you, you can live a happy, fulfilling, and prosperous life. But if you allow the people you deal with *personally* to be morally flawed, it will affect your life negatively on a daily bases—and *that* is a metaphysical absolute.

I could give example after example showing why morality is based on intent, but I think it would just be just way too repetitive. So I'll just ask you to think of some examples for yourself and apply the standard of Intent. What you'll discover is that you won't be able to find *a single example* where morality *is not* based on intent. But please go ahead and make the attempt.

Chapter 4: Politics

The word "politics" is derived from the word "poly" meaning "many," and the word "tics," meaning "blood sucking parasites"—Larry Hardiman. Now, I know very little of Mr. Hardiman, but he sure did sum it up quite concisely in my opinion. But seriously, what is politics? In essence, it's how human beings deal with one another beyond a personal scale. Yes, it's as simple as that. And how many ways are there for human beings to deal with one another? Only two: Force or Persuasion. It will *always* come down to one or the other—period! I challenge you to think of *just one* example were it does not come down to force or persuasion—it cannot be done (Included in the definition of force is also the *threat* of force because it's essentially the same thing. And fraud's also included because it's a form of *indirect* force). So, we as humans must decide which it will be. If we want to live in a *moral* society there's only one choice: persuasion.

This is what I refer to as the 'Paradigm of Peace'. A person who lives under a paradigm of peace doesn't resort to the use of force, or hire their government to use force against those who have forced no one. As long as you leave them alone, they'll leave you alone. Whereas a person who lives under the 'Paradigm of War' will live as an aggressor and either initiate force themselves, or they'll hire the government to do it for them. Either way, they've chosen to live as a predator, and as such, have violated a prerequisite of morality. These people believe they're justified in the use of force because they don't think human beings will be moral unless you force them to be moral. But as I've already shown in the first three chapters, you cannot force someone to be moral i.e., you cannot legislate morality. The government can attempt to legislate *behavior*, but not morality. Morality can only exist where the initiation of force is prohibited. Once again, if someone is *forced* to do something, they have not committed a moral act. They can be forced to 'do the right thing' (as *you* see it. Or as the government sees it), but they cannot be forced to be moral.

So, is it ever *moral* for the government to force someone to 'do the right thing'? No, because as I've already proven in the first three chapters, *force* is the antithesis of morality—the two are mutually exclusive. In order for something to be *moral* it must be freely chosen. However, is it ever *right* for the government to force someone to 'do the right thing'? Yes, but only under extremely limited *legal* circumstances. I'll go into more detail on this topic in the last chapter on 'Exceptions to the rules, and odds & ends'.

I would also like to point out that the two ways for humans to deal with one another (force or persuasion) can also be summed up by comparing the political philosophies of the Founding Fathers and Karl Marx. All cultures, societies, nations, states, cities, towns…etc., *must* come from one perspective or the other—period! Either the political premise of the Founding Fathers—that every man has "the Right to Life, Liberty, and the pursuit of Happiness," or the Marxist political premise "From each according to his ability, to each according to his need." Either you're free to live your life as you choose (as long as you don't violate another's rights), or you are forced to be your brother's keeper (fellow citizens). These are the *only two* political premises that exist—period! All known civilizations throughout history (except for the beginning of the United States) has had the same basic political moral premise: "from each according to his ability, to each according to his need"—whether they recognized it or not. And this has also become the basic moral premise of the United States as well—whether Americans recognize it or not.

The United States of America was the first, and so far the only, country to establish *as law* the politics of persuasion *over* the politics of force. Although there were inconsistencies and contradictions (slavery, the subjugation of the native population, the subjugation of women…etc.), for the first time in history the precedent of *unalienable individual rights* was established (although only for white males of course). Individual rights are based on the premise that human beings have the *right* to live in *any* manner they choose as long as they do not initiate force against others. And what is a "right"? As usual, I'll go to Ayn Rand for the definition: "A 'right' is a moral principle defining and sanctioning a man's freedom of action in a social context."

The founders of the United States understood that the only way to violate another mans rights was by the initiation of force; and they expressed this thought perfectly at the beginning of The Declaration Of Independence when they wrote: "We hold these truths to be self evident, that all Men are created

these Ends, it is the Right of the People to alter or abolish it, and to institute new Government…etc"—The Declaration of Independence. The *Constitution* was written as a legal document to secure man's unalienable rights to life, liberty, and the pursuit of happiness, as expressed in the Declaration of Independence; but unfortunately, Americans at large have forgotten this. And because Americans at large have forgotten this, so have their politicians.

One of the reasons this has happened may sound simplistic, but it's still, nevertheless, true. When elected to public office, these politicians take an oath to uphold the *Constitution* of the United States, *not* The Declaration of Independence. In my opinion, this seemingly little thing makes all the difference. Nowhere in the Constitution does it say we have the "Right to Life, Liberty, and the pursuit of Happiness." Nowhere does it say we have any "unalienable" rights at all. It does state we have rights, but it does not state they're unalienable. This was a huge mistake. To some this might just sound like arguing semantics, but because that one word was left out, a black hole of servitude was inserted. When taken out of the historical context of the Declaration of Independence, The Constitution can be the legal basis of communism, socialism, or just about any other form of government you can think of; all you would need is enough votes to make it so—which is *exactly* what has been happened since the beginning of the 20th century. But when taken in conjunction *with* the principles set forth in The Declaration of Independence, it's only basis can be freedom and capitalism. To be *human* is to possess unalienable rights, and as the Declaration states: "That to secure these Rights, Governments are instituted among men." Until the American people demand government officials take an oath too *not only* uphold The Constitution, but The Declaration of Independence as well, unalienable rights will not be recognized.

How to secure unalienable rights was one of the sticking points when The Constitution was originally written. Many of the founders wanted a Bill of Rights, many didn't. The ones that wanted a Bill of Rights wanted it because they thought it would be the only way to guarantee unalienable rights. They thought that the only way to secure them was to write them down for all to see. But the other side argued that writing them down would be a mistake because there was no way you could write down *all* the rights possessed by men, and that if you attempted to state each one, many would be left out. They believed that the phrase "Life, Liberty, and the Pursuit of Happiness" encompassed all rights, and would be good enough to secure them. In a way, I think both sides were somewhat correct. The Right to Life, Liberty, and the Pursuit of

Happiness, if looked at as a general guiding principle, really does cover all unalienable rights, but its strength is also its weakness. By not explicitly stating what these rights are, it's left open for debate. After all is said and done though, I fall on the side that says it's impossible to explicitly state all the rights held by human beings, and that it would be ridiculous to even make the attempt. Noah Webster also thought that attempting to state all Rights held by men would be disastrous. And to prove it, he sarcastically added to a proposed Bill of Rights the following: "Congress shall never restrain any inhabitant of America from lying on his left side in a long winter's night, or even on his back, when he is fatigued by lying on his right." Obviously, he thought it was ridiculous to even attempt to state all the rights possessed by man.

Since a Bill of Rights *was* written, and then became a part of the Constitution through amendments, the side that wanted rights explicitly stated, won. But looking back at the last 100 years, I'm not sure this was a good thing for the cause of liberty. Because, as those who fought against a Bill of Rights argued, there would be no way to write down all the rights possessed by men, and if they weren't all written down, they would not be respected.

Just for a few quick examples, look at the right to privacy and the right to private property. Many people who want to push their own personal "moral" agenda believe that the Constitution does not protect the right to privacy (mostly conservative Republicans). There are also many who do not believe the Constitution protects the right to private property (mostly liberal Democrats). And since the Constitution doesn't state these two rights explicitly, they argue they don't exist. Of course this is absurd if you look at it from a historical perspective. If anything, the Founding Fathers were adamant supporters of the right to privacy and property. As a matter of fact, the original Declaration of Independence was written: "The Right to Life, Liberty, and Property," and Jefferson later changed it to "The Right to Life, Liberty, and the Pursuit of Happiness" because it was more all-encompassing. Although the Ninth Amendment states: "The enumeration in the Constitution of certain rights shall not be construed to deny or disparage others retained by the people," this doesn't mean the government is recognizing these un-enumerated rights. Of course the question asked about the ninth amendment is, once again: What are these other rights? It really is an enigma because, once again, how do you name them all? But one thing is for sure, those who believe that if it's not written in the Constitution it's not a right, are winning the legal argument. In most cases the Ninth Amendment no longer really holds much sway. In practical application, it's become a mute amendment, except for the possible exception of abortion.

So, what about the rights *explicitly* stated in the Constitution? Do we as Americans posses them? Not even close! In regards to the *First* Amendment though, I think the government has done a fairly good job of respecting the right of free speech and the right of the people to peaceably assemble, but certainly *has not* remained neutral concerning religious affairs. However, I'm afraid the right to free speech may be in jeopardy. According to a recent survey, roughly 50% of Americans are willing to give up their right to free speech for the sake of "security." I'm not sure if this is because of the recently enacted war on terrorism, but whatever the reason, it's yet another blow to the cause of freedom. One thing history has shown us is that once a right is given up, the only way to get it back is through some form of revolution. Hopefully, Americans will wake up before it's too late.

So what about the *Second* Amendment? Do Americans have the right to "keep and bear arms"? Well, since a "Right" by definition, means being able to do something *without* having to first ask permission, then no, the government does not recognize the right to keep and bear arms. We can fill out the proper paperwork and hope the state, county, city…etc., grants us *permission* to "bear arms," but if they don't, then you can't—it's that simple. Since it's up to the government in one form or another to grant you permission, then by definition, it is no longer recognized as a right.

How about the Thirteenth Amendments ban on involuntary servitude? Do you posses the right *not* to be forced into servitude? At this point, I'm not going to get into the argument on why forcing me to pay taxes, and then giving those tax dollars to someone else *is* involuntary servitude, I'm just going to point out the military draft. If the draft *isn't* involuntary servitude, what the hell is? Of course we don't have a draft right now, but it's already been ruled constitutional if the government wants to bring it back. So in my opinion, it will just be a matter of time before it's reinstated.

So here we are at the beginning of the 21st century and our government simply no longer recognizes unalienable rights—period! Our "unalienable" rights can be voted away by a simple 51% majority, or taken away by a judge's capricious decision. I can easily prove this by asking a simple question: Can you name *just one* unalienable right that cannot be taken away by the government? Think long and hard about it because it cannot be done. Even if we just consider the unalienable rights *explicitly* stated in The

Declaration of Independence ("Life, Liberty, and the Pursuit of Happiness") it cannot be done. Do you possess the unalienable right to Life? Only if you do everything the government expects from you. If you do not, the government will first take away your "unalienable" right to the pursuit of happiness. It will then take away you're "unalienable" right to Liberty by throwing you in prison. And if you resist, it will take away your "unalienable" right to Life by murdering you for resisting. Here are some specific examples to prove my point.

Once again, the very fact that the government can institute a military draft proves it does not recognize unalienable rights. The military draft violates *every single* unalienable right possessed by *any* human being *without exception!* How can you possess the "unalienable Right to Life," if the government can send you off to war, and quite possibly your death, if, and when, it sees fit? How can you possess the "unalienable" right to "Liberty and the Pursuit of Happiness" if the government can throw you in prison, or murder you if you resist, for not fighting in a war that you think is completely immoral or unjustifiable? How can you possess *any* unalienable rights if you are a *means* to the government's ends? You cannot, and you do not.

Or how about the Automatic Income Tax Payroll Deduction? How can you possess the unalienable "Right to Liberty and the Pursuit of Happiness" if the government can take your wages *by force of law* before you even see them? As a matter of fact, the income tax *itself* is a violation of unalienable rights. The basic premise underlying the income tax is extortion. The government tells its citizens if they pay it tribute, they'll be left alone. But if they don't, they'll either go to jail or be murdered for resisting to pay. That's called extortion! But it's much worse than regular extortion because when the government does it—*its legal!* I would also like to point out the absurdity of the government telling us that the Income Tax is "voluntary." Give me a break! To anyone who says the Income Tax is voluntary, I challenge you to not to pay it and see what happens.

And how about property taxes? How can you have the unalienable right to "Liberty and the Pursuit of Happiness" if the government can take your property *by force* if you do not pay what it says you owe? Aren't we truly *renting* from the government?

Americans are not free, and haven't been free for a long time, and the sooner they realize this, the better. But why has this happened? Simple, Americans at large have decided that *security* is a higher value than freedom (consciously for some, subconsciously for others). What they don't understand is that, without freedom, security is not even possible. They're incrementally giving up their freedom for a *false* sense of security, not *real* security. They've decided to give up their individual sovereignty and independence in favor of a socialistic, paternalistic, and egalitarian form of government. They've accepted the cradle to grave, diapers to dentures mentality that pervades the modern world. They've decided that life is just too Goddamn hard, and that it's much safer to just be one of the collective Borg. Sure, some Americans haven't given up the fight for freedom and independence, and that's why America is still a great country. But since the majority has, the battle is swiftly being lost.

You cannot be *free* if the majority in your society do not value freedom! You cannot be *free* if the majority in your society will not permit you to be free! You are not *free* if you have to ask permission to live your life as you choose! Freedom consists of being able to make the *wrong* decisions as well as the *right* decisions. Freedom consists of being able to make mistakes, and then (hopefully) learn from them. That is as long as *your* mistakes do not violate another's freedom. If they do, then and only then, is it okay for the government to become involved. Freedom consists of developing your own moral character *regardless of outcome,* and leaving others free to do the same. You cannot have security without freedom because, sooner or later, it's *your* security that will be sacrificed to supply another's. Without freedom, neither security nor morality is even possible. But it also makes it impossible to judge another's moral character because you can never know what choices they would've made *without* being coerced. Of course, you can guess, but it will always be just a guess, you'll never know for sure.

Besides accepting security as a higher value than freedom, Americans have also succumbed to the 'good intentions' mentality of government interventionism. Both major political parties value good intentions over freedom. The good intentions of the majority takes president over the freedom of the minority. If the majority has the good intention of making sure that the elderly are taken care of in their old age, then they simply force the minority (people who agree with their cause, but not their means) to be beasts of burden for their fellow senior citizens—*by force of law.* If the good intentioned majority believe all children should have access to a basic education, then they simply force the minority (people who agree with their cause, but not their means) to be beasts of burden for their fellow citizens children—*by force of law.* If the good intentioned majority believe the poor should to be fed, clothed, housed...etc., they simply force the minority (people who agree with their cause, but not their means) to be beasts of burden for their fellow poor countryman, and in time, the entire human race—*by force of law.* And on, and on, and on, it goes. Never ending because no matter how far human beings advance as a species, no matter how high the average standard of living becomes, good intentions will always be a part of man's nature, and wealth will *never* be distributed equally among humans. Besides that, all of the examples given in this paragraph are absolute violations of the 13th Amendments ban on involuntary servitude.

Now, I'm not saying good intentions are a bad thing, they're neither good nor bad, but amoral. It's the way they're implemented *into* society that determines whether they'll have a positive (moral) or a negative (immoral) affect *on* society. And as to the equal distribution of wealth, we *as humans* well *never* be equal when it comes to personal possessions because we *as humans* will always have different values. One man's highest value may be having a large family, while another man's highest values may be having a small family so he can save enough money to retire early. These two men may work at the same job and make the same amount of money, but because the one man has a large family, he'll have to spend a lot more money supporting his family—while the other man will spend a lot *less* money supporting *his* family. Each man has *freely chosen* his own way of life and values. So why should the man who chose to have only *two* children be enslaved through taxation (involuntary servitude) to educate the *eight* children of the other man? Isn't this is an injustice? Yes, those eight children need be educated, but it's the parent's responsibility to do so. And if the parents don't have the resources to do so, they shouldn't have had the children in the first place! Now, if the people in their society want to help them educate their children, they should do so, but they should do so in the only *moral* way of doing so— through *voluntary* contributions. However, nobody should be *forced by law* to do so. No man should ever be *forced by law* to be another man's beast of burden—period! No man should ever be *forced by law* to subsidize another man's values. This is where 'good intentions' go bad.

A good modern example of the 'good intentions' mentality is what happened when hurricane Katrina struck New Orleans. In fact, it's a microcosm of what's wrong with modern America. This is also a perfect example of how we've become a nation who's basic moral premise is based on "need" (or as Marx put it "from each according to his ability, to each according to his need"), and not on freedom (as the founding fathers put it "the Right to Life, Liberty, and the Pursuit of Happiness"). Why should the tax payers of the entire United States be forced to pay for the irresponsibility of the people living in places such as New Orleans? Most of this disaster could have been easily avoided if they would've just been rational and responsible in the first place. Allow me to explain.

To begin with, the state of Louisiana receives more money from the United States government for the Army Corps of Engineers than any other state in the nation. And what did the politicians of Louisiana (people the voters of Louisiana put into office) do with all that money? They spent it on things other than the levees—*even knowing that a category 5 hurricane hits their coast every half century or so!* But that's only the beginning. The people *knew* the hurricane was coming 5 days in advance; they *knew* it was a category 5 *at least* 2 days in advance; they *knew* the levees were only built to withstand a category 3 hurricane; they *knew* they lived next to the ocean *and* that they were *below* sea level; and I even heard about a survey that was taken before Katrina hit that showed that roughly 300,000 residents of New Orleans said they wouldn't leave the city *no matter what size hurricane struck!* So it seems to me, poor or not, they *knew* what was coming and freely chose to stay; they *knew* what was coming and freely chose to spend their tax dollars elsewhere; they *knew* what was coming, but chose to deny reality. With all that, why should the rest of America be forced to pay for the irresponsible choices (to the tune of at least $3000 per household last I read) that were made by the people of Louisiana? I think this is a perfect example of what Henry David Thoreau was articulating when he said: "It may be that he who bestows the largest amount of time and money on the needy is doing the most by his mode of life to produce that misery which he strives in vain to relieve."

Another example would be how the American government forcibly extracts money from its citizens to send to the needy in Africa (or anywhere else for that matter). Of course it's good to help people in need, but *in the long run*, are we helping them, or are we hurting them? Allow me to explain. With the constant barrage from the media about Global Warning, most Americans should now be fairly aware of how the climate changes over time. One region of the planet may be a perfect environment for humans for thousands of years, but then the climate may slowly, or sometimes not so slowly, change (Ice Ages would be an example). So when the climate of a particular region changes for the worse, is it wise for human beings to continue to live there? If human beings are living in an area of Africa that has become barren and subject to long periods of drought, why are they still there? Wouldn't they be better off if they moved on? In America, what happens when a region loses jobs? Simple, people move to other regions of the country that have jobs. So why aren't Africans doing the same as related to loss of food and water? Do you see where I'm going with this? If the world community would quit sending supplies, these people would *have-to* move wouldn't they? Or as the late comedian Sam Kinison put it: "Why aren't we giving them what they *really* need—luggage!." Aren't we just exasperating the problem by helping them live where conditions are no longer suitable for human survival? In other words, if we're going to *really* help them, shouldn't we help them move to an area with a more suitable climate? By constantly sending them food and water, aren't we just keeping them where they really shouldn't be? And once again, isn't this precisely what Thoreau was talking about when he said, once again: "It may be that he who bestows the largest amount of time and money on the needy is doing the most by his mode of life to produce that misery which he strives in vain to relieve."

And you also have to keep in mind that most of the money and resources we send go to corrupt immoral regimes and not to the people who really need it. And then those corrupt governments use the money and resources to buy military equipment, make payoffs, and oppress the very people we're trying to help. So this is yet another example on how the road to hell is paved with good intentions.

Getting back to internal American politics, when San Francisco was devastated by an earthquake at the turn of the 20th century, did the federal government force everyone in the United States to rebuild it? No, it was rebuilt by private citizens with private money. When Chicago was destroyed by the great fire of 1871, did the federal government force everyone in the United States to rebuild it? No, it was rebuilt by private citizens with private capital. Even things like the 1893 Chicago Worlds Fair were financed by private means. My point being that people make choices, and those choices should not be subsidized by forcing every other citizen in the United States to pay for them. That's not freedom, but Socialism, Communism, Statism, Collectivism...etc. And all of those forms of government are immoral because they don't meet the prerequisite of morality—freedom.

Yes, I think the rest of America should help out, but no, they should not be forced too. By having the government force the responsible to pay for the irresponsible, we're subsidizing irresponsible behavior; and by subsidizing irresponsible behavior, we're creating a nation of more irresponsible people. Of course it's okay if the government gets involved in *emergency* situations, but once the emergency is over, government involvement should be over as well. And of course, once again, that's what the 13th Amendment's ban on involuntary servitude is all about.

You see, we all want basically the same things. We all want children to be taken care of, the elderly to be taken care of, people to have access to quality healthcare, people to be happy, people to make enough money to be happy, people to have a nice home, people to get the best possible education, people to have quality food, people to have clean water…etc. But it's how we, first as individuals, then as a society, go about achieving these noble ends that determines whether morality will be an ever-*expanding* part of society, or an ever-*contracting* part of society. Unfortunately, our current trend of rejecting freedom in favor of "security" is leading us down the ever-*contracting* path of morality.

When it comes to politics, both Democrats and Republicans believe in good intentioned Big Government. The only difference between the two is that Democrats believe the government should force people to do the right thing *economically,* while the Republicans believe the government should force people to do the right thing when it comes to personal moral issues. Democrats are big government socialists who don't want to admit they're socialists because they would lose elections (falsely, most Americans still cling to the idea that they value freedom). Democrats still cling to the absurd notion that they are pro freedom, so they don't like to be called socialists (although they agree completely with the socialist agenda). Republicans are big government authoritarians who don't want to admit they're authoritarians because *they* would lose elections (falsely, most Americans still cling to the long lost idea that they don't like being told what to do or how to live). Republicans are constantly espousing the value of freedom while denying American citizens the very thing they espouse. In general, Democrats believe people have the right to personal freedom, but not economic freedom; and Republicans believe people have the right to economic freedom, but not personal freedom. *Both* political parties only believe in freedom when it's in line with what *they* believe to be the moral position. If freedom doesn't coincide with their moral beliefs, they simply outlaw it. Now don't get me wrong, *neither* party is for *complete* economic or personal freedom, but in general, they fall on those sides of the issue.

So what do I mean by *economic* and *personal* freedom? Pretty much exactly what those words imply. *Economic* freedom consists of being able to make *economic* choices without the threat of physical coercion from the government. Any time the government comes between you and another in the economic realm, it's taking away economic freedom. Minimum wage laws are a perfect example. If a person *freely chooses* to work for another, whether it's an individual or corporation, it's absolutely none of the government's business what the agreed upon wage should be. As long as both parties enter the agreement of their own free will, there's absolutely no justification for government intervention—period! The only *legitimate* reason for government involvement would be if one side tried to use force or fraud against the other. If that's the case, it's *incumbent* upon the government to step in and stop the physical threat. But it's *never* incumbent upon the government to take sides and *force* one party or the other into an economic agreement they don't want or agree with. Social Security, Welfare, subsidized housing, giving other governments money as a matter of foreign policy, or any other time the government *forcibly extracts* money from one citizen to give to another citizen (or non citizen), it's a violation of economic freedom—period! And once again, it's also a violation of the 13th Amendment's ban on involuntary servitude.

Personal freedom consists of being able to make *moral* decisions without the threat of physical coercion from the government. Lying, cheating, adultery, taking drugs, smoking, sexual acts, gambling, drinking alcohol, pornography, prostitution, and any other behavior that does not physically effect anyone *except* the people who *choose* to be involved, are cases of personal freedom. Whenever the government passes laws trying to legislate morality, it's taking away personal freedom. Now, I'm not saying these behaviors are moral, or even good activities, only that these behaviors are a matter of personal preference, and that it's not the governments job to advocate particular values or virtues. It's the government's job to protect individual rights; which means letting each person choose their own values and virtues *without* the threat of force from others—including the government itself.

Most Americans seem to be under the delusion that the Constitution was written to limit the freedom of the people, when in fact, it was written to limit the *power* of the government. The philosopher Ayn Rand expressed this point perfectly when she wrote: "The reason we have a government is to protect citizens from criminals. The reason we have a Constitution is to protect citizens from the government." Speaking for myself, I do my best not to associate with people who lie, cheat, steal, take drugs…etc. But even so, I certainly don't want the government telling me what's moral or immoral in the personal realm.

People in government are usually *the last* people who have any credibility when it comes to telling others about ethical behavior. Like most people, I'm perfectly able to choose who I associate with in my personal life; but if I have a *low* moral character, I'll pay for it by having to associate with others of low moral character. Obviously, those with a high moral character will want to have as little to do with me as possible. If I have a *high* moral character, I'll be rewarded by being able to associate with others of high moral character. It's that simple. But it's up to us *as individuals* to determine exactly what a *high* or a *low* moral character consists of, not the government.

For example: Many people believe gambling is immoral. I myself am not a gambler, but I don't think it's an immoral act. It may become an immoral act if taken to extremes though. If a man gambles away his family's grocery money, it certainly becomes an immoral act. However, if he gambles away discretionary income while fulfilling his personal responsibilities, it's *not* an immoral act. It may be a waste of money, it may be stupid, but should wasting money and being stupid be outlawed?

The same goes for drinking alcohol, taking drugs, prostitution…etc. These are all personal moral issues and should be out of the realm of government legislation. Please remember there's a difference between *these* types of behavior, and behavior such as murder, theft, fraud…etc. In the latter cases of behavior, freedom is being taken away from someone. In the former cases of behavior, nobody's freedom is being taken away. This is truly what it all comes down to. When you take away another's freedom, you're taking away their ability to choose, and when you take away another's ability to choose, you take away *any* chance for morality.

In a political context, this is the difference between being *governed* and being *ruled*; and over the last century, Americans have lost their ability to distinguish between the two. A good government *governs*, a bad government *rules*. A good government *governs* by protecting everyone's right to live their life as they choose; a bad government *rules* by either taking away your right to live your life as you choose, or by letting others take away your right to live your life as you choose. A good government *governs* by maintaining equality under the law; a bad government *rules* by taking away equality under the law by passing legislation that benefits one citizen at the expense of another citizen. A good government *governs* by making sure all of its citizens know that *justice* will be served; a bad government *rules* by maintaining a legal system of *injustice*. A good government *governs* by passing objective laws that protect innocent citizens from criminals; a bad government *rules* by passing subjective laws that protect criminals from being held accountable by innocent citizens. A good government *governs* by protecting the productive from the un-productive; a bad government *rules* by forcing the productive to pay for the unproductive. Americans are now *ruled*, not *governed*!

So, getting back to economic and personal freedom, which is more important? Although they are both equally important in relation to morality, economic freedom is more important because it's the more practical. When you look at economic freedoms alongside of personal freedoms, it becomes obvious why economic freedom is more important. Let me give some examples.

There have been many laws passed over the years that take away personal freedoms. For a quick example, just look at laws against various sex acts between consenting adults. In many states, anal and oral sex are still against the law. But how is the government going to charge you with this "crime," let alone prove it, without using the other person involved as a witness? Thus, the crime is virtually unenforceable. Whatever people do in their own bedroom is between them. To think that they're only going to have missionary-position sex because all other forms of sex are prohibited is ridiculous. The government can pass all the laws it wants concerning sex, but it really affects people very little (except of course for the economic cost of trying to enforce such idiotic laws).

How about gambling? Once again, it's going to be hard for the government to stop people from gambling because it will take somebody in the gambling circle as a witness. So unless it's done in a public place, there's really no way to stop citizens from gambling. If my friends and I get together for a night of poker, the fact that there is a law against it means absolutely nothing. So on the practical side, it really has no affect on 95% of gamblers.

The same goes for most other types of personal freedoms as well. The fact that unconventional sex, gambling, prostitution, drugs, or any other "crime" consenting adults participate in is against the law, really doesn't mean much to the 95% who participate in such behavior—because 95% of the time the government has no way of proving, or even knowing, who's doing it. 95% of the time these crimes go undetected. Once again, I'm not saying that these are moral behaviors, only that people have the right to participate in them if they choose to; and that it's a complete waste of time, money, and resources for the government to attempt to stop people from participating in such behavior *knowing* it's only going to catch a small percentage of those involved.

Now let's look at *economic* freedom. Unlike personal freedom issues, economic freedom issues are easily detectable and enforceable by government. Take something like the Automatic Income Tax Payroll Deduction. If I'm not born into wealth, I'm probably going to have to get a job. And when I do get a job, the company I work for will take a portion of my earnings to give to the government *before they even pay me*. There's really no way for me to get around paying it. So in essence, if I want to eat, I'll *first* have to pay. This includes such things as Social Security, Medicade, Medicare and various other programs that take away economic freedom in favor of some form of egalitarian "societal good." But is this so-called "societal good" an *actual* good? Hardly. Of course there's a feeling of security people get when they *believe* (not *know*) they're going to be taken care of when they retire, but that feeling of security is far outweighed by the loss of economic freedom and personal responsibility forfeited by the individual.

In my own case, the government steals roughly $160.00 a week from my earnings because it's assumed I'm too stupid, ignorant, or just plain lazy to save for my own retirement. Do I have a choice in the matter? No. Could I do better investing the money than the government? IT DOESN'T MATTER! I, like everyone else, should have the freedom to choose for myself—PERIOD! If some people can't handle the realities of every day life, and of growing older, and they *choose* to join some form of collective, fine, they should join. But don't stick a gun to *my* head and force *me* to join. Don't take away *my* freedom because *you* can't handle it!

I would also like to ask a question concerning Social Security. I just received my latest statement and have realized something: The money I've paid in Social Security could've already paid off my home. That's right, my second biggest financial obligation (after taxes of course) could've been paid off by the time I was forty! Think about what kind of security that could've brought me. Would I be more "secure" having my second biggest monthly payment *paid in full*, or by having a small retirement fund in my name that I may or may not receive in the future? In my opinion, there's not even an argument. Of course *you* may feel differently, but why should *you* have the freedom to choose but not *me*?

There are many more cases like these, but I think just those two examples alone prove why economic freedom is more important than personal freedom (the only possible exception being that of free speech). I'm also not saying *all* Republicans are for economic freedom, or that *all* Democrats are for personal freedom. There are many variations of thought among individuals, and the lines are becoming more blurred all the time. Only that, in general, they fall on those sides of the issue. Amazingly, they both live under the delusion that *they* are pro-freedom, while the *other* is anti-freedom, but in reality, *both* are anti-freedom.

In modern America, the entire Democratic philosophy can be summed up in a single sentence: 'Give a man a fish and you feed him for a day, but teach him how to steal the fish of others through the voting process, and you feed him for a lifetime'. Obviously, Democrats believe in the *false* "economic equality" theory of freedom. Democrats believe stealing is perfectly justifiable *and moral* as long as 51% of the voting population agrees to it—which of course usually means less than 25% of the entire population.

The entire *Republican* philosophy can also be summed up in a single sentence: 'People should have the freedom to do whatever they want with their life—as long as *we* believe it's moral'. As long as you're living your life in a manner Republicans agree with, they'll let you live it. But if you cross the line into what they believe to be wrong or immoral, they'll use the power of the government to attempt to stop you. So in essence, if freedom doesn't coincide with what they believe to be moral, they'll simple ignore the entire concept of freedom.

Another way to look at it is that Democrats value freedom over responsibility, while Republicans value responsibility over freedom. Democrats want people to be as free as possible—even if that means not holding them accountable for their actions, *and* forcing others to pay for the consequences of those actions. Republicans, on the other hand, hold responsibility as such a high value that they're willing to sacrifice freedom. Neither political party seems to understand that freedom and responsibility are opposite sides of the same coin, and that in the long run, one cannot be sacrificed for the other without sacrificing both.

And yet another way to look at it is that Republicans want government to be our daddy, while Democrats want government to be our mommy. Of course this doesn't apply in every single case, but in terms of a general overall philosophy, it applies perfectly. Republicans want government to be a moral authority figure. Like the father of our youth, they want government watching over us with the rod of punishment to make sure we act correctly in the personal realm. Of course this is how it should be when we're children, but once we're adults, we're adults, right? As children and adolescents, we simply cannot make most ethical decisions for ourselves because we don't have a large enough base of knowledge and understanding to do so. But once we become adults, it's our own personal responsibility to do so, not the governments.

Illicit drugs would be a good example here. It's our parents responsibility, when we're children, to lay down the law when it comes to using drugs. Drugs can destroy the mind and arrest mental development; therefore, it's a parent's responsibility to keep their kids off drugs. But is it the government's responsibility to do such things for adults? No. If it's up to the government to stop people from hurting themselves (or I should say *potentially* hurting themselves), why haven't Republicans been working to outlaw lying, cheating, smoking, obesity, dangerous sports, drinking of alcohol, excessive use of prescription drugs, gambling, or a million other harmful, or potentially harmful, behaviors? These behaviors can be *proven* to be as destructive as drugs, prostitution or other "crimes" between consenting adults, so where's the cry for new legislation from Republicans?

As *adults* we have the *right* to engage in harmful, or potentially harmful, behavior *as long as* that behavior *is not* physically affecting others in society whom don't want to be involved. If a man smokes marijuana in his own home, it's none of the government's business—period! But if the man smokes marijuana and gets into his car and drives on public roads, it becomes the government's business. If a man wants to pay a woman for sex, and the woman freely accepts, it's none of the government business—period! But it must be done on one or the others *private* property. If done on *public* property, then and only then, does it become governments business. If a group of men meet at a friend's home to spend the night gambling, it's none of the governments business—period! But if force or fraud becomes a part of the game, then and only then, does it become government's business. If two or more people get together to have sex, regardless if it's oral sex, anal sex, missionary position sex, or up-side-down backwards sex, it's none of the governments business—period! But if it's done in public, or if one is *forced* to participate, then and only then, does it become governments business. Only *after* the threat of force or harm takes place is the government obliged to take action, never *before* it takes place. That's what individual rights are all about.

And once again, I'm not saying any of these behaviors are moral, only that it's up to the *individual* whether or not he or she is going to participate in them. And remember, just because you have the *right* to do these things, doesn't mean you *should* do these things. Patrick Henry addressed this point perfectly when he said; "He who does not govern himself wisely will be governed by despots. The greatest way to lose our liberties is to exercise our freedom irresponsibly." I couldn't agree more!

I guess about now your probably thinking: "Ok Mr. Smarty pants, if I can't vote for Republicans because they're immoral for taking away *personal* freedom; and I can't vote for Democrats because they're immoral for taking away *economic* freedom: who am I suppose to vote for? Who'll allow me *complete* freedom so I can be as moral as I can be, and others can be as moral as they can be? Is there any political party that will give me *both* economic & personal freedom"? Yes there is: The Libertarian Party. The Libertarian party is the *only* political party that believes human beings have the *right* to both economic & personal freedom, or in others words—freeliberty. But it needs to be pointed out that allowing others the freedom to live their lives as they choose is only one part of being moral. Just because a person is a Libertarian *does not* make them a moral person. They can be as immoral as the next guy. But what separates the Libertarians from other political parties is the fact that they believe every human being has the *right* to both economic & personal freedom; which means they will not initiate force against other citizens to achieve political ends. So at least in the political realm, they cannot be evil. Being evil and being immoral are not one in the same. Being evil is much worse than simply being immoral. Being evil, in the political sense, begins with the initiating of force. Both Republicans and Democrats basic political philosophy begins with being evil; they both believe might makes right; they both believe that the way to solve problems is with the force of government; they both believe that without forcing humans to act as they want them to act, society would fall apart i.e., they both ultimately reject persuasion in favor of brute force. And as I have already shown, the initiation of force is the antithesis of morality.

But *would* society "fall apart" if the government stopped initiating force against its own citizens? Hardly. In fact, it would flourish. And the first 125 years of this country bears that fact out. Before the American government started using the initiation of force against its own citizens as a matter of public policy, Americans had created the highest standard of living in the world. True freedom will do that. To think everyone would just sit back and watch as our society fell apart is ridiculous. The only reason we're still a great nation at this point in history is because we're living off the inertia of our past freedoms. And that's why we need to get back to a Libertarian form of government. Since the initiation of force would be banned if the government was run by Libertarians, evil (at least in the political sense) would cease to exist. Of course some *individuals* in government would still commit acts of evil, but at least the *government itself* wouldn't be committing acts of evil as a matter of public policy.

Since Libertarians are the only political party that prohibits force as a means of dealing with others, they are the only political party that allows morality to exist on all fronts. Since liberty for all is their only guiding principle, they believe people have the right to be immoral if they choose to be immoral, but they *do not* have the right to force their immorality on others. You see, that is *precisely* what freedom is all about. If human beings have the *right* to "Life, Liberty, and the Pursuit of Happiness," then they have the *right* to be wrong, they have the *right* to make mistakes, they have the *right* to commit acts that are harmful, or potentially harmful, to themselves. But once again, they *do not* have the right to commit acts that are harmful to others (acts of evil).

In essence, Libertarians are the only political party whose members understand that morality is based on choice, choice is based on freedom, and therefore, morality is based on freedom. Like the founding fathers before them, Libertarians believe *all* humans have the *right* to life, liberty, and the pursuit of happiness; which means the right to self-determination; the right to self-actualization; the right to self-realization; the right to self-defense…etc. In other words, the right to live your life as you choose—unobstructed by others in your society, or by an all-powerful government. But they also understand that *everyone else* possesses these rights as well. And that, as much as they may disagree with another's choices, they *do not* have the right to make those choices for them; they *do not* have the right to infringe on anyone else's right to life, liberty, and the pursuit of happiness; and most importantly, they *do not* have the right to hire the government to violate anyone else's rights for what *they* believe to be a good, or just, cause.

Human beings have the right to seek happiness in any manner they choose *as long as* they are not violating another human being's right to do the same— period! If someone seeks happiness through religion, through philosophy, through exercise, through family, or even through sex, drugs, and rock n roll, *they have that right*—no matter how much you or I may disagree with their decision; no matter how much you or I can prove to them drugs are not the path to happiness; no matter how much they may harm themselves in the long run, they have the *right* to be wrong—period! Let me give a quick example coming from my own perspective.

After reading the next chapter it will become obvious that, overall, I don't see religion as a positive force in human relations. As a matter of fact, you'll see that I think religion in general is not only immoral at times, but evil as well—and I can prove it. But even though this is the case, it doesn't give me the right to stop people from practicing any religion they choose to practice. And it certainly doesn't give me the right to take my evidence to the government and lobby to have another man's religion outlawed. No matter how much I think religion destroys a human being's ability to use their mind effectively, I have no right to vote away *their* right to hamper *their* mind if they choose to do so; I have no right to stop them from hurting themselves; I have no right to stop them from living in their self-imposed mental mousetrap. If I want freedom for myself, I must grant others freedom. If I want justice for myself, I must grant others justice. And if I want to be left in peace, I must grant others peace. It really is that simple.

So what it all comes down to is that the Libertarian Party is the only political party that will grant *everyone* freeliberty. Although there are some things in the official Libertarian platform that I disagree with, they're still the only political party that will leave people alone to live their lives as they choose, and this is why I will continue to vote for them unless, or until, there's a better choice. So let me give an admittedly overly simplistic, yet accurate analogy as to why you should vote for them as well.

To begin with, imagine for a moment that you decide you want to be a sheep farmer. Next, imagine that you're looking for a place to locate your farm. After all, you must live somewhere right? You have basically three choices: You can live in the midst of wolfs (Democrats), coyotes (Republicans), or deer (Libertarians). If you live in the midst of wolfs, you'll lose roughly 50% of your herd annually because that's what the wolfs will take. If you live in the midst of coyotes, you will lose roughly 40% of your herd annually because that's what the coyotes will take. And finally, if you live in the midst of deer, you won't lose *any* of your herd because deer won't take any of your herd—if you leave *them* alone, they'll leave *you* alone.

So which will it be? I think the choice is obvious. Of course this analogy is overly simplistic, but in essence, it's dead on. Both Democrats and Republicans believe they're entitled to take and (or) re-distribute roughly half of what you produce—and that they're morally justified to use force to get it. After all, they're part of society too aren't they? So don't they have a right to exist—even if it's at your expense? *They* obviously think so. The only difference between the two being the percentage of your income each believes the government is entitled to take and (or) re-distribute.

So what it ultimately comes down to is that both major political parties believe initiating force against others is not only morally acceptable, but a moral imperative. And they believe this because they don't understand the prerequisites that morality is based upon. Whereas libertarians understand that in order to have a moral society, force must only be used in defense and as a last resort, and never offensively and as a first resort (like it is today). Libertarians understand that in order for the government to give, it must first take. Libertarians also understand that to use the power of government to force *one* man to be responsible for *another*, is to destroy all the values that make it possible for human beings to not only prosper, but to survive as well.

You may be saying to yourself right now: "But why should I waste my vote on a Libertarian? After all, they're not going to win anyway." Well, I say why should you waste your vote on a Republicrat? After all, the differences between the two major political parties aren't much more than superficial. Both are for bigger and more intrusive government, the only difference being where and how much it will intrude. This is easily provable by simply looking at the results of the last couple of decades. As the Democrats and Republicans have played musical chairs with the Senate, Congress, and the Presidency, our nation has slipped deeper and deeper into debt. While both political parties have been clamoring over how the government wastes money and needs to be more efficient, our national debt skyrockets. This year's deficit alone (2007) will reach roughly 350 billion dollars, and our total debt will surpass nine trillion dollars—and all the Democrats and Republicans do is blame each other! Roughly twenty years ago our *entire government budget* was less than what our deficit alone will be this year. Not only that, but Americans pay more *just in interest on the debt* than they paid to run the entire government a little over 20 years ago. Americans should be outraged!

Just imagine if you ran your family in this way. The Rebulicrats have turned us, and our children, into lifelong beasts of burden and Americans keep voting for them. I just can't believe it! Every man, woman, and child is indebted to our ever-expanding gluttonous government leviathan for roughly $35,000 each, and roughly 15% of every dollar we pay in taxes now goes to pay *just the interest* on that debt. That's 350 billion dollars per year wasted! And the debt grows by an average of a billion and a half dollars *every single day*! The average family of four, not including their own accumulated debt, owes the government roughly $140,000—and that appears to be the good news! According to an older issue of USA TODAY (10/4/04), the entire government debt obligation for the near future will exceed $53 trillion, or a whopping $470,000 per household! That's per household! Your government's not only ruining your children's future, but your children's children's future as well. The American populous really needs to come to grips with the fact that the Republicrats *are* the problem!

But when you vote for Libertarians, you're voting for the values that made this country the most prosperous in human history: freedom, personal responsibility, justice, unalienable rights, limited government, and equality under the law. When you vote for the Republicrats, you're voting for the same old thing: forced involuntary servitude, irresponsibility, injustice, government granted rights, unlimited government control, and inequality under the law. The actions of the government over the last few decades *alone* bears these facts out.

If you still think you're wasting your vote voting for Libertarians, look at it like this. As far as I know *not one time in history* has the outcome of a presidential, congressional or senatorial race ever been decided by a single vote (this may also be true of state races but I'm not sure). So in essence, on a national scale your *one vote* simply doesn't matter. This is why I always laugh when I hear someone say something like "Although I would like to see Mr. Libertarian become president, I'm not going to vote for him because I'm afraid Mr. Republican might loose to Mr. Democrat if I do." Or the reverse "I'm afraid Mr. Democrat might loose to Mr. Republican if I do"; as if their single vote would make the difference between which Republicrat wins—it's ridiculous! These people bitch and moan about the state of political affairs in modern America, and then turn around and vote for the very people who have caused the problems in the first place. Instead of voting for what they know is right, they vote for the "lesser of two evils"; and if they *know* they're voting for the lesser of two evils when *they know* there's a moral alternative, then they have no moral right to complain; they're getting the exact government they're voting for. And *they* think *I'm* wasting *my* vote?

And it also comes down to the fact that I simply couldn't sleep at night if I knew I was deliberately voting for the lesser of two evils. And at the end of my life I'll know that my vote was never wasted because I always voted, not only for freeliberty, but my conscience as well. I'll know I was not part of the problem, but part of the solution. Will *you* be able to say the same? When America takes the final step (Socialized Medicine) into becoming a stagnating socialist nation, will you be saying "What could *I* do about it"? Or will you stand proud knowing you fought against it? When the greatness of the United States of America is nothing more than a distant memory, are you going to be remembered as a hero who stood up for freedom, or are you going to be remembered as one of the ignorant apathetic masses who claimed they didn't know any better? The way you vote will ultimately determine which. Unlike voting Republicrat, if you vote Libertarian your vote will ultimately make a difference because you'll be one of the early brave few who stood upon principle and steered America back on the path toward freedom. You'll be at the forefront of the paradigm shift back toward the values that made America great in the first place.

What most people just don't seem to understand is that freedom will ultimately win out because it *must* win out—there's no *moral* alternative. If human beings are to not only survive, but prosper as a species, freedom must be at, or near, the top of our list of values. Because as I've already proven: morality is based on choice, choice is based on freedom, and therefore, morality is based on freedom. In order for human beings to *survive* as a species they must *thrive* as a species; and in order to thrive as a species, they must be free. Or as Louis Rukeyser put it: "Ambition and creativity are not cultivated in captivity."

Listen, sooner or later we must be technologically advanced enough to survive whatever nature throws our way: Whether climate destroying asteroids, mega-tsunamis, volcano eruptions, ice ages…etc. Human ingenuity is dependent upon human beings being free to be able to pursue paradigm shifting answers to questions that relate to the betterment and survival of mankind. And at this point in history, at least in the political realm, only the philosophy of the Libertarian party complies with this requirement.

A good example to look at is space exploration. If we're to survive as a species, sooner or later we must colonize space. As a matter of fact, *all* living organisms on earth are dependant upon humans colonizing space for their long-term survival. I hate to be the bearer of bad news, but our sun simply isn't going to last forever. And sooner or later we must be able to get as far away as possible from it in order to survive. And this isn't just my opinion— its fact. As unbelievable as this may sound, I was once talking to a religious man about this and he dismissed what I said and simply replied "God won't allow that to happen." I'm sorry, but if mankind sits around waiting for God to save it, mankind will simply disappear as a species. You can believe whatever nonsense you want, but it will be men of science, not religion, who will ultimately save mankind. But even though what I just said is true, it still doesn't give me (or the government) the right to force anyone to pay for space exploration. It can only be done *morally* through voluntary contributions.

Now I would like to give some common sense advice on how to make politics much simpler for the average person. It's my opinion that many people get frustrated and give up on politics because of how complicated some issues seem to be, but that doesn't have to be the case. Nearly all complex political issues can be broken down by simply thinking about them on a personal level, and then expanding out. I call this Inductive Political Reasoning.

For example: If it's not good on a family level, then it's not good on a state or national level. If it's not good for your family to go into debt, then it's not good for the government to go into debt. If it's not good for your family to waste money, then it's not good for the government to waste money. If it's not good for your family to keep busting its budget, then it's not good for the government to keep busting its budget. If it's not good to allow your family members to get away with lying and manipulating, then it's not good to allow politicians to get away with lying and manipulating. It really is that simple. And it also works on the positive side as well. If it's good for your family to be fiscally responsible, then it's good for the government to be fiscally responsible. If it's good to hold your family members morally accountable, then it's good to hold politicians morally accountable. If it's good to be prepared for *neighborhood* thugs, then it's good for government to be prepared for *international* thugs…etc. Allow me to give a perfect example concerning fairly recent foreign policy.

When Saddam Hussein invaded Kuwait most of the world was outraged—and rightly so. So the world community combined its forces and kicked him out of Kuwait, but was that the end of the story? Of course not. Bullies, whether small time or big time, don't end their ways just because they might lose one fight, they simply find others to bully. In Saddam's case, he just went back to bullying his own people. And as outrageous as this may sound, that was good enough for the world community. In essence, the world community just told this murdering, torturing, sadistic dictator to, in essence "just go home and we'll call it even"—UNBELIEVABLE!

Saddam's downfall came when he agreed to let inspectors into Iraq to make sure he had no weapons of mass destruction, and then reneged on the deal. As soon as he stopped the inspectors from doing their jobs, he became prone to an attack, and of course President Bush took advantage of the opportunity. But my question is: Why was he allowed to remain in power in the first place? This is where Inductive Political Reasoning should have been applied. Suppose your neighbor attacked your home, killed some of your family, stole some of your belongings, and then when the police came, they just told him to go home. Would that be good enough for you? Of course not. So why was it good enough on a world scale? The moment Saddam's troops invaded Kuwait he relinquished any right (if he had any in the first place) to remain Iraq's leader. As a matter of fact, he relinquished any right he might have had to remain a free man. It's bad enough when a leader kills his own people, but when he kills people in other nations, life in prison should be the absolute *least* punishment he should receive by the world community. Anything less would be an absolute travesty of justice. Now, that doesn't mean it was the United States *duty* to invade Iraq, only that it was a morally justified invasion *if* America chose to do so. My point being that, using Inductive Political Reasoning, we can see that what's moral in the *little* picture is also moral in the *big* picture.

So in essence, Inductive Political Reasoning gives us a standard to judge local politics, state politics, national politics, and geopolitical world events. If it's morally justified to bring the perpetrator of a crime to justice when he violates *your* rights, then it's morally justified to bring a political leader to justice when he violates the rights of others as well. It's called being consistent. So whenever you're trying to figure out what action your government should take in world affairs, just ask yourself what type of action should be taken if the exact same thing was happening to you. If it's moral on a small scale, it's moral on a large scale; and if it's immoral on a small scale, it's immoral on a large scale. It really is that simple.

But let's look at it from another angle. Instead of using *inductive* type reasoning, let's use *deductive* type reasoning. If you think it's moral for the government to initiate force, then why isn't it moral for private citizens to do so? Remember, I'm not talking about using force in *defending* rights, I'm talking about the government *initiating* force when no ones rights have been violated. When it comes to morality, you cannot have it both ways without being inconsistent or contradictory. Either the initiation of force is moral or it's not; and if it's moral for multiple people to get together to initiate force, then it's moral for an individual to initiate force. So obviously, it's immoral to initiate force on all levels and should not be tolerated by anyone—except for *very limited* legal situations which I'll be discussing in a moment.

Now I would like to address some public policy issues coming from a position that doesn't violate the prerequisites of morality (reason, freedom and intent) or the Universal Code of Conduct (Do not murder, steal, lie or cheat. And treat others the way you want them to treat you. I'll be discussing these principles, along with where they originated, in chapter 6). But please keep in mind that even if some of these actions don't violate the Universal Code of Conduct or the prerequisites of morality, it doesn't necessarily make them moral or even right. It's just a starting point.

I'll begin by pointing out that, politically speaking, any time one citizen is being *forced by law* to supply a material good or service to another citizen, it's an immoral act by the government because no one is entitled to *anything* someone else is *forced* to give. The reason I say "politically speaking" is because I'm speaking in a strictly political context. It's not immoral if the government uses force to secure legal contracts or uphold objective law because in those cases nobody's freedom is being taken away except for the person who had already violated someone else's rights in the first place; in fact, it's the right thing for the government to do. But when the government uses force against a person who *hasn't* violated anyone else's rights (as in a political context such as social security, welfare, minimum wage…etc) it's immoral. This is also where inductive political reasoning can be used. If it's immoral *for you* to take something by force (i.e. steal) then it's immoral *for government* to take something by force (i.e. steal). I'll never understand why this is so hard for most people to understand. I guess it's because politicians have done their very best to keep the issues as complicated as possible in order to remain in office and in power, but that doesn't mean we have to let them get away with it. So let's proceed issue by issue applying our consistent moral standard to issues of public policy.

Socialist Security (that's right, lets call it what it is): Like all so-called "entitlements" Socialist Security was based on good intentions. So obviously it meets the prerequisite of intent. It may also be, or at least argued, that it's a reasonable approach to the problem of making sure the elderly are taken care of in their old age. So it also meets the prerequisite of reason (although it's not reasonable enough for many of us). But even though it meets those two prerequisites, it certainly does not meet the prerequisite of freedom. If people are *forced* to join, then their freedom is being taken away from them; and if their freedom is being taken away from them, it's out of the realm of morality—no matter how reasonable, or how good the intentions seem to be. If I'm not mistaking, I think it was Booker T. Washington who summed this idea up quite nicely when he referred to slavery by saying: "feeding and clothing me is not a good enough excuse for taking away my liberty." I wholeheartedly agree!

Also keep in mind that Socialist Security also violates the second principle of the Universal Code of Conduct. When you forcibly take something from someone who does not want to give it, it's called stealing. It doesn't matter if it's being done "for their own good"; it doesn't matter if 99% of the people vote for it; it doesn't matter if "society" thinks it's a good thing to do—stealing is stealing. If we're going to be honest with ourselves we should *at the very least* begin by admitting that *it is* stealing and go from there. Just because the majority has been psychologically conditioned not to see it as stealing, doesn't change the fact that it is. When the average recipient gets back everything he paid into it within the first 5 years of collecting, and is on program for an average of 15 years, where does he think that extra ten years of money is coming from—The Tooth Fairy?

I would also like to point out that, even if it could be argued that Socialist Security has done more good than bad for society at large (which it cannot), it's still not *moral* public policy. The end *does not* justify the means. If it does, then there's no way of having any type of consistent moral standards. If the end justifies the means, then principles, values and virtues are thrown out the window. *Freedom* cannot be a value because it should be taken away at any time, or for any reason, for what 51% of the population believes to be a "social good." *Honesty* cannot be held as a virtue because sometimes it may get in the way of achieving a so-called "social good." And *integrity* cannot be held as a virtue because it can also get in the way of what the majority may consider a "social good."..etc. Principles, values and virtues are things we live by in order to live a successful, consistently moral life. If the end justifies the means, they're not only meaningless, but worthless. Socialist Security *by its very nature* violates everyone's "Right to Life, Liberty, and the Pursuit of Happiness" if they are *forced* to join—period! And that is why it's immoral.

All other so-called "entitlements" can be thought of in the same moral light as Socialist Security; as being in the realm of "good intentions", but none the less, still immoral because freedom is being sacrificed at the alter of a short-term so-called social good. The reason I say a "short-term" social good is because that's exactly what it ends up being. Once the government becomes involved in social problem solving, it becomes entrenched in a status quo system that doesn't *solve* problems, but perpetuates itself. Whether we're talking about welfare, medicade, medicare, subsidized housing, food stamps…etc, doesn't matter. When you create hundreds of thousands of full-time bureaucratic government jobs to fix problems that are better fixed in the private sector, you're setting up a paid middleman who uses up the precious resources it receives because, simply put, *that's it's very nature!* Instead of actually *solving* the problems they were intended to solve, these bureaucracies turn into nothing more than self-perpetuating entities who's jobs are not to solve the problem they were set up to solve, but to keep themselves employed and empowered. If they actually solved the problem, they would put themselves out of work! For most of us, this is just common sense. However, for those employed in the 'good intentions government business', their very livelihood, integrity, and self-esteem is based on them avoiding this fact. Upton Sinclair hit the nail on the head when he said: "It is difficult to get a man to understand something when his salary depends on him not understanding it."

This is why, whenever possible, good intentioned work should be done in the private *voluntary* sector, and not the public *compulsory* sector. People who do voluntary charity work come from a completely different paradigm. Since their subsistence doesn't depend on hordes of people being in need or in poverty, they're much more likely to come up with solutions that will actually work to help needy people in the long term and not just in the short term. It really is common sense (or at least used to be). Who is more likely to end poverty? Hundreds of thousands of volunteers who deal with the needy on a charitable face to face level every day, or hundreds of thousands of government paid bureaucrats who's very livelihood is dependant on people being in need? The answer is obvious.

I would also like to give another reason why private charity should prevail over compulsory government programs. When government bureaucracies took over work that used to be done by private charities, it took away one of the greatest experiences human beings can ever have—the feeling of joyful benevolence one gets when they help others in need. Give an impoverished family a turkey dinner at Thanksgiving, a poor girl a doll at Christmas or a poor boy a bicycle in the spring, and you'll know exactly what I mean. There aren't many things that make you feel as good. Of course people can still be involved with local charities, or give to the needy even if government is doing it; but history has proven that when human beings think the government is taking care of the needy, they're much less likely to get involved; and they're also much less likely to think there really are people out there in need. But even more than that, when nearly 50% of a person's income is being legally plundered by the government, there's not much left over for people to give.

And then of course there are other good intentioned laws that are passed for social engineering such as Affirmative Action, minimum wage, the 40 hour work week…etc. But these also don't fit into our criteria for what's moral because the government is forcing businesses to comply with these good intentioned programs as well. And by forcing them, it's taking away freedom; and by taking away freedom, it removes them from the realm of the moral. But it also creates an environment of resentment among those who are being forced to do something that they think is none of the government's business in the first place, and is at times, even immoral. For example, what kind of government tells its citizens something is immoral, and then turns around and tells them to do it anyway? In essence, that's what Affirmative Action does. It tells people that the way to end discrimination is by discriminating; it tells people that the way to fight racism is by means of racism; it tells people that the way to right a wrong, is to use a wrong to make it right; it tells people that the way to make things fair for some people, is to make things unfair for other people; it tells people that because some people are the victims of racism, it's morally acceptable to allow the victims to victimize others by using government mandates that are based on the ability to discriminate based on race; it tells people two wrongs make a right; it tells people that the way to make up for injustices committed on people in the past, is to commit injustices on people in the present—and all of these things are blatantly wrong and immoral. If discrimination based on race is wrong, then it's wrong. You simply cannot have it both ways. But as usual, the government, and proponents of Affirmative Action, attempt to anyway. Allow me give a perfect modern-day example.

As of this writing (2006) there's a battle going on in Michigan over whether or not to keep allowing race (Affirmative Action) to be used as a criteria for hiring government employees, college admissions…etc. The overwhelming majority of Michigan voters want to get rid of Affirmative Action, but the overwhelming majority of special interest groups want to keep it. These special interest groups are so enamored with keeping it that they're doing everything in their power to keep it completely off the ballet so people won't even get a chance to vote on it—even though there were more signatures collected to put it on the ballet than any other proposal in Michigan history!

Anyway, there's been numerous protests by University of Michigan students who want to keep the policy of Affirmative Action because they believe (wrongly) it's the only way to rectify past injustices. As I watched these protests on television, and read about them in local newspapers, it hit me: if these protesters are so concerned with "social justice" then why don't *they* simply give up *their* spot at the university? I mean, it's the perfect solution, right? By doing this, *they* can put their money where their mouth is (in other words, be consistent in applying their values); their spots would then go to people who are now benefiting from Affirmative Action; and the people who were kept out in order to make room for the Affirmative Action applicants can attend as well. This way, no injustices will be committed against anyone. Perfect solution, right? Fat chance!

The problem here lies in the fact that the protesters who act as though they're so concerned about "social justice," only want it applied *if it doesn't affect them*—what hypocrisy! They clamor about the importance of "diversity," but of course only if it's applied to others and they're watching safely from the sidelines. It seems to me the only "diversity" Affirmative Action proponents want is the diversity to live by one set of standards while the rest of society is forced to live by another. Sorry, but it just doesn't work that way.

I would also like to point out that the very people who claim to value diversity, only seem to value it if it has to do with "multiculturalism" and skin color. In essence, they only seem to see things through skin-colored glasses. When it comes to *the most important aspect* of diversity there is, the diversity of ideas, the silence is deafening. As long as American Universities remain monopolistic bastions of liberalism, they're all for "diversity" when it comes to other, less important, issues of diversity.

Since I'm on the topic of Affirmative Action, I guess this would be a good time to take a look at the morality of Civil Rights. My problem with the Civil Rights Act of 1964 lies in the fact that, if government would've just followed the principles set forth in The Declaration of Independence and The Constitution, the Civil Rights Act wouldn't have been necessary in the first place. After all, all blacks wanted was to be treated equally under the law. If they would've stood up for their unalienable rights, instead of so-called civil rights, I would've had no problem with it.

The problem with *civil rights* lies in the fact that, in many cases, they take away the freedom of others. It's one thing to demand equality concerning government policies, it's quite another to demand people in the private sector treat you equally. It's one thing for the government to stop you from riding in the front of a public bus, using a public restroom, drinking at a public drinking fountain, going to a public school...etc. It's quite another for a private citizen to stop you from riding on *their* privately owned bus, using *their* privately owned restroom, drinking from *their* privately owned drinking fountain, going to *their* privately owned school...etc. If a bigot only wants white people to eat at his privately owned restaurant, that's his prerogative— period! Do I think it's moral? Do I think it's right? Do I think he's an idiot? No, no and yes. But in a free society a person has the right to be wrong, the right to be immoral, and the right to be an idiot—that's what freedom is all about. He's not taking away the freedom of an African American; he's exercising his right to do business with who he chooses to do business with. He's simply exercising his constitutional right of association. Do I think he should act in this way? Of course not, but it is his *right* no matter how *wrong* he is.

The Civil Rights movement *began* as a movement to counteract *government* actions, not the actions of private citizens, but along the way, its policies changed. In essence, it went too far. Demanding equality under the law is one thing, but demanding that the government take the freedom of others away because they don't treat you "equally" goes far beyond that. Once again: Morality is based on choice, choice is based on freedom, and therefore, morality is based on freedom. When government takes away freedom, it's taking away the ability to be moral. The more freedom it takes away, the less morality will exist—period!

I would like to make one more point before I move on. Isn't it better to have a free and open society so we know who the racists, bigots and sexists are? In a *free* society these people are easily identifiable by their actions. In the *un-free* society of modern America, these people easily hide themselves among the masses. Either way, they're still there! In a *free* society, we can simply identify them and not support them financially. In the *un-free* society of today, it's hard to identify them, so we support them financially all the time. I would much rather bring everything out in the open so we can make an effort to change the irrational minds of our fellow countrymen rather than keep their true thoughts and feelings hidden behind a wall of ignorance. Positive change can only come about by negatives being exposed, and negatives will only be exposed in a truly free society.

Now let's look at suicide and assisted suicide. Suicide is one of those issues that's so transparently a case of freedom and personal autonomy that, anyone who wants to outlaw it, simply doesn't understand what freedom is. Now once again, don't get me wrong here. I'm not saying people *should* commit suicide, only that in a free society, it's a viable *and* moral choice in some cases. As a matter of fact, this is the most basic of all choices (You know, "to be or not to be? That is the question"). If we have the "Right to life, liberty and the Pursuit of Happiness," we have the corollary right to end ones own life, liberty to end ones own life, and if ending ones life on our own terms is what will make us die happy, the pursuit of how to do it rationally.

For example: If I have only a few months to live, and if my quality of life is miserable, and if my life savings are being depleted, am I going to hang around wearing diapers and drooling all over myself until everything is lost and my loved ones inherit nothing? Hell no! In my opinion, that's one of the stupidest and immoral things I could possibly do. I don't care what religious mumbo-jumbo the majority believes about suicide, they have no right to force me to live by their man-made religious dogmas—period! Just as *they* have the right to believe it's immoral, *I* have the right to think that sometimes it's the moral thing to do. This is a choice that only the individual can make.

I would also like to make another quick point about suicide. I remember when growing up adults use to say that suicide was "selfish," and for whatever reason, that stuck with me until I got older. But once I really started thinking about it, it hit me how wrong that opinion really is. I mean, exactly how can suicide be "selfish" when it eliminates the "self." It's actually the most *self-less* act a human being can commit. It's yet another example of the religious minded twisting the meaning of words around in order to fit into their dogmatic paradigm. But I'll save religion for the next chapter.

So how about *assisted* suicide? Well, it really is quite simple (and this is a universal principle as well): If you have the *right* to do something, then you have the *corollary* right to ask someone to help you do it, or to hire someone to help you do it. If we have the right to commit suicide, then we *must* also have the corollary right to ask for help in committing suicide. Of course that doesn't mean we have the right to *force* someone to help, only the right to ask. If both people freely consent, and if it's made perfectly clear that both people are freely consenting, then the government has absolutely no right to intervene—period!

I like drawing an analogy between assisted suicide and the second amendments right to keep and bear arms. If we have the right to self-defense, then we must also have the corollary right to the means of self-defense. And since at this point in history the most reasonable means of self-defense is a loaded gun, we have the right to own a gun—period! There's simply no way of getting around the logic. Assisted suicide is the same. If we have the right to commit suicide, then we must also have the corollary right to the most rational and humane means of committing suicide. And since doctors probably know what the most humane ways are to commit suicide, we have the right to ask for their help. However, if the doctor doesn't want to help because he believes it's immoral, we have no right to force him to help.

Of course some people will say that there's no right to commit suicide, but they're just plain wrong. Many of these are the same people (and on this point I agree with them) who think it's moral and humane to kill animals that are suffering. Just exactly how they come to the moral conclusion that it's "humane" to put a dog out of it's misery when it's needlessly suffering, but *not* humane to let a human being end his life if he is also needlessly suffering is beyond me. And besides, how stupid is it to think we can actually stop people from killing themselves if that's truly what they want to do. I mean, if someone *really* wants to commit suicide there's no way they can be stopped anyway, right?

Last but not least, let's see if suicide and assisted suicide conform to the three prerequisites of morality, and to the Universal Code of Conduct.

To begin with, are suicide and assisted suicide *reasonable* actions to take under certain circumstances? Absolutely. Of course many people believe they are immoral actions, but that doesn't make them unreasonable actions. There's a big difference between the two. Reasonable people can differ on what they believe to be moral or immoral, but that does not necessarily make one or the other less reasonable. So yes, they both conform to reason.

Next we need to determine if anyone's freedom is being taken away from them. Or rather, is someone being forced to do something they don't want to do? If all the people involved freely choose to be involved, then of course nobody's freedom is being taken away. So yes, it conforms to freedom. But what if the government forces someone to stay alive until a "natural" death takes place? Then freedom *is* being taken away, so the government's actions are no longer in the realm of the moral. It would also be taking away the individuals right to the pursuit of happiness because they wouldn't die happy knowing their last wishes were not fulfilled. So no matter how you slice it, suicide and assisted suicide do not violate the prerequisite of freedom.

The hardest part to determine, as always, is Intent. Does this person think he's doing the moral thing? Does this person think he's doing the right thing? Of course since we're not mind readers we can never know for sure, but I think under the circumstances, they should be given the benefit of doubt, don't you? After all, if they didn't think they were doing the right or moral thing, they wouldn't be doing it would they? So yes, the prerequisite of intent is also met (as best as can be known that is). Since all three prerequisites are met, then suicide and assisted suicide can be considered moral actions under certain circumstances. Plus, neither action violates anyone else's rights, or the Universal Code of Conduct.

Now let's look at sex "crimes" committed between consenting adults— beginning with prostitution. Should prostitution be against the law? No, not if we're going to have a *free* society. It doesn't matter if the majority consider it immoral, what matters is that in a free society people have the right to partake in activities the majority consider wrong or immoral *as long as* those involved are not forcing it on others. In other words, you have the right to be wrong and the right to be immoral, but you *do not* have the right to be evil; because when someone is being evil, they're *forcing* their will on others. Once again, I'm not saying that prostitution is moral, only that it's a matter of freedom and nobody else's business. People have the right to pay for sex if that's what they choose to do. Whether you or I consider it immoral is inconsequential in a free society—period! And since it doesn't violate anyone else's rights, the prerequisites of morality, or the Universal Code of Conduct, people should be allowed to do it without government interference.

And by the way, I have an actual solution to prostitution (at least 95% of it). Just think about the problem logically. I would say that at least 95% of prostitutes do it for the money. And if this is true, then the real culprit is lack of money, right? Well, since the overwhelming majority of Americans call themselves Christians, and Jesus said that in order to be his disciple you must give all your possess to the poor, why don't prostitutes and Christians just get together? This is truly a match made in heaven. If Christians simply did what Jesus told them to do, there would be no need for women to become prostitutes in the first place. But no, they would rather throw them in jail. Just think about how ridiculous this is for a moment. I mean, can a human being sink much lower than becoming a prostitute? You really have to be in some dire circumstances to sink that low don't you think? But instead of *helping* them, we throw them in jail! It's even more ridiculous when you consider how much money we spend trying to stop people from doing something they're going to do anyway. And it's *even more* ridiculous when, even after these women get caught, they're back on the streets plying their trade *the very next day*!

No, I don't think woman should be prostitutes, but I also don't think our politicians should prostitute themselves either, but we allow them to do it all the time. And if you look at the big picture, all the prostitutes in America put together do less damage to our country than just 10% of our politicians whoring themselves out. At least when a prostitute does it, it's at her *own* expense; when elected officials do it, it's at the expense of *every single* American. The immorality of the prostitute is *nothing* compared to the immorality of special interest prostitutes in Washington. She's only selling her *body* for money; they're selling their *soul* and *country* out for money. Which is worse?

If prostitution were legal, it would not only be *safer* for the prostitutes, but *safer* for their clients as well; it would not only be *healthier* for the prostitutes, but *healthier* for their clients as well. But none of that even matters. What matters *morally* is the fact that individual rights are being violated by the government; and if individual rights are being violated by the government, the government is being immoral.

Now, how about laws against sodomy (anal and oral sex)? In my opinion, these laws are the most ridiculous of all. To pass laws based on ignorant religious dogmas created by men thousands of years ago is quite simply one of the dumbest things a nation or state can do. These were the same people who believed the earth was flat, that the sun revolved around the earth, that human beings could live to be nearly 1000 years old, that people who commit adultery should be stoned to death, that lazy drunkard sons should be stoned to death, that women should not be permitted to speak in church…etc. Do I have to go on? I'm sorry to break the news, but a *just* God simply wouldn't punish everyone in a society just because some people are having oral sex. But of course that's exactly what the God of the Bible does by "visiting the iniquity of the father upon the children and the children's children to the third and the forth generation." Just because some religious people may consider any kind of sex, except for procreation, immoral, doesn't mean it is. And it sure doesn't give them the right to hire the government to outlaw it. It's also ridiculous to have these stupid laws on the books because how often are they even enforced? When's the last time you read about someone going to jail because they committed the "crime" of sodomy?

Last but not least, sodomy does not violate anyone else's rights, the prerequisites of morality, or the Universal Code of Conduct in any way. So even if you believe it's immoral, it's none of your, or the government's, business if others are doing it in the privacy of their own homes.

Next let's look at homosexuality and gay marriage. Once again, just because some people, or maybe even most people, think homosexuality is immoral or just plain wrong, doesn't mean it is, or that they have the right to use the government to outlaw it. This is yet another issue of personal freedom and autonomy. And once again, this is yet another one of those ignorant religious dogmas passed down through generations because people actually believed God would punish everyone for the so-called "sins" of the few, but of course this is ridiculous if you believe in a *just* God.

I'm also amused when a right wing religious fundamentalist resorts to the silly "God created Adam and Eve, not Adam and Steve" argument. How childish. But let's run with it anyway. Ok then, if God created Adam and Eve and not Adam and Steve, then who created Steve? I thought we were all created in Gods image and by God? Well apparently some human beings weren't created by God. So who created them?

And when it comes to gay marriage, what's the big deal? So what if two men or two women want to get married, who does it hurt? It simply amazes me that people are so freaked out over such a non issue. After all, it's my understanding that only about 5% of the population is gay. And if this is true, then let's say half of them want to get married. So here we are at the beginning of the 21st century passing legislation that's intended to effect maybe 2% of the entire population who aren't even hurting anyone else? Give me a break! If two men or two woman get married, it violates nobody else's rights in anyway whatsoever—period! That's why they have the right to do it.

Now they're trying to pass the so-called 'Marriage Protection Act' legislation. But please tell me exactly how two people of the same sex getting married "destroys" marriage? Exactly how is this legislation going to "protect" *my* marriage? Or even *yours*? It's yet more meaningless political posturing. Now, if you *really* want to protect the sanctity of marriage, then only allow people to get married one time. After all, isn't this what their God Jesus taught? Didn't he say that when people got married they became one? And that no man could separate what God brought together? Maybe they need to actually read the book they're supposed to believe in. But of course legislation will never be passed limiting marriage to only one time, will it? And why not? Because many of the people supporting the so-called 'Marriage Protection Act' are on their second, third, and even forth marriages! If they think marriage is so "sacred" why do they do it so many times? *They* are destroying the sanctity of marriage all by themselves (and by the way, I would never support any type of legislation limiting the number of times someone can get married. People have the right to get married as many times as they wish, that's called freedom. I just brought it up to show the hypocrisy).

There's also one more thing you should think about. In case you didn't know, only a few short decades ago interracial marriages were illegal in many states as well. And the Supreme Court itself didn't stop that nonsense until 1967. And guess what, the same type of arguments that were being used then to fight interracial marriage, are being used now to fight Gay marriage. So please keep that in mind when considering this issue.

Last but not least. Even though many (if not most) people are against same sex marriage, they have no right to stop others from doing it because it doesn't violate anyone else's rights, the prerequisites of morality, or the Universal Code of Conduct. They may believe it's wrong, they may even believe it's immoral, but they still have no right to hire the government to stop others from doing it.

Now let's take a quick look at Polygamy. As with Gay marriage, even if most people are against it, it should be the choice of the individuals involved. If one man wants to marry two women, so what? If one woman wants to marry two men, so what? If one man and three women want to get married, so what? As long as everyone involved does it of their own free will, it's nobody else's business—period! It doesn't mean I think it's moral, it doesn't mean *you* think it's moral, it only means *the people doing it* think it's moral.

The amazing thing to me is the fact that people actually believe that if there's a law against polygamy, people won't participate in the polygamist lifestyle—give me a break! Anyone who has the inclination to have multiple wives isn't going to really care if they can get married *legally* or not—they're still going to do it. It's not as if these people are going to say to themselves: "O golly gee, since we can't get married, I guess we can't live together either." An official piece of paper or not—they're still going to do it. So even if you believe it's morally wrong, it's still going to take place whether you like it or not. And if nobody's getting hurt, what business is it of yours anyway?

And if you believe it's morally justifiable to stop multiple people from getting married, then isn't it also morally justifiable to stop multiple people from living together *as if* they were married? It seems to me, if you want to involve the government in order to stop one practice, to be consistent, you must involve the government in order to stop the other as well. If it's such an important moral issue, how can we allow either, right?

Of course opponents will next argue: "Well, where will it all end? Are we next going to allow human beings to marry animals"? Now, this is where it really begins to get ridiculous. Of course human beings cannot marry animals—marriage implies consent. If a being cannot consent, it cannot get married—period! I know this is going to sound far out, but just imagine for a moment that other intelligent life forms exit out there somewhere besides human beings. And let's say in the future a human being and one of these life forms fall in love and want to get married. Should they be allowed to get married? Of course they should. *Consent* is the only thing that really matters. Sure, this scenario is way out there, but so what? It still illustrates that *mutual consent* is the only thing that really counts when it comes to marriage.

Last but not least, polygamy doesn't violate the rights of others, the prerequisites of morality, or the Universal Code of Conduct. Therefore, like it or not, it should be left up to the moral discretion of the individuals involved and no one else.

Now let's look at a topic that's so taboo that it rarely ever gets discussed: the selling of body organs. Every single year thousands of human beings die in America because selling body organs is prohibited—it makes absolutely no sense at all. Here we have human beings dieing by the thousands because we don't have enough people donating their organs; and why don't we have people donating their organs? Simple, because they get nothing for doing it. *Every single person* involved in the process of organ donation (doctors, hospitals, the recipient…etc) profit from this procedure except for the person who gives the most, the donor! What kind of a screwed-up system is this? If the families of deceased loved ones received some financial compensation for the donation, most people would sign up immediately. As a matter of fact, there would no longer be a waiting list. It would actually create an abundance of available organs; which in turn would lower costs; which in turn would save even more lives. It's a win-win situation for everyone involved. So why isn't it being done? Simple, because society is stuck in the ancient, nonsensical, illogical, immoral, backward paradigm of altruism instead of self-interest when it comes to the selling of body organs.

People seem to believe that giving body organs is such a noble thing that anyone who would even think of selling theirs is a greedy, selfish, immoral low life, but this notion is ridiculous. Why is it immoral for a person to want their family to get some financial compensation if they die? Is it better for a poor family who might have just lost their main source of income to get nothing and go on welfare? And what if they don't have insurance? Is it better that they get absolutely nothing, or to get maybe 5 or 10 thousand dollars for their loved ones healthy heart or lungs? The doctors are making thousands of dollars from the operation; the hospitals are making tens of thousands of dollars from the operation; and the recipient is getting something that is truly priceless—the gift of life. So why doesn't the person who makes *the whole operation possible* get anything? It's ridiculous! In a free society people have the right to sell their body organs if they choose to do so. And as long as everyone involved (patients, hospital, doctors…etc.) *choose* to be involved, it's none of the governments business! At this point in history the government might not recognize it as a right, but in time it will, because it certainly is.

As for myself, I would love to donate my organs, but I won't as a matter of principle. The way I look at it is like this: I could donate my organs and maybe save one or two lives, or I can try to bring awareness to this issue and change the system, and in the long-run, save countless numbers of lives. In my not-so-humble opinion, there's not even an argument here. Of course I would donate my organs to a loved one, but that really has nothing to do with this issue. This issue, once again, is all about freedom. And how, once again, freedom can solve problems much better than good-intentioned busy-body government bureaucrat's who obviously haven't given the issue much thought.

Last but not least, since selling ones body organs doesn't violate anyone else's rights, the prerequisites of morality, or the Universal Code of Conduct, people have the right to do it. It's an individual moral choice that no government has the right to impose itself upon—period!

Next let's look at the so-called 'War on drugs'. The war on drugs is yet another good-intentioned government program that is more aptly named the 'War on Rights' or the 'War on Freedom' than it is the 'War on Drugs'. Once again, in a free country people have the right to take any drug they want *as long as* they're not violating anyone else's rights. Does that mean I think it would be moral to do so? Of course not, but there's a lot of things I don't consider moral that are legal. So why don't we outlaw them? If people have the right to hurt themselves, i.e. the right to smoke themselves to death, the right to drink themselves to death, the right to eat themselves to death…etc, they also have the right to ingest whatever drugs they want. Once again, I'm not saying they should, or that it's moral, only that it's their right as long as they're not hurting others.

But let's look at in from another angle. How many innocent lives will be lost, and how much money are we going to spend on this nonsensical war on drugs before we realize what a waste it actually is? It's my understanding that roughly only 7% of drug dealers and users are actually caught. So statistically speaking, the war on drugs is a complete and absolute dismal failure. Wouldn't we be better off using our limited resources to stop dealers from selling to children? With the amount of money we spend trying to stop *adults* from hurting themselves, which is impossible to do, we could probably put an undercover police officer in every school in America. Considering the limited resources we have to work with, wouldn't this be a better use of our money? And consider this: In 1998 there were more people in prison in California *alone* than in Great Britain, France, Germany, Japan, Singapore and the Netherlands combined! And why are there so many people in prison in America? Because of the so-called 'War on Drugs'. It's absolutely ridiculous that over half of our prison population is incarcerated for non-violent illicit drug offenses when there are so many more important crimes and issues to be addressed.

For example: How many thousands of *innocent* people are in prison right now, and how many thousands of *guilty* people are on the streets right now, simply because there is no money for DNA tests? In my opinion, we're spending way too much money trying to stop people from hurting *themselves*, and not nearly enough money stopping people from hurting *others*. We only have so much money, so why aren't we spending it more wisely? We've got to start prioritizing law enforcement based on how much harm is being done to others, rather than on how much harm people are doing to themselves. Or maybe a better way to look at it is to ask yourself: Would I rather live next to a person who smokes pot, gambles, occasionally goes to prostitutes, and commits victimless crimes; or next to a rapist, child molester, murderer, thief…etc? To me, the answer is obvious. And by the way, statistically speaking, you're *already* living next to someone from the first group of people—you just don't know it.

I would also like to ask why, when it comes to the war on drugs, we're outlawing *potential* deaths caused rather than *actual* deaths caused? The last time I saw statistics, roughly 350,000 Americans die each year as a *direct result* of smoking; 100,000 Americans die each year as a *direct result* of drinking alcohol; and less than 4000 Americans die every year as a *direct result* of *all* illegal drugs combined. If saving people from themselves is the responsibility of the government, it's obviously going after the wrong people. Instead of outlawing things that may *potentially* cause death (illicit drugs), why aren't we outlawing things that *actually* cause death (smoking and alcohol consumption)? Once again, statistically speaking it's not even close as to which group kills more Americans. We either have the "Right to Life, Liberty, and the Pursuit of Happiness" or we don't. If we do, then the War on Drugs violates all three rights without exception.

And just look at how much corruption is caused by the War on Drugs. It seems like every week I read about more police officers lining their pockets with drug money or even the drugs themselves. And these are just the cases we hear about. What about all those cases we don't hear about? What about all the officers who never get caught? It's just way too tempting for some of these people. Of course I'm not justifying it, but when you're putting your life on the line every day; when you're seeing that what you're doing isn't even making a noticeable dent in the problem; when you're barely making enough money to live a decent life, but you see scumbags bringing home more money in one week than you make in an entire year, I guess just too many people find it hard to resist taking a little off the top. Of course they shouldn't, but they still do. In my opinion, it's yet another case of good-intentioned government policies *causing* bigger problems than they're actually fixing.

Last but not least, since taking drugs does not violate anyone else's rights, any of the prerequisites of morality, or the Universal Code of Conduct, people have the right to do it—even if you or I think it's wrong and (or) immoral.

Next let's look at abortion, and then second-hand smoke. The reason I like to put these two together is because they're kind of unique based on the fact that they do physically affect another's life. Although I think woman have the right to get an abortion, there's no doubt in my mind that she's ending a life. So I guess the question is: When does the fetus change from being a *potential* human being to being an *actual* human being? People who make the argument that the moment the sperm enters the egg it's a human being, are really being silly in my opinion. Is an acorn an oak tree? Is an egg a chicken? Is an apple seed an apple? Of course not; they're all potentials, but not yet actuals. So the answer that must be determined is: During a pregnancy, at what point in time does the fetus change from being a *potential* human being to being an *actual* human being?

Of course "life" begins at conception, but when do we grant the fetus human rights? Not being an expert in this field, I don't know. But I do know that I have no problem with a woman getting an abortion in the first trimester if she wants too; but then again, I think it's immoral of her to keep doing it as some type of birth control. And on the other end of the spectrum, I think it's not only irresponsible, but immoral for a woman to get an abortion in the latter stages of pregnancy. However, if it's medically needed to save her life, then it's acceptable. As always, it really comes down to what's reasonable in a given situation. I think it's reasonable for a woman who becomes pregnant by accident, or by no fault of her own (faulty contraception, rape, incest…etc), to be able to get an abortion if she chooses too. But I also think it's unreasonable for a woman to wait until she's six months pregnant to get an abortion. Morally speaking, like with everything other issue, every case must be judged on its individual merit.

It's the same with second-hand smoke. Since second-hand smoke can physically affect another's life, we do have a conflict of interest when it comes to rights. Does a person have the right to smoke? Absolutely. But does a person have the right to smoke if it's affecting another person? This answer can only be derived through property rights. If someone is smoking on their own property, or on another's property who allows smoking, then the smoker has the right to do as he pleases. But if the smoker is on another's property who doesn't allow smoking, then he doesn't have the right to smoke—it's that simple. However, the conflict of rights gets much more complicated when we start considering *public* property. When it comes to public property, it really comes down to the vote of the people. However, I would have to say that if smoking is being done on the inside, it may be causing harm to others, so yes it can be banned. But, if it's being done on the outside, I don't think it can be reasonably argued that another person's health is being directly affected. So in essence, as long as they're on private property or outside, people should be free to smoke if they wish to.

As to the government making it illegal to smoke in privately owned places such as bars and restaurants, that's a complete violation of individual rights. If a person or corporation wants to allow smoking in their privately owned establishment, they have that right—end of story! This is a clear-cut case of property rights. Unlike *public* (government owned) property, where all Americans have an equal say in how it is used, what type of rules apply, and where people have no choice but to use it continuously, or even every now and then, people *don't* have to use someone's *private* property. No one is forcing you to go to a bar or restaurant where smoking is allowed; no one is forcing you to go to a hotel were smoking is allowed; no one is forcing you to go anywhere smoking is allowed—just like no one is forcing you to go to someone's private residence. If you don't like how a privately owned business is run, don't go there. There are plenty of other places you can go, so go to them. It's called Freedom and the right of association.

Last but not least, smoking doesn't violate anyone else's rights (exceptions given), the prerequisites of morality, or the Universal Code of Conduct. So yes, people have the right to smoke.

Now let's turn our attention to the Second Amendment and the right to keep and bear arms. In essence, there are four reasons why *all* human beings (not just Americans) have the right to keep and bear arms. In no particular order of importance they are:

#1) Hunting: This category is self-explanatory so I really don't need to go into much detail. In essence, since human beings have the right to attempt to survive, and since sometimes the only way to survive is by hunting, human beings have the right to hunt. And since the most efficient way of hunting at this point in history is with a gun, human beings have the right to own a gun. Or maybe a better way of putting it is: If human beings have the right to hunt (which means to supply one's own food), then they have the corollary right to the *means* of hunting; for instance, a loaded gun. You simply cannot have one without the other.

#2) Self-defense: Until people who want to ban guns come up with a better way of defending oneself against the criminal element, guns will be the overwhelming weapon of choice. If human beings have the right to self-defense (which of course they do), then they must also have the corollary right to the *means* of self-defense—which at this point in history is a loaded gun. Once again, you cannot have one without the other.

#3) Defense against foreign nations: Although most modern Americans don't think of gun ownership in this context anymore, it was extremely important in the past, and may indeed be just as important in the future. Just because America is on top now, doesn't mean it will remain on top. History is full of civilizations that believed they would last forever, but didn't. Just look at it this way. If you wanted to invade other countries, where would you begin: A country like the United States (armed citizenry), or a country like England (unarmed citizenry)? All things being equal, the choice is obvious. After you defeated the English military, the war is over, you win! But if you somehow defeat the American military, the war would be just beginning. A well armed populous has always been an important deterrent for any would-be aggressive nation, and it will continue to be so far into the foreseeable future.

#4) Defense against one's own government: As an American, I find it simply amazing that there are people living in this country who are so ignorant of history that they don't understand this crucial point. The Declaration of Independence confirms this fundamental idea by explicitly stating that when our rights are endangered by our government "it is the Right of the people to alter or abolish it." Having a well armed citizenry helps keep an ever-expanding, rights-violating government in check. It's our last line of defense against the Hitlers, Stalins, and Husseins in our own government.

So until gun grabbers can find ways to guarantee food for all, safety from criminals for all, safety from foreign invasion, and safety from government itself, every human being has the right to keep and bear arms...*even if* that right is not always recognized by the government.

I would also like to make another crucial point here concerning any governmental attempt to ban guns. When the Founding Fathers wrote the Declaration of Independence, The Constitution, and The Bill of Rights; the idea that the government had the power to ban guns was so foreign that I challenge *anyone* the find a *single quote* from a single person of influence of that time period who even mentions such an absurd notion—it cannot be done. The Second Amendment was *actually* written as way to guarantee the American people the ability to defend themselves against their own government and foreign powers; however, it had *nothing* to do with the right to defend oneself against the criminal element, or to hunt food. These rights, along with countless others, were so basic, obvious, and readily understood, the founding fathers would've considered it absurd to even mention things so self-evident.

This was the point Noah Webster was making when he said, once again: "Congress shall never restrain any inhabitant of America from lying on his left side in a long winter's night, or even on his back, when he is fatigued by lying on his right." In other words, it would be ridiculous to even attempt to put on paper all the rights possessed by man. Just for a few examples, think about these:

> -Nowhere in the Constitution does it say you have the right to defend yourself.
> -Nowhere in the Constitution does it say you have the right to get married.
> -Nowhere in the Constitution does it say you have the right to have children.
> -Nowhere in the Constitution does it say you have the right to hunt.
> -Nowhere in the Constitution does it say you have the right to get an education.
> -Nowhere in the Constitution does it say you have the right to drink alcohol.
> -Nowhere in the Constitution does it say you have the right to own a pet…etc.

My point being that many of the most important rights possessed by mankind are not explicitly stated in our founding documents because they fall under the banner of the unalienable "Right to Life, Liberty, and the Pursuit of

Happiness" as expressed in The Declaration of Independence. However, everyone also knew that these rights existed *long before* the Declaration of Independence was ever written. Thus, the unalienable right to keep and bear arms existed long before any government was even in place, and as such, it cannot morally be taken away by any government—no matter what the Supreme Court determines. What it all comes down to is we, as human beings, have the right to defend ourselves—period! And inherent in the right to defend oneself is the corollary right to the means of self-defense, which at this point in history is a loaded gun.

Last but not least, gun ownership does not violate anyone else's rights, the prerequisites of morality, or the Universal Code of Conduct. So yes, people have the right to keep and bear arms.

Now let's look at another currently hot political issue: Flag burning. Flag burning is yet another one of those acts that most of us consider reprehensible and disgusting, but once again, it's nothing more than a matter of property rights. If a person is burning their own flag, they have the right to do so. If they're burning someone else's, they don't. If they're doing it on their own property, they have that right. If they're doing it on somebody else's property, they don't (that is unless they have permission from the owner of course).

And when it comes to *public* property, it's a simple matter of law. For example: When the Supreme Court ruled that flag burning was protected by free speech, it made the correct call. In that particular case, a young man took a flag off a building and burned it while protesting. But instead of going after him for theft, destruction of private property, public endangerment…etc, over-zealous prosecutors went after him for the emotionally charged issue of desecrating the flag. They tried to make political hay and set precedent instead of going after him for laws actually broken. In my opinion this clown got off scot-free because of hubris and political pandering by those on the right. If they would've gone after him for actual laws broken, instead of patriotic zealotry, they could've easily won.

But I look at the whole issue this way. To me, the flag is not only the symbol of our nation, but *the* symbol of freedom. As a matter of fact, I would say that of all the symbols around the world, the American flag is universally recognized as the symbol of freedom more than any other; and the fact that people are still allowed to burn it shows that it really does stand for freedom. If the Supreme Court banned flag desecration they would've been taking away the freedom of the desecrator, which is why it would've been the wrong thing to do.

And since the flag desecrator isn't violating anyone else's rights, the prerequisites of morality, or the Universal Code of Conduct, he has the right to do it—no matter how wrong, immoral or disgusting we believe it to be.

Now let's look at the debate over the term "under God" in the Pledge of Allegiance. Does the term violate the first amendment's ban on government respecting an establishment of religion? Let's read the first amendment to find out: "Congress shall make no law respecting an establishment of religion, or prohibiting the free exercise thereof...etc.." This sentence can be broken down into two parts: the primary and the secondary. The primary states: "Congress shall make no law respecting an establishment of religion." So, if Congress made a law requiring children to attend school (which it did); and if schools promote or require students to say the pledge (which some do); and if the words "under God" are in the pledge (which they are now); then Congress *has* made a law "respecting an establishment of religion," the logic is irrefutable.

The secondary part of the statement reads: "or prohibiting the free exercise thereof." This means the government cannot make laws stopping you from practicing any religion you wish. Put the two parts together and it means the *government* must remain neutral concerning religious beliefs, but each *individual* can believe whatever they wish. It really is that simple. Contrary to the beliefs of many religionists, the secondary part of the first amendment does not negate the primary part of the first amendment.

So in 1954 when the words "under God" were inserted into the pledge, was Congress "respecting an establishment of religion"? Absolutely! But worse than that, it was respecting an establishment of a certain kind of religion: Judeo/Christian Monotheism. Hindus don't believe in a monotheistic God. Buddhist's don't believe in a monotheistic God. Taoist's don't believe in a monotheistic God. Pagans don't believe in a monotheistic God. Atheists don't believe in a monotheistic God. I would even argue that Christians themselves don't believe in a monotheistic God (the trinity). And while I'm at it, the people who wrote the first books of the Bible didn't believe in a single monotheistic God either. Please read it for yourself. They believed there were *many* gods, but they just *followed* one.

Of course "under God" respects an establishment of religion, just look at what President Eisenhower said when it was signed into law during his administration: "From this day forward, the millions of our school children will proclaim in every city and town, every village and rural schoolhouse, the dedication of our nation and our people to the Almighty." He certainly wasn't talking about *Bruce* Almighty was he? Of course not, he was talking about the God of the Bible. If that's not *respecting* an establishment of religion, what is?

But it's also easily proven by just asking a couple simple questions: Would it be alright with Christians or Jews if Congress inserted "under Allah" or "under Gods" into the pledge? Of course not. And why not? Because words have meanings. Whether or not anyone wants to admit it, the term "God" itself implies a certain religious point of view; just like the term "Allah" implies a Muslim point of view. You simply cannot get around that fact. So when congress made a law inserting "under God" into the pledge, made "in God we trust" our nations motto, and put "in God we trust" on American currency, it was *absolutely* respecting an establishment of religion. But worse than that, it wasn't just *respecting* an establishment of religion, it was *establishing* it as well.

This is what the overwhelming majority of Americans don't seem to understand. The Constitution goes *way beyond* just telling the government not to *establish* religion, it tells the government not to even *respect* an establishment of religion—and that requirement is much more stringent. In fact, that's why the way this debate is even referred to is fundamentally flawed and biased toward favoring the religious. *Both* sides mistakenly refer to this part of the Bill of Rights as the "establishment" clause, which places the argument in the context of whether or not the government can *establish* religion. But this is a huge mistake by people who want the government to remain completely neutral when it comes to religion. *They* should refer to it as the "respecting" clause. This would put the argument square on the side of those who want a separation of church and state because as I said earlier: The Constitution goes way beyond just telling the government not to *establish* religion, it tells the government *not to even respect* an establishment of religion; and that requirement is much, much more stringent.

Just think about this. When the founders got together to write the Bill of Rights, the very first thing they debated was the best way to keep government from taking sides in religious affairs. It was *that* important to them. And they could've easily just wrote "congress shall make no law establishing religion" and been done with it. But they didn't, they went much further. They wrote "Congress shall make no law *respecting* an establishment of religion" (emphasis mine). And as I said earlier, that restriction goes way beyond just telling Congress it cannot establish religion; it tells Congress it cannot even *respect* an establishment of religion. If they weren't so adamant about it, why would they go to that extreme? But obviously Congress no longer goes to this extreme because it respects and establishes religion all the time by passing laws that respect and establish religion. And by respecting and establishing *by law* the belief in Monotheism as our nation's official type of religion, the United States government is telling Atheists, Agnostics, Buddhists, Hindus, Taoists…etc, that they are wrong in their beliefs. The United States government has no right, knowledge, or authority to make such a claim or judgment.

Last but not least, the pledge was written by a Baptist Minister *without* the words "under God" in it. So what gave anyone, especially the government, the right to change it in order to conform to their own limited, intolerant, dogmatic point of view? As a writer, I would be outraged if someone in the future took it upon himself to change what I had written to mean (or even imply) something different. If the Minister wanted a reference to God in the pledge, he would've put it in there, after all, he was a Minister! If it wasn't good enough *as it was written* the government should've looked elsewhere for a religious pledge of indoctrination.

Now let's look at prayer in public schools. The reason prayer doesn't belong in public schools is basically for the same reason I've already mentioned—it violates the first amendment. The moment the United States Congress *made a law* forcing children to attend public schools that said prayers, it was "respecting an establishment of religion." It's one thing if a child prays in school on his own accord, it's quite another if the school sets time aside for prayer because then it begins "respecting an establishment of religion." There's simply no way of getting around that fact.

Now, some proponents of school prayer will say that prayers have been in public schools ever since the United States has had public schools, and they would be correct. However, back in those days the United States government (Congress) had nothing to do with public schools. So yes, they did say prayers in public schools, but the day Congress passed laws making education compulsory, was the day it began "respecting an establishment of religion."

One thing that's always amazed me about this issue is the fact that, if a student wants to pray 100 times a day, who can stop him? As long as he's not disrupting the classroom, nobody is even going to notice. So the argument truly isn't about *praying* in public schools, it's about *establishing* prayer as government policy in public schools, i.e., it's about the majority forcing its beliefs on the minority. And speaking of the majority, I would also like to point out that even though the majority in America *call themselves*

"Christian" they certainly don't do what Jesus said to do concerning prayer. According to the Bible, Jesus only said *one* thing about praying: "And when you pray, you are not to be as the hypocrites: for they love to stand and pray in the synagogues and on the street corners, in order to be seen by men. Truly I say to you, they have their reward in full. But you, when you pray, go into your inner room, and when you have shut your door, pray to your father who is in secret, and your father who sees in secret will repay you." So why do Christians insist on turning prayer into a public event? This is yet another case when Christians completely ignore what Jesus supposedly said.

Last but not least, proponents of school prayer argue that as long as the prayer being said is "non sectarian" it's not a violation of the first amendment. Of course this is ridiculous for the same reasons I've already given in the last few paragraphs. But even without those arguments it's still ridiculous. Fact is, there is no such thing as a "non sectarian" prayer. *Every single prayer* comes from some point of view. No matter how it is said it will always leave someone out, or take a side. Any prayer that would even be *remotely* considered nonsectarian would be absolutely meaningless. A truly non sectarian prayer would have to not only have to acknowledge God, but the Gods as well. And what about the Tao? Or Buddhist metaphysics? Once every sect was included, it would be absolutely meaningless to any believer of any particular sect. But if you think you can write a nonsectarian prayer, go for it. I challenge anyone to try.

Now I would like to address the issue of teaching 'Intelligent Design' alongside of The Theory of Evolution in biology class in public schools. To begin with, let's be honest with ourselves here. We all know that Intelligent Design Theory is truly not the real issue. It's simply a feeble attempt to sneak Creationism into the public schools through the back door. In essence, Creationists (i.e., the religious) keep losing their court battles to get creationism taught in public schools, so Intelligent Design was dreamed up as a "viable" alternative. However, since the issue is extremely important, I'll spend a little time on it now.

To begin with, Intelligent Design isn't even a theory. A theory must have *at least some* physical evidence in order to be called a theory, Intelligent Design has none. For example: Evolution is a theory because physical evidence was first observed (Darwin at the Galapagos Islands, fossils, skeletons…etc.) and then the theory was formulated. As far as I know, the only thing Intelligent Design has going for it is its flimsy premise. The basic premise of Intelligent Design is that life is just too complex to have begun on its own. Or as some others have put it: "Life is so complex that the odds against it beginning without being purposefully designed are so great that it would be a statistical impossibility." But if this is true, wouldn't it also be true of the designer? Wouldn't the designer be too complex to exist without a designer? If *life* cannot simply exist by its very nature, and out of a natural process, then neither can the designer, right? Thus, the premise collapses back upon itself. If life *must* have an intelligent designer, then the intelligent designer *must* have an intelligent designer as well. There's simply no way of getting around the logic.

I also have another problem with the so-called "odds" argument. To anyone reading this, what are the odds against *your* existence? If I didn't know you existed (assuming that since you're reading this you exist), I could use the "odds" argument to prove you don't exist. Just think about it. What were the odds against your parents meeting, liking each other enough to have intercourse, and then successfully giving birth to you? Of all the partners, or potential partners, your parents could have mated with, they chose each other. The odds against your being created were overwhelming. And then we must add to the equation the odds of both sides of your *grandparents* meeting, liking each other enough to have intercourse, and then successfully giving birth to both sets of parents. Once again, the odds were overwhelmingly against it. But that's still not good enough, because not only would your parents, grandparents, great grandparents, great great grandparents…etc. have to have gotten together, but every generation of your ancestors as well would've had to meet, like each other enough to have intercourse, and then successfully give birth. If all this is added up, the odds against *your* coming into existence were, as proponents of Intelligent Design put it "a statistical impossibility." But obviously, since you're here, it must have happened. So what's the difference, statistically speaking, in the odds of *you* existing on an individual scale, and *life* existing on a universal scale? I would say the odds are probably pretty equal.

Another problem with the "odds" argument is that it doesn't take enough information into account when determining the odds. Most astronomers think (although it's yet to be proven conclusively) that there are billions of planets in the universe that have all the right conditions for life to exist on them. In other words, they say that, statistically speaking, life *must* exist elsewhere. But they arrived at this conclusion by first studying the ingredients necessary for life (biology), then by studying our planet (geology), then by studying other planets and stars (astronomy)…etc. And only after studying many different branches of science did they come to the conclusion that there are almost certainly billions of planets in the universe that have the capacity to create and sustain life. And how did Intelligent Design proponents come to *their* conclusions? Simple, they began with the belief in God, and then came up with a way to get God into the public schools without officially getting God into the public schools—through "Intelligent Design." They use all the same flawed arguments that theologians have been using forever to "prove" creationism true, but then just simply leave out God the creator, and insert an intelligent designer. Either way, it's not science, and there's no evidence.

You cannot begin, as Creationists and Intelligent Design proponents do, by saying "since evolutionists cannot explain in every minute detail the mechanisms of evolution (how life began, where life began, when life began…etc.), then obviously a designer must have done it." Just because our scientific knowledge at this point in time cannot explain every minute detail, doesn't mean there must be supernatural or super-intelligence behind everything. Are we going to go back to when everything that was unexplained at the time must be caused by God or the Gods? "Yes son, that loud sound you here (thunder) is God expressing his anger." "Yes son, God is mad at us so he's throwing lightning bolts at the earth from heaven." "Yes son, those lights in the heavens are Gods. That one is Jupiter, that one is Mars, that one is Venus, that one is…etc." "Yes son, your mother is sick (a virus) because she sinned against God and she is being punished." "Yes son, the Tsunami that killed over 200,000 people was an example of Gods wrath. After all, didn't you notice that it only struck non Christian, ungodly countries?."..etc. In the past, whenever something was unknown it was simply attributed to God and then dismissed. Only in relativity recent history has mankind turned to its own mind and said "I don't know why, let's use the scientific method to find out."

My next question is: Why aren't the proponents of Intelligent Design Theory arguing in favor of Intelligent *Designers* Theory? The most obvious answer is because they're trying to prove there's only *one* God (Monotheism), and not *many* Gods (Polytheism). But theoretically speaking, multiple designers make a lot more sense than a single designer. To begin with, multiple designers would be members of a species; and if they're members of a species, they violate no laws of nature. On the other hand, if it's a *single* designer, it violates *all* natural laws. Intelligent Design proponents cannot point to a single living being and say "that's the only one of its kind;

there are no others (obviously they cannot use an example of a animal going extinct because *it was* a member of a species). Since they have no examples in nature to point too, their Intelligent "Designer" Theory is significantly less plausible than multiple designers because every single living organism ever observed in nature is, or was, a member of a species. A 'Monospecies', for the lack of a better word, is a contradiction in terms. Or in other words, "monospecies" do not exist. This just shows, once again, that their true agenda is really all about proving monotheism true and nothing more.

Now let's look at it from another angle. What about the limits on the mind concerning the accumulation of knowledge? There's not a single example in nature that Intelligent Design proponents can point to and say "that species has no limits on its ability to accumulate and store knowledge." As far as we know, the human mind is capable of storing more knowledge than any other species. As a matter of fact, no other species even comes close; but look at how limited the human mind is. One person may be extremely knowledgeable compared to other human beings, but the amount of knowledge he possesses is miniscule compared to the knowledge mankind has accumulated overall. One knowledgeable man may be able to build or invent something on his own, but that invention was the end result of a series of knowledge accumulating events strung together over vast amounts of time. A book cannot be written without language; algebra cannot be learned without first learning about numbers; an engine cannot be built without the knowledge of how to forge steel…etc. In essence, most of the knowledge we possess is based upon the accumulated knowledge of others.

Or it can be looked at like this. A doctor may be extremely knowledgeable about the human body, but that doesn't mean he can tell you what ails a cat; a heart surgeon may be able to operate to save the life of a human, but that doesn't mean he can operate to save the life of a dog…etc. My point being that it's the accumulation of knowledge from multiple minds over great lengths of time that's responsible for most of what we now know. So theoretically speaking, which is more plausible: A single designer with a mind that was capable of storing unlimited amounts of knowledge, who then used that knowledge to design every single living organism on earth; or multiple minds that specialize in particular areas of "life" knowledge who design just a piece of the life puzzle—with the end result being all life on earth? From a purely *scientific* viewpoint, the answer is obvious. There's absolutely nothing that's ever been observed that falls under the first category, but we know by how humans accumulate and disseminate knowledge that the second category is not only possible, but we see it happen *every single day.* Now, do I believe this is how life on earth began? Of course not. However, at least with multiple designers we're not violating any natural laws and it conforms to reality as we know it to be. Thus, Intelligent Designers Theory should become the standard among Intelligent Design proponents. But will it? Of course not. It won't because Intelligent Design proponents are out to prove the existence of God, not Gods.

I would also like to address another point concerning Intelligent Design. Intelligent Design proponents say that if you look at life on a microscopic level, it's so complex it must have been intelligently designed. But the problem with this line of thought is that just about *everything* looked at on a microscopic level looks like it was intelligently designed. If it didn't, it wouldn't make sense. Just look at some viruses at a microscopic level. Or better yet, look at a snowflake. If you were able to show someone living a few centuries ago what a snowflake looked like up-close, and if they didn't know what it was, they would swear it was man-made because many look too complex and symmetrical to be a natural phenomenon. It just doesn't seem like something that looks so complex, beautiful, and symmetrical could have come into existence naturally, but we *know* they do. We *know* they were "designed," built, and brought into existence by a natural process and not by an intelligent designer. So if we see complex things or systems occur all the time in nature, and by a natural process, why should we attribute a designer to the ones we don't yet fully understand? That wouldn't be scientific, would it?

In essence, science is science and beliefs are beliefs. No matter how Intelligent Design proponents (i. e. Creationists) try to wrap up their beliefs in the guise of scientific terms, they are still only beliefs. And unsubstantiated, unverifiable, unprovable beliefs simply don't belong in a science class—*especially* a biology class.

Also, if we're going to teach Intelligent Design in *biology* class, don't we have to teach it in *astronomy* class as well? After all, the same Intelligent Design premises can be applied to both can't it? If Intelligent Design proponents argue that on a *micro*scopic level things are so complex that they must have been intelligently designed, then shouldn't it be argued that things on a *macro*scopic level are so complex that they must have been intelligently designed as well? If the *universe* isn't complex, what is?

And what about any other natural science class? Don't these people believe a designer designed everything? How about teaching Intelligent

Historical Design Theory in history class? Don't the *overwhelming majority* of human beings believe a designer (God, if we're going to be honest with ourselves) intervened throughout history? Shouldn't Intelligent Historical Design be taught alongside of "secular" history class? As Intelligent Design proponents put it "why should only one side be taught? Shouldn't we teach both theory's equally and let people decide for themselves which is true"?

Or how about Intelligent Mathematical Design Theory? Shouldn't it be taught that some things in math are so complex they must have had a designer as well? Aren't things like addition, subtraction, multiplication and division pretty complex? Or better yet, how about algebra, geometry, calculus and trigonometry? Or even better, how about equations such as PIE or E=MC squared? Shouldn't it also be taught, as theory, that these things are just way too complex to have come into existence on there own? That they're just too perfect to have come into existence without being created by a Designer? If Intelligent Design can be taught in biology *as a theory*, then it can be taught *as a theory* in nearly every other class as well. There's simply no way of getting around that fact.

If this happens, it will be the beginning of the end of *all* objective science. Put Intelligent Design in a philosophy class, in a mythology class, or it in a comparative religions class, but keep it as far away from any science class as possible or it will help take us into a new Dark Age.

Another quick point I would like to make about Intelligent Design (and even Creationism for that matter) that proponents don't seem to understand is: Even if it were somehow proven that life was intelligently designed, it still wouldn't prove an omniscient, omnipotent, omnipresent God did it. As I point out in the next chapter, it may just be a life form much more advanced than human beings. Do I believe it? No. However, that conclusion would be infinitely more rational, reasonable, logical and plausible than the "God" hypothesis.

Now let's look at the death penalty. Do I think it's proper for the state to put people to death under certain circumstances? Absolutely. If it's proven beyond a shadow of a doubt that a person committed a murder, the only *just* thing to do is take the life of the murderer. I know people worry about putting an innocent person to death, but that's why I say "beyond a shadow of doubt." If there's *any* doubt at all, the most the person should get is life in prison. But I would also like to ask a question about the death penalties affect on *innocent* people. How do most innocent people die *as related to* the death penalty? Are they put to death by the state, or do they die at the hands of murderers who've already served their time, are out on furlough, escape from prison…etc.? If you look at the numbers, it's not even close. A thousand times more innocent people have died because murderers *were not* put to death by the state as opposed to being put to death by the state. As a matter of fact, I don't know of a single case in the last fifty years where it's been proven an innocent person was put to death by the state—not one! But I could easily give example after example of where innocent people died at the hands of already convicted murderers who were let out, furloughed, murdered others in prison, or who had people murdered while they were still in prison. So looking at the big picture, if we truly want to save *innocent* lives, we would be taking the lives of the guilty.

And then of course we have the "the death penalty doesn't detour crime" crowd. This is a perfect example of 'tell the big lie long enough and people will begin to believe it'. Of course the death penalty detours crime. Only someone completely lacking in common sense could say otherwise. To begin with, if a murderer is put to death, he sure as hell isn't going to commit any more crimes, is he? So it certainly does detour him doesn't it? Next, just think of it logically. If a criminal knows for sure he'll get the death penalty for murdering someone, what action is he more likely to take? If he's robbing a store, is he *more* likely to shoot the clerk *knowing* he will get the death penalty? Or is he *less* likely to shoot the clerk *knowing* he will get the death penalty? In most cases the answer is obvious. Of course there will always be criminals who will shoot the clerk no matter what, but even if just 10% of criminals are *detoured* by knowing they will be put to death (the percentage is actually much higher, but I'm deliberately being conservative) it would save *thousands* of lives annually. In other words, it would *detour* thousands of murders each and every year. However, as I mentioned earlier, the main reason for the death penalty is not because it's a deterrent, but because it's the *only* course of action that will serve justice i.e., it's the only *just* thing to do.

Now let's look at foreign policy. I hope most of my opinions on foreign policy should be obvious by now. Earlier in this chapter I pointed to just one example of a rational foreign policy in regards to Saddam Hussein. So using Inductive Political Reasoning, like in Saddam's case, we can approach other cases in foreign policy logically as well. Like I mentioned earlier, what works in the small picture works in the big picture as well. We should treat immoral foreign nations the same way we treat immoral neighbors or other citizens— according to the concept of justice. If a foreign nation acts like a thug, treat it like a thug. If a foreign nation treats you justly, treat it justly…etc. It really is that simple.

The main problem with America foreign policy today is that we've become so entrenched around the world we're actually creating more problems for ourselves than solutions. Just like with domestic policies, our elected officials don't seem to have ever heard of The Law of Unintended Consequences. For a quick example, let's look at the situation in the Middle East. The main reason America is hated so much by the Muslim community around the world is because of our direct involvement in the Middle East—especially Israel. We give billions of dollars in aid to Israel every single year, and what do they do with the money? Buy, and build weapons. And who do they use those weapons against? Muslims. Is it any wonder why they hate us so much? Now, I'm not saying Israel is wrong for defending itself *or* that Muslims are right doing what their doing. What I'm saying is: IT'S NONE OF OUR BUSINESS! The Jews and the Palestinians will probably never have peace because that's what happens when people take their religions seriously. The Jews believe God gave them the land they call Israel, the Palestinians don't—period! Nothing we can do as Americans can change that situation. But what we *can* do is remain neutral and just let them fight it out among themselves. By involving ourselves in their stupid, barbaric, neanderthalistic religious war, we've made ourselves a target for religious fanatics, and that's exactly why the World Trade Center was attacked. And unless we change our foreign policy it will happen again and again.

At this point, I would like to draw an analogy between the Muslim world and Israel, and between the Americas and Asians. Now this is going to be a little complicated, so please bear with me.

Since we live in a nation were the majority of the people believe in the Bible, we usually support Israel's point of view more than the Palestinian point of view. So I would like you to put yourself in a Palestinian/Arab/Muslim's shoes for a moment so I can set the stage for my example.

Let's say you're a Palestinian/Arab/Muslim living in the Middle East at the end of World War II. The Germans just spent the last few years trying to wipe out the entire Jewish population (to the tune of millions of innocent people). So white Europeans (people coming from a historically Judeo/Christian Biblical point of view) decide that Jewish people need a homeland. But instead of giving part of *Germany* (you know, the very people who committed the whole atrocity) to the Jewish people, they decide to give the Jews the land they controlled two thousand years ago. Problem is, there are already people living there. So the historically white European Christians (and Americans of course) simply decree that although Israel hasn't existed for two thousands years, they're going to return the land to the Jewish people and recreate it.

Now, here you are. As a Palestinian/Arab/Muslim, isn't it going to piss you off that these outsiders are going to bring a nation back into existence that hasn't existed for two thousand years—especially in your own back yard! Wouldn't you be wondering why *you're* being punished for something that white Christian Germans did? Wouldn't you be wondering what the hell the people in Palestine had to do with what happened in Germany? I know I would. My point being that if I were in their shoes, I would feel the same way they do. I wouldn't like it done to me, so why would I think they would like it done to them? So here's they rest of the analogy.

Through the study of DNA we know for a fact that Native Americans are of Asian descent. We know that over ten thousands years ago they came across the Alaskan ice bridge from Asia to America and colonized a land where there were no human beings. And then roughly five hundred years ago, Europeans showed up and forcibly took the land from them. Now, don't get me wrong here. I'm not making any moral judgments, I'm just stating a indisputable, historical fact.

Anyway, let's say a hundred years from today the United States is no longer the world's only super-power, but China is; and Native Americans go to China and say "Listen, we want our land back. The entire world knows that Asians were the first to colonize America; that people of Asian decent were in America at least ten thousand years before the Europeans, and that they stole our land from us. If people of white European ancestry can go back *two thousand* years and recreate Israel for the Jews, why can't China (Asians) go back *two hundred* years and give *us* the land of *our* forefathers? If it was moral for white Europeans to do it for Jews, then it's moral for Asians to do it for the native tribes of North America. In fact, it's moral to do it for the native people of Central and South America as well."

Now, I'm not saying *I* believe this would be a moral thing to do. I'm just saying that using the same logic that was used to recreate Israel, can be used by Asians to recreate the Cherokee nation, the Sioux nation, the Iroquois nation, the Aztecs, the Incas, the Mayans…etc. If it's moral to go back *two thousand* years in order to right a wrong, then it's certainly moral to go back just *two hundred* years in order to right a wrong. Do I think it should be done? Of course not. I'm just trying to show why people in the Middle East are so angry at America, Europe, Christians and Jews. They see what happened as an injustice, just like *you* would see the Chinese giving America back to its former native population as an injustice. Would you be pissed off if the Chinese gave America back to the Indians? Of course you would. So why do you think the Palestinians would feel differently?

Getting back to foreign policy, it's my opinion that we're doing exactly what the Roman Empire did—spreading ourselves too thinly around the world. And it will be *our* downfall as well. It would be nice if we could solve all of the world's problems, but we can't. We can only do what we used to do as a nation; set a good example and hope the people of the world follow it. Am I an isolationist? No, but I do think there are just some things we don't need to be involved in. We simply don't have the ability (or power) to be the world's policeman. And even if we did have the ability (or power), there's nothing in the constitution that says it's our government's job to force its citizens to pay for it through taxation. Here's yet another example of where our good intentioned government has gone way beyond its proscribed duties.

In regards to foreign affairs concerning *economic* matters, *justice* should be the prevailing standard as well. The debate between "Free" Trade and "Fair" Trade is extremely complex, but once again, *justice* should be our prevailing standard. Should the world be one free market place? Absolutely! But the problem here lies in the fact that in no country in the world are its citizens "free," not even the United States. And if their citizens aren't free, then it's not a free market, is it? "Free Trade" implies freedom; which means you cannot have Free Trade unless all parties involved are Free, but this simply isn't the case, is it? So until all parties involved are truly free, there simply cannot be "Free Trade."

The way I see it when it comes to any economic matter and morality, I try to do my best to support people who support my values and virtues (Freeliberty, Justice, Peace, Integrity…etc). Of course this is impossible to do all the time, but I do at least make the attempt. Which means I make some economic decisions based not only on price and quality, but on other factors as well. For example: If I have the choice to buy a product from a family member for say $100 dollars, and someone I don't know for $90 dollars, as long as I don't have some type of moral problem with the family member, I'll spend the little extra to buy from them. The same goes for friend vs. stranger, local vs. national, American vs. foreign…etc. In essence, all things being nearly equal, I'll support those who support me.

In my opinion, the lack of this practice has become a huge problem in the United States. Just a few decades ago our society wasn't burdened with the high taxes and debt we now have, so it might have been a lot easier to justify buying foreign made products back then. But now, when you buy foreign made products, the money which would've gone to our government through taxes, is supporting the government in which the product is made. For example: The last time I saw statistics, over 40% of the price of a new Ford Taurus is taxes; meaning that taxes paid through the entire build process (suppliers, dealers, manufacturer…etc.), is nearly half the price of the car. So if a Ford Taurus costs $26,000, roughly $12,000 of that goes to support Americas infrastructure (schools, roads, Social Security…etc). However, if you buy a *foreign* built automobile, the only tax money that goes to American infrastructure is the sales tax, which is only a few thousand dollars.

So, if half the cars sold in America have foreign nameplates, and half of those are foreign built, we're losing tens of billions of dollars in tax revenues each and every year. If, on average, 16-17 million automobiles are sold in America every year, and if roughly 25% of those cars are now foreign built, and if we lose just $5,000 in tax revenues on each vehicle, that would mean, conservatively speaking, that we're losing *at least* $20,000,000,000 (4,000,000 x $5,000) each year in government tax revenues—*and that's just from the sales of automobiles!* My point being that for every dollar you think you may be saving buying a foreign car, you're having to make it up in higher taxes, less economic freedom, and a more intrusive overbearing government. So all things being equal, is it really worth it? Now, I'm not talking so much about small products or goods (although some might argue those as well), I'm talking about large purchases such as cars and the like. I'm just trying to show the *real* cost of buying such foreign products on America's economy and infrastructure.

Another point I would like to make while on this topic is that, while Americans continue to buy things that *depreciate* in value, foreigners continue to buy things that *appreciate* in value. While Americans are buying things that have short-term value, foreigners are buying things that have long-term value. Even if you look at durable goods such as automobiles, they'll only have value for as long as they're being used (maybe ten years?), but after that, they're almost valueless. So while Americans are using dollars to buy things that *lose* value, foreigners are using those dollars to invest in American real estate, American businesses, American stocks and bonds, Treasury notes…etc, i.e., things that have current value *and* future value. So we may be living the good life now, but if this trend continues, how well are our children going to be living in the future? If our government seems corrupt now, how corrupt is it going to be when more and more foreign interests are plowing money into lobbying efforts in Washington? I don't know if it's true, but I read somewhere that there are now more foreign lobbyists in Washington than American lobbyists—unbelievable! Fact is, the more foreigners own in this country, the more say they'll have in our government. I for one don't think it's a good thing.

Now let's take a look at "hate" crimes. To begin with, the problem with banning so-called "hate" crimes is that it's completely unconstitutional. In most, if not all hate crimes, it's the assailants right of free speech that's on trial. When a person is convicted of a hate crime, it's because the perpetrator of a *real* crime calls the victim names while committing the crime. When a "white" person attacks and robs a "black" person and calls them names in the process, the name calling is considered a hate crime. When a heterosexual physically attacks a homosexual and calls him names in the process, the name calling is considered a hate crime…etc. What hate crime advocates have done is made free speech a crime. And this "crime" is for simply having and expressing a point of view. In fact, it's more like a "thought" crime than a "hate" crime. Although we might not like what some people say or think; even bigots, racists, homophobes and anti-Semites have the right to their own opinion and to free speech—no matter how wrong they may be.

And besides, just because someone calls someone else names, doesn't mean they "hate" them. I remember getting into many fights growing-up where I called people names all the time (and they called me names as well), but it had nothing to do with "hate." I remember getting into a fight with a kid who cut in line at the drinking fountain and calling him names. He was a big kid who was a little overweight and I called him "fat ass." But that was only after he called me a "skinny little runt." Either way, I didn't call him a fat ass because he was overweight, and he didn't call me a skinny little runt because I was skinny. I called him that because he cut in line, and he called me that because I said something about him doing it. My point being that when people call other people names, it's usually in order to push the other persons buttons in some way, and not necessarily because they "hate" them.

Just think about it. If, for whatever reason, you're arguing with someone, what are you going to do? Are you going to call a fat man a "skinny runt"? A skinny man a "fat ass"? A black man "honky"?…etc. Of course not, that wouldn't make any sense. You're going to call them something that will get their goat. My point being that "hate" usually has little or nothing to do with their actions in these cases.

Another thing hate crimes do is tell society that some people have more value than others. If my son gets assaulted by a thug, the thug gets 5 years in prison. But if the same thug beats up a minority and calls him a name in the process, the thug gets 10 years! Does that make sense? Thus, the criminal is being punished for exercising his right of free speech. When someone gets murdered, raped or assaulted, is that crime worse because they were called names in the process? No, certainly not. If free speech can be made a crime while committing another crime, then in time, it can be made a crime all by itself. Are we willing to take that risk? Are we willing to give up the right of free speech? I for one, am not.

And besides, when did it become unconstitutional to hate? Don't human beings have the right to hate? I'm not saying it's a good thing, only that people have the right to hate if they choose to hate. Now, if their hate causes them to cross the line of violating another's rights and committing a crime, then no, they don't have that right. But the crime is in the violation of another's rights, not in the "hate," i.e., it's the murder, theft, assault…etc, that can *and should* be punished, not the person's opinions, biases or bigotries. If opinions, biases and bigotries are to be punishable, then we are all criminals and should all be punished.

Now let's take a look at Unions. As a blue-collar worker who has worked for over fifteen years as a Union member, and over a decade without a Union, I think I'm uniquely qualified to give an opinion concerning Unions. As of this writing (2007) Unions have really been taking a beating, and for good reason. It seems to me that they've turned into little more than self-perpetuating entities that, in many cases, only seem to be out for themselves and for workers who should've been fired years ago; but that doesn't mean they're no longer necessary or obsolete. It simply means they need to go back to basics. Like spending their time helping the actual *working* man and quite wasting time fighting for non-workers in the Union and for socialist political causes (after all, we're called auto *workers* right? By definition, we are there to WORK). If a person doesn't want to work, they're not living up to their job obligation, and therefore, the Union has no obligation to protect them—period!

So what it all comes down to is that the Union needs to quit protecting people who don't want to work, and who, in actuality, are not only hurting the *real* workers, but the Union itself. I estimate this percentage to be roughly 10% of the Union workforce (at least the autoworker workforce). This small percentage actually does great harm to everyone else because:

#1) People who actually work have to make up the slack of the non-workers.

#2) Quality suffers because it's usually the 10% who cause the majority of the quality problems, and because of the Union, they're rarely held accountable.

#3) Autoworkers get a bad reputation in the public's eye when they hear about what these human parasites get away with *on the job!* And when this happens, it causes many of them to purchase foreign made vehicles out of a sense of justice, and I can't really blame them.

#4) By having this type of work environment, it actually encourages the good workers to become bad workers because in many, if not most cases, the bad workers get rewarded. How? Simple, because less is expected from them. If you're a *good* worker, you have more work added to your job, but if you're a *bad* worker, you'll be put on an easy job. If you're a *good* worker, most supervisors will use your pride against you because they know you'll try to do the job no matter how much they add on to it. If you're a *bad* worker, most supervisors will simply put you on an easy job and then leave you alone because they don't want the hassle of dealing with a bad employee. Thus, bad workers are rewarded and good workers are punished. And when the bad is rewarded, over time, everyone else loses. If the Union would simply allow the company to fire these human parasites, everyone else would benefit and be much better off.

With that said, I also think it's just a matter of time before Unions make a comeback. As a matter of fact, I'm surprised it's not already happening. It's my opinion that many companies are treating their employees worse and worse every year that goes by. Just look at pay ratios. 40 years ago the average CEO made something like 30 times what the average worker made, now they make something like 300 times what the average employee makes. Of course the CEO is much more important than any individual worker to the company—but 300 TIMES more important? I don't think so. Of course a good CEO should be rewarded for success, but today, even CEO's who run their companies into bankruptcy receive obscene payouts. It's my opinion that both the United States government and corporations are destroying the American middle class, and because of this, it's only a matter of time before Unions make a comeback.

I would also like to make another point here. Why is it that all around the world the average top executives make roughly 25 times the average worker, but in America, they make roughly 300 times the average worker? If pay is to be based on merit, the CEO of Toyota should be making many times what the CEO's at Ford, Chrysler and GM make shouldn't he? But it's not even close. The CEO at Ford makes many times more than the CEO of Toyota even though Toyota is making billions while Ford is losing billions. Is this not a double standard? Of course people have the right to make as much as they can, and companies have the right to pay whatever they want; but in my opinion, things have really been getting out of hand lately. A question from the movie 'Wall Street' applies perfectly here: "how many yachts can a person ski behind"?

In my opinion, part of the measure of a nation's wealth is how well the people on the bottom of the economic scale live. And this is why I'm for capitalism and free markets. The "bottom" in America live as well as many middle class people in the rest of the world, and that's because of freedom and capitalism (at least what we still possess of them). Although someone has the right to make as much as they can, that doesn't mean people in a society should pay them whatever they want. For example: I think it's morally repugnant that the former CEO of the New York Stock Exchange can make over a hundred million dollars in compensation (plus $144,000 *a month* in retirement). I also think it's morally repugnant that a basketball player can make 20 million a year; or that a movie star can make 25 million for a single film; or that a singer can make millions for a single song…etc. But it's not the fact that these people make that kind money that's morally repugnant, it's the fact that Americans value them to such a high degree that they're *able* to make that kind of money that's morally repugnant. And this is yet another reason why America is going the way of the Roman Empire.

Now, many on the political right argue that these business leaders deserve their high pay because they've "earned" it. They'll argue, for example: "Lets say a company hires a new CEO and then after a couple of years the company's profits soar 1000%. If the company is making hundreds of millions of dollars more after the new CEO took over, why shouldn't he get a big piece of that pie? After all, isn't he responsible for all those new profits"? Now, on the surface this may seem like a good argument, however, if we look at the big picture, it may not be a good argument after all. Let's say a CEO takes over a company at the bottom of an economic downturn. His company may make great profits over the next few years or so, however, did *he* create those profits because of his business savvy, or were those profits created because of simple market trends and he just happened to be in the right place at the right time?

If a real estate agent began his carrier in the early 1990's, and he made a fortune by the year 2000, was it his genius that created all those big commissions, or was it just the fact that he was lucky enough to come along during a real estate boom that created all those big commissions? This applies to the stock market as well. If a stock broker made millions in commissions during the late 1980's, was it his brilliance that created that wealth, or was his wealth created by him just being in the right place at the right time? Can't it be argued that in both these cases that it was more likely market forces that created their wealth than their own abilities? Now don't get me wrong here, I'm not saying there are no great wealth creators, because there are. All you have to do is look at someone's carrier *long-term* to see if they're a true wealth creator (a good example would be someone like Warren Buffet). However, there's absolutely no doubt that many people who become rich just happen to be in the right business at the right time. And if that's the case, do they really *deserve* to make such outrageous amounts of money? It's something to think about.

Last but not least for this chapter, I would like to address the ongoing debate over whether or not The United States of America is a "Christian" nation. There's absolutely no doubt that the majority of the founding fathers called themselves "Christians," but did they create a Christian nation? For this answer we must look at our nation's founding documents. When we do, we find that *not one time* in The Declaration of Independence, Constitution, Bill of Rights, or the Federalist Papers is "Christianity" evened mentioned— *not once.* You would think that if the founding fathers were creating a Christian nation they would've mentioned it at least once in its founding documents, wouldn't you? But they don't. The deliberate omission is the only argument I really need to prove they didn't create a Christian nation. After all, they certainly could have. And many states actually did write Christianity into their constitutions. Some even fought to have the preamble to the Constitution changed. One state wanted: "We, the people of the United States, humbly acknowledge Almighty God as the source of all authority and power in civil government, The Lord Jesus Christ as the governor of all nations, and His reveled will as of supreme authority, in order to constitute a Christian government...do ordain and establish this Constitution of the United States." Certainly *Christians* wanting to create a *Christian* nation would've used a preamble like this instead of what they actually used, wouldn't they? So why didn't they? Obviously, although self-professed Christians, they knew the dangers of a monopolistic theocratic government, so they simply didn't want to create a strictly Christian nation. They wanted as much freedom of conscience and religion as possible.

Of course there was much influence from the Judeo-Christian *moral* tradition, but when it came to the founder's *political* perspectives, they were influenced much more by the Greco-Roman tradition than by the Judeo-Christian tradition. Even such concepts as "Republic" and "Democracy" come straight out of ancient Greece. Certainly nothing in the Bible leads one to think government should be based on a Constitution. The fact that this side of the story is almost completely ignored in our society (outside of a University setting, that is) just proves once again that the "winner" writes the history. Since most people in America consider themselves Christians, they pretty much dictate what, and how, history is taught—deliberately downplaying the influence Greco-Roman ideas had on the founding fathers, and deliberately overplaying the influence of Judeo-Christian ideas. But once again I'm getting off track, and that's a whole different book. So let's get back to determining if the United States was, or is, a Christian nation.

The problem here begins with determining what it means to be a "Christian." I would assume that being a Christian means believing Jesus was the Christ and following his teachings. So let's see if America was founded on the teachings of Jesus by quoting some of his basic moral teachings and principles.

How about "Love thy enemy"? Is this a moral principle followed by Americans? No. Was it ever? No. How about "love thy neighbor as thyself"? Is this a moral principle followed by Americans? No. Was it ever? No. How about "if a man steals your coat, give him the shirt off your back as well"? Is this a moral principle followed by Americans? No. Was it ever? No. How about "do not resist him who is evil; but whoever slaps you on your right cheek, turn to him the other as well"? Is this an American moral principle? No. Was it ever? No. What did Jesus teach about divorce? "What therefore God has joined together, let no man separate" and "whoever divorces his wife, except for immorality, and marries another woman commits adultery." It doesn't sound to me like Jesus was to keen on allowing people to divorce. We certainly don't follow any of these teachings in America, do we?

Now let's look at some of his teachings on the accumulation of wealth. "No one can be my disciple who does not give up all of his possessions," "sell all possessions and give to the poor," "Do not lay up for yourself treasures on earth," "avoid greed in all its forms," "it is easier for a camel to go through the eye of a needle than it is for a rich man to enter the kingdom of God," "blessed are the poor."..etc. Are any of these teachings on wealth practiced by Americans? No. Have they ever been? No. How about what Jesus says in Mathew 6:19-34? I won't write the whole thing out here because it would take too long, but please read it for yourself. In essence, Jesus teaches the *exact opposite* of the traditional "Protestant work ethic," and also disparages accumulating wealth once again. Jesus not only says: "No one can serve two masters; for either he will hate the one and love the other, or he will hold to one and despise the other. You cannot serve God and mammon." And what is mammon? Wealth! He then goes on to say don't worry about getting ahead in life: "Therefore do not be anxious about tomorrow; for tomorrow will take care of itself." Do Americans think like this? No. Have they ever? No. When it comes to accumulating wealth, Americans are, and always have been, the most anxious people on earth. *I* don't see anything wrong with it, but Jesus certainly did.

Last but not least, Jesus said to "be perfect as your heavenly father is perfect." So what does being "perfect" mean? Well, according to Jesus, wouldn't it mean to follow his teachings? I mean, what else could it possibly mean? So, do Americans follow the teachings of Jesus? No. Have they ever followed the teachings of Jesus? No. Are our laws based on the teachings of Jesus? No. So to conclude that America was founded on the teachings of Jesus is not only wrong, but completely wrong.

And add to that the New Testament teachings that came after Jesus. The book of Acts describes how wonderful the early church was: "Not one of them claimed that anything belonging to him was his own; but all property belonged to all." Does this sound like a moral, economic, or political principle America was founded on? Or how about this from Corinthians: "Let no one seek his own good, but that of his neighbor." Does that sound like a moral, economic, or political principle America was founded upon?

1st Timothy tells us "money is the root of all evil" and that rich people need to be "rich in good works" and be "ready to distribute." Aren't these teachings more communistic than capitalistic? So please tell me exactly what "Christian" principles the United States was supposedly founded upon, because they're certainly not the ones I've read about in the New Testaments I own. I do see the *Judeo* influence on America from the Judeo/Christian tradition (Old Testament principles such as do not murder, steal…etc), but I fail to see the *Christian* influence. Remember, Christians refer to them as the "Old" and "New" Testaments for a reason.

So no, America is not, and never was, a Christian nation. It's simply a nation full of *so-called* Christians. Not only that, but in fact, America became the greatest nation in history *in spite of* its Christian heritage, *not* because of it. America became the most *militarily powerful* nation on earth because it did the *exact opposite* of what Jesus taught to do concerning using physical force.

And America became the *wealthiest* nation on earth because it did the *exact opposite* of what Jesus taught to do concerning the accumulation of wealth. Isn't that ironic? If you don't believe me, simply read the teachings of Jesus on both subjects.

I would also like to point out that when Christians attempt to use the argument that the intention of the founding fathers was to create a government that "guaranteed freedom *of* religion, not freedom *from* religion," they're only telling part of the story. Obviously there's no country in the world where people are completely free from the influence of some type of religion; and that's alright because people have a right to their own beliefs and opinions. But there's a big difference between *private citizens* and the *private sector* taking sides in religious matters and the *government* taking sides in religious matters. No, the founders didn't attempt to free people *from* religion, in fact, most mistakenly saw religion as a moral necessity. However, *they did* attempt to free people *from government* "respecting" or "establishing" religion. And this isn't just my interpretation, it's explicitly stated in the First Amendment.

I would also like to bring something else to your attention. Have you ever noticed that the religious leaders who claim there's no such thing as the Separation of Church and State, are the very people who DEMAND a separation of church and state when it comes to paying taxes?

Now I would like to write about a few other observations I have concerning Jesus, Christianity and politics. To begin with, it never ceases to amaze me how Christians treat their sacred text like a salad bar—picking and choosing what they like and ignoring the rest. Of course this technique is used by adherents of *all* religions, but once again, since I live in America, I'll focus on Christianity.

To begin with, I would like to know why fundamentalist Christians are so selective concerning the things they condemn. They go after homosexuals like a starving pit-bull goes after a raw piece of meat, but they never even mention what Jesus condemned over and over again—hypocrisy! Why is this? Could it be because they're such hypocrites themselves when it comes to actually following the teachings of Jesus? It sure looks that way to me. The same goes for what Jesus said about divorce. Why is it so ignored by the majority of Christians? Allow me to give a couple of examples of "picking and choosing" and how Christians interpret his teachings to fit their own personal/political agendas. I put these here, and not in the chapter on religion, simply because they directly affect American politics.

Let's begin with this from Jesus: "render unto Caesar the things that are

Caesar's, and unto the Lord the things that are the Lords." This saying has been used, or should I say *abused*, throughout history as a moral conditioner to keep the masses in line in order to support those in power; including, and maybe especially, the church. In other words, it's been effectively used as a way keep the populous from uprising in order to keep them like docile little sheeple so they can be fleeced when the powers that be see fit. Contrary to the opinion of the majority of Christian theologians throughout history, when Jesus said "render unto Caesar the things that are Caesars, and unto the Lord the things that are Lords" he wasn't giving the governments around the world carte blanch authority or permission to tax it's citizens into lifelong slavery or involuntary servitude; he was simply being ambiguous in order to put off his capture by the Roman authorities until the time he saw fit. It really had nothing to do with taxes.

But exactly what is "Caesar's" anyway? And why should he (government) be entitled to nearly half (or more) of what we earn? Please explain to me why it's moral for the government to take from those who produce in order to give to those who do not? Isn't that stealing? Isn't America supposed to be based on individual rights, freedom, personal responsibility and equality under the law? Or do we now go by Marx's communist creed of "from each according to his ability to each according to his need"? Our immoral, incompetent, irresponsible government is spending this great nation into oblivion, and the clergy keeps telling us that rendering unto Caesar is the moral thing to do? GIVE ME A BREAK!

While on the topic of taxes, I would also like to know why the teachings of John the Baptist are so ignored by Christians. When the tax collector and soldier came to John to be baptized they asked him, in essence, what they had to do to be saved. He told the tax collector to "Collect no more than what you have been ordered to." He said this because he knew tax collectors usually took more than the proscribed amount and kept the extra for themselves. And to the soldier, who were also policemen of the day, he said "Do not take money from anyone by force, or accuse anyone falsely, and be content with your wages." Do not take money from anyone by force? Isn't this statement the equivalent of saying that taxes are to be voluntary? It sure sounds that way to me. Obviously John the Baptist understood that *freedom* is the basis of morality, and that the initiation of force is not a moral act. So if this is what John taught, isn't it probably what Jesus taught as well?

Over and over throughout the New Testament Jesus taught peaceful resolutions to human conflicts. In other words, he never resorted to initiating force against other human beings, and never tells anyone else too either. Of course he did resort to *violence* when he overturned the tables of the moneychangers in the temple, but violence and initiating force are not the same. Violence does not necessarily violate the prerequisites of morality, while the initiating of force does. So please keep in mind that they are different.

My point being that Jesus probably thought more like John the Baptist than anyone else. He studied with John, he preached with John, he spent a lot of time with John, he taught the same message as John, he was baptized by John, and John may have even been Jesus' teacher and mentor (Jesus didn't even start preaching until after he met John the Baptist. And in case you didn't know, there's even a middle eastern religion that believes Jesus hijacked John's place in history). Jesus even said of John: "Among those born of woman, there is no one greater than John the Baptist." So when all these things are added up, it's logical to conclude that Jesus was most likely against the initiation of force just like John. All evidence points to the fact that, politically speaking, Jesus was a Libertarian. I could go on and on, but this is probably as good a place as any to start to wrap this chapter up.

So what can average Americans do to turn this country around? Of course they can vote to bring about change, but with so many Americans now collecting some type of government check, it may be too late for that. So perhaps it's time for Americans to rein in its ever-expanding gluttonous government leviathan by refusing to pay all their taxes? Perhaps it's time for a revolution of the producers? Even the Declaration of Independence itself says that when government becomes destructive "it is the Right of the people to alter or abolish it." Thomas Jefferson also wrote: "The tree of liberty must be refreshed from time to time with the blood of patriots and tyrants," and "A wise and frugal government…shall refrain men from injuring one another, shall leave them otherwise free to regulate their own pursuits of industry and improvement, and shall not take from the mouth of labor the bread it has earned." Since our government is no longer following Jefferson's advice on not taking the bread labor has earned, perhaps it's time for those who labor to follow Jefferson's advice on refreshing the tree of liberty? When nearly half of the average Americans hard earned wages are legally plundered by an out-of-control, rights violating, behemoth government that no longer adheres to the principles set forth in The Declaration of Independence and The Constitution, maybe, just maybe, the day of reckoning is at hand. I for one, welcome it.

Chapter 5: God, Religion, and Morality

I guess the only way to begin this chapter is to ask the question: Does "God" even exist? This is one of mankind's enduring questions, and as long as there are human beings, this question will be asked, answered, and debated upon. But to me, this question isn't important because it will *never* be answered satisfactorily to all because of the nature of the question. Of course people coming from a particular religious perspective will disagree, but that's only because they're coming from their own particular religious perspective. The truly important *moral* questions are: If God exists, how should we live? And: If God *doesn't* exist, how should we live? But these two questions can also be summed up in *one* question: How should we live? I'll answer this question in chapter 6, but for now let's get back to God.

So, does God exist? I hate to even answer this question because *morally*, it's truly not an important question. Whether or not God exists should have no bearing on how we act as human beings, we should live our lives ethically either way. I also hate to answer this question because if I do, one side or the other will simply dismiss everything else I say based solely on the answer to that one unanswerable question (well, to be more exact, I should say *unprovable* question). But since this chapter is partly based on the subject of God, I'll have to give my opinion. Before I do though, I would also like to point out that most people will consider much of what I'm about to write as blasphemy, but this couldn't be further from the truth. It's impossible to blaspheme something that has no identifiable identity. If I knew God's identity, then and only then could I possibly blaspheme Him, Her, It, or Them. But until I do, nothing I say can possibly be blasphemous.

Just look at it like this. Let's say there's a man out there somewhere named "Mike" that I've never met. But every day I met people who tell me about

Mike and about Mike's opinions, characteristics, ethics…etc. In essence, I only know what other people have told me about Mike, and what's been written about Mike. Then I start talking to people outside of my own community and realize something else: Mike is not "Mike" in their communities! Depending on where you are, "Mike" goes by many different names, has different identities, and in some places, there are multiple Mikes! And not only that, but wherever I go, people give Mike different characteristics, *and* they all give differing opinions of what Mike expects from me. Knowing all of this, how could I possibly say *anything at all* about Mike, positive *or* negative? So in essence, unless God identifies himself, herself, itself or themselves to me, nothing I say about him, her, it or them, can possibly be blasphemous.

Now, if I believed the God of the "Old" Testament was God, or the Jesus of the "New" Testament was God, or Allah of the Quran was God, or Vishnu of the Hindus was a God…etc, and I deliberately spoke badly of him, her, it or them—then yes, that would be blasphemy. But since I don't, it simply cannot be blasphemy—period!

Since all religions view God(s) differently, how can I even begin to answer such an overly simplistic question on his, hers, its, or their existence? However, since most people reading this book will live in America, I'll use the definition the majority uses here. The one of an all knowing, all powerful, everywhere at all times, always good, God. So, do I believe in a *living* being that knows *everything*, that can do *anything*, that is *everywhere* at all times, and that is *always* good? A *living* being who existed before existence? A *living* being who was never born, who will never die, who has no mother, father, grandmother, grandfather, or absolutely no genealogy at all, in fact, there aren't even others of his own species? Do I believe in a God that exists *outside* of all laws of nature and goes *against* all laws of nature? No, not me. Do I believe in any other type of God or Gods? Absolutely not, and I certainly don't believe in any God I've ever read about. I've studied all of the worlds major religions and many of the minor ones and I've yet to find one that stands up to reason, logic, and critical scientific scrutiny. If God exists, he sure isn't the God of any religion I've ever studied. But maybe this is why I haven't found him. I've spent my life searching for the God of Reason, but no such God exists. There are only Gods of faith and belief. Maybe if I had found a religion who's God valued reason and rationality above all else, then yeah, maybe I would've been for him. But I've yet to find any religion who's God or Gods holds reason and rationality as his highest value and virtue. And this is obviously because; the *men* who made up the worlds religions were not very reasonable or rational—at least not by today's standards.

I call myself both an atheist and an agnostic. I'm an atheist in the sense that I don't believe there's a Cosmic Puppet Master of the universe pulling the strings of our lives and making things happen in accordance to some omniscient circumscribed design. If I believed in God, it would be closest to the God of Deism. The God of Deists created the world, but assumes no control over it. Basically, he started things off, but now only watches from afar; the world is exactly what we as humans make of it—he leaves *everything* completely up to us. As far as I'm concerned, this belief in God is the only legitimate (but not completely rational) belief left. Anyone who believes a God is taking part in daily earthly affairs is simply playing psychological mind games and fooling themselves. I could write an entire book systematically disproving the existence of an all-controlling God, but it's not up to me to disprove God, it's up to believers to prove he exists. It's only possible to prove a positive, not a negative. But what I've learned over my life is that no amount of evidence I give to a believer will ever be good enough if he insists on believing in some type of supernatural power. So the argument remains, and will remain, in a stalemate because of the nature of the question.

I would also like to point something else out in regards to Atheism. Although it's said that *statistically speaking* atheists only make up a small percentage of the population, in reality, they make up the overwhelming majority of the population. Let me explain why. To be an Atheist means: "to not believe in God or the Gods." And although most people say they *do* believe in God or Gods, if you look at it more closely, it's a much more complicated issue *and* they're extremely particular in their beliefs. A Christian believes in the God of Christianity, but he certainly doesn't believe in the God of Islam. A Muslim believes in the God of Islam, but he certainly doesn't believe in the Gods of Hinduism. A Hindu believes in the Gods of Hinduism, but he certainly doesn't believe in the God Mormonism. A Mormon believes in the God of Mormonism, but he certainly doesn't believe in the God of Shintoism…etc. So although most people say they believe in God or Gods, they only believe in their particular religion's God. Which means, in essence, the overwhelming majority of the time they're actually atheists. The only time they're not Atheists is in regard to their own version of God.

But it gets even more complicated than this. A Christian will argue that he believes in the same God as Jews, while Jews will say Christians believe in a different God. Muslims say they believe in the same God as Jews and Christians, while Jews and Christians say Muslims believe in a different God. Mormons say they believe in the same God as Christians, while Christians say Mormons believe in a different God…etc. All these different religious groups may believe in *a* God, but they *obviously* don't believe in *the same* God. Thus, while I'm an atheist 100% of the time, they're atheists 99% of the time because they only believe in their own religion's God and they dismiss the rest as nonexistent or not the "true" God.

Getting back to the tiny *agnostic* part of myself, I look at it like this. I'm an agnostic in the sense that I don't know if a being supreme to humans exists, or if it had something to do with the beginning of life on earth. Maybe a being supreme to humans had something to do with the beginning of life on earth, maybe it didn't (although there's certainly no evidence of it). But just because a being is supreme to humans, doesn't make it *the* Supreme Being; it doesn't make it the omniscient, omnipotent and omnipresent being written about by religionists. It could just be a form of life supreme to us as humans. Is it possible? Yes. Is it probable? No. Do I believe it? No. Can I disprove it? Of course not. Once again, you cannot prove a negative. So in this small sense, I'm agnostic.

Before I go on, I would like to make an important point here concerning agnosticism. As I wrote in the Forward of this book, although I've been an Atheist my entire life, I've sometimes hid in the, comparatively speaking, more comfortable world of agnosticism. It seemed like the more reasonable thing to do because, well, after all, "you cannot *prove* God *doesn't* exist" right? But over the years I've come to realized how ridiculous this position really is.

Most agnostics say they're agnostic because it cannot be proven one way or the other whether or not God exists. But the problem with this position is that in order to believe it, you must then give equal credence to *all* positions in-between all the extremes. In essence, if life on earth is on one extreme, and an all-knowing, all-powerful God is on the other extreme, then everything in the middle is possible, right? So if you're agnostic concerning "God," then to begin with, you must also be agnostic toward all positions concerning things such as angels, demons, witches, warlocks, extra terrestrials…etc. If you believe that *it is possible* that an all-powerful, all-knowing being exists; then you must also believe that *it is possible* that beings exist that have much greater powers than humans, but less powers than God. The logic is irrefutable. This is where many human *beliefs* come in. The belief in the devil, demons, spirits, angels, aliens, ghosts, witches, warlocks, voodoo…etc, are all beliefs that fall in-between the extreme of God (or the Gods) on the one end, and life on earth as we know it, on the other end.

So to be logically consistent, an agnostic must be agnostic toward *anything* where beliefs are concerned. If *it is possible* that God exists and involves himself in human affairs, then *it is also possible* that other powerful beings exist and involve themselves in human affairs as well. But are most agnostics agnostic toward other human beliefs? Not the ones I've met. It's my experience that most agnostics are extremely rational and logical concerning irrational and illogical human beliefs. Most are extremely skeptical towards ghosts, evil spirits, horoscopes, astrology…etc.—and for good reason. If there's no proof of these things, why act as though they exist, or that they're even probable or possible.

So my comment to agnostics is: If you believe *it is possible* that an all-knowing, all-powerful, ever-present being exists; then you must believe *it is possible* that beings (and other completely unprovable things) exist that are in-between the *unlimited* entity called "God" and the *limited* entities we know of on earth. In essence, to be logically consistent, you must believe that *anything* is *at least possible* that comes from our imagination. Do most agnostics believe this? Of course not, because it simply wouldn't be reasonable. So why is it *reasonable* to believe it's possible that an *unlimited* being exists, but *unreasonable* to believe that it's possible that unproven *limited* beings exist?

Was that a little confusing or what? You'll probably have to read that whole line of reasoning a few times before it really sinks in, but it's well worth the time because it's so logically sound. If you would like a couple of easier examples, try these: If we know that a class of animals exists called 'felines', and we know that at one end of the scale we have domestic cats, and at the other end of the scale we have Bengal Tigers, then *any sized* feline in the middle of those two extremes is possible. If we know that a class of animals exists called 'canines', and at one end of the scale we have Chihuahuas, and at the other end of the scale we have Great Danes, then *any sized* canine in the middle of those two extremes is possible. So if you're agnostic toward the belief that an all-powerful, all-knowing, unlimited, immortal being exists; then to be logically consistent, you must also be agnostic toward all beliefs that exist between the absolutely limited and the absolutely unlimited of the extremes—which means there can never be anything that is not possible. And since reason dictates that many things are simply not possible, holding this belief is not only illogical, but irrational as well.

I would also like to make another point about agnostics. It's my opinion that many, if not most, agnostics simply don't want to admit that they're *really* atheists. In fact, many atheists don't even want to admit out loud that they're atheists; but in my not-so-humble opinion, this is a huge mistake. I've asked some agnostics about this and many have said basically the same thing: "what if there really is a God? Or a heaven and hell? Do I want to take that chance?." But this position is truly ridiculous if you think about it for a moment. If there really is a God, wouldn't he already know exactly what you think? You're certainly not pulling the wool over *his* eyes, right? After all, he's God! So why remain silent about what you really think or believe? The only people you're really hurting are people who think and believe as you do, and why would you want to do that? You already belong to one of the most hated, vilified and distrusted groups in America, so why not show some support for those you really agree with?

As a matter of fact, a fairly recent survey (University of Minnesota) published in the April 2006 issue of 'American Sociological Review', found that atheists are not only the "most distrusted" minority in America, they're also the group that most parents would least want their children to marry. My whole point being that atheists and agnostics really need to stand up and say what they truly think or others are going to continue to view them in a negative manner—without even knowing who they really are! In fact, this happens to me all the time. I worked with a man for two years before he said to me "You're not an atheist. You don't do drugs, you don't steal, you don't lie, you don't party all the time…etc.." He, like most people, equated being an atheist with being immoral, or being a hedonist. And he did this because most non-believers usually keep their mouths shut about what they truly think, so nobody seems to know that non believers can be good, honest, moral human beings just like anyone else. So please speak up about what you truly think or we'll continue to be viewed in a negative manner. With that out of the way, let's move on.

Now, to those of you who ask: If there's no God, how did everything come into being? I answer: I have no idea. But I'm certainly not going to just make something up and pretend it's true like religionists do. In essence, I agree with the Objectivist view called 'the primacy of existence' and the Objectivist axiom 'Existence exists'. Astronomers say the universe came into existence roughly 15 billions years ago, and by using scientific techniques such as triangulation, the study of light and sound waves…etc., are able to prove it. But what existed *before* the universe as we know it? Who knows? What phenomena *caused* the universe to come into existence as it now exists? Who knows? We may as well just start with what we know exists and go from there. We know the universe exists. We know galaxies exist. We know stars, planets, asteroids, moons, trees, oceans and life exists, so why not just begin there? In essence, existence exists *by its very nature,* and it's always been around in one form or another.

What do we gain by saying a "God" had to create it? Because if *existence* had to be created, then to be consistent, so did God. If existence can't just exist by its nature, than neither can God. To believers I say: You can't have it both ways. If existence had to be created by God, then God had to be created by Super God. If God had to be created by Super God, then Super God had to be created by Super Duper God. It's a never ending regression. So instead of having an infinite regress, we may as well just begin with what we know exists and go from there. Existence exists, and it's always existed in one form or another—period!

Another way to look at it is like this. Nobody knows what existed before existence as we now know it. So we must choose one of two premises: Either life (God) existed before matter, or matter existed before life. It must be one or the other. If you believe in the first premise (life before matter) you cannot point to a single example of where life existed before matter *and* the premise violates all laws of nature. But if you agree with the second premise (matter before life) you can point to millions of examples every single day, *and* they violate *no* laws of nature. So the premise that life (God) existed before matter is a lot more flawed and illogical than the premise that matter existed before life. It may seem complicated, but it really is quite simple.

Of course there's always the law of cause and effect, but do I know the *ultimate* cause? Of course not, do you? If you say yes, then you don't know the difference between *knowing* something and *believing* something. You may *believe* God is the ultimate cause, but you do not *know* it. I'll go into more detail on *knowing* and *believing* later in this chapter.

The reason I entitled this chapter 'God, religion, and morality' is because most people around the world believe that the three are inextricably connected, but are they? No (although they usually are by intellectual default). Of course anyone coming from a particular religious viewpoint will disagree, but once again, that's only because they're coming from their own particular religious viewpoint. To prove the three can be mutually *exclusive,* and don't have to be mutually *inclusive,* all we have to do is ask ourselves a couple of questions: Can a human being be moral without believing in God? And: Can a human being be moral without believing in any particular religion? The answer to both questions is a resounding YES! Morality, however you want to define it, can only come from a mind that's willing to put forth the mental effort to discover it for himself—religious or not. This doesn't mean anyone attempting to discover it will automatically be moral, only that morality cannot exist *outside* of a reasoning mind. Morality is based on having the freedom to choose and the choices we make. It's not based on a belief in God, or on a belief in any particular religion. It's based first on our thoughts, then on our actions. It's based on the choices that we, whether we believe in God or not, make as individuals.

To prove this, all you have to do is look at history. Much of the evil perpetrated throughout history was perpetrated by individuals who believed in God. There's also no doubt that religion was, and still is, one of the major, if not *the* major, causes of war and bloodshed throughout the world today. Believers can be the most evil humans alive, just as atheists can be the most moral humans alive. But believers will ask: "Doesn't morality come from God"? No, it doesn't. It comes from a mind that's advanced enough to choose to identify that there is right and wrong, good and evil, just and unjust…etc. And when a mind can combine all these concepts together into a coherent whole, it's identified as 'morality'. If there's no mind capable of bringing morality into existence, then morality will not exist—period!

Or ask yourself this: If God died tomorrow, would morality still exist? Of course most people would say this is an absurd question, but please honestly think about it. If you do, there can only be one answer: Of course it would. Would you go out and start raping and pillaging tomorrow if you knew God died? Of course not. Would you quit taking care of your children? I don't think so. Would you simply drop all of your values and virtues? Probably not. So obviously human beings can be moral without God. And this would also apply to "meaning." Believers use the ridiculous "if there is no God, life has no meaning" argument for the existence of God, but the above paragraph answers that question as well.

And to those of you who believe in the God of the Bible, think about this. The Bible *itself* confirms you can have morality without God. What was happening *before* God supposedly gave Moses the Ten Commandments? Was everyone running around raping and pillaging? Were people abandoning their children? Did people just accept murder as a metaphysically given? Of course not. In fact, they couldn't even have made it to Mt. Sinai without there being moral standards that were practiced and accepted by the majority of the population. So at least biblically speaking, codes of morality existed long before God gave the people any moral codes to live by. So obviously morality can exist without God.

Of course, I cannot prove morality doesn't *originate* from God, just as believers cannot prove morality *does* originate from a God. In order to prove something true or false we must begin with the concept of identity. Since "God" has no identifiable identity, how can anything about him, her, it, or them, be proven true or false? Simply saying that God is omniscient, omnipotent, omnipresent, and omnibenevolent *does not* mean there's an entity with such characteristics in reality. Saying that God is love, just, jealous, or any other descriptive word, also doesn't mean there is such an entity in reality. There's no way for me to *prove* God doesn't exist if we can't even agree on *what* God is.

This is one of the strategies (consciously or subconsciously) theists have used for millennia in order to maintain the belief in the existence of God. Without having to give a specific, absolute, and verifiable definition of God, theists have made it impossible to prove he doesn't exist. This is also why the definition of God has changed over time. Historically speaking, the God of today's Christian is a far cry from the 1st century's Christian, which was a far cry from the God of the "Old" Testament, which was a far cry from…etc. In modern times, people speak of a "personal" God; whereas in the past, there was no such thing as a "personal" God, only *the* God. In the past, God was defined as a being who could do anything. Now, many people define God as a being who can do anything *that's possible to do*. Those definitions are miles apart from each other. So my point is, if the identity of God is unknowable, always changing, or continually ambiguous, it's impossible to prove he, she, it or them don't exist. Since God is defined differently at different times and in different places, there's really no way to even begin the argument on his, her, it, or their existence. But then again, believers really have no choice here do they? I mean, if something doesn't exist, how can they identify it?

But lets say for the sake of argument that somehow (or maybe 'miraculously' would be a more appropriate word) we all agree that God exists and on his identity. Then comes the questions: What does he want from us? And: How do we know it? Every religion in the world gives a different answer to these questions. And not only do they give different answers, even people belonging to the same religion give different answers. Christianity in America *alone* has at least 400 different denominations (I've also read that worldwide there are more than 20,000), and every one of them believe differently in many aspects of their religion.

Of course all religions have things in common, but that can be said of *any* two differing viewpoints when we're discussing things on such a grand scale. The only way we could ever know God's opinions is if God himself told them to us; and of course, this is what most religions are all about—people claiming to speak for God. But the problem with this is, unless God speaks to each and every one of us individually (assuming that it's even God of course), we have to take someone else's word for it, i.e., put our faith in another human being. And if we put our faith in another human being, we're not putting our faith in God, are we? So unless God speaks to us personally (once again, assuming it's even God), how can we know he spoke to *anyone* in the past? Simple, we can't. Whether we're talking about Abraham, Moses, Jesus, Paul, Mohammed, Nanak, Arjuna, or any other human being who claims to have spoken to God, or for God, doesn't matter. We cannot *know* God revealed *anything* to *anybody*; we can only choose to believe the people we choose to believe.

Personally, I don't believe "God" revealed anything to anyone because, obviously, I don't believe in God. Human beings simply had thoughts that made more sense to them than the ideas they had been previously exposed too. In essence, "revealed" knowledge was simply the human mind making connections and coming up with original thoughts. And after this happened, the person would attribute the phenomenon (thinking) to be a "revelation" from God instead of something that came out of his own mind. As a matter of fact, I would even go as far as to say that "revealed" knowledge and "thought" are one in the same. Instead of God revealing knowledge to humans, they simply started figuring things out for themselves in their own minds, i.e., they started thinking. And many times when this would happen it would be like the "Eureka!" phenomenon. We've all had the experience of an idea or a thought just popping into our heads haven't we? Well, that's what I'm talking about. In the past, people would interpret the "Eureka!" phenomenon as a "revelation" from God; while today, we understand it to be just one more aspect of how humans think and how the mind works.

So what about people who say they talked *directly* to God? Did God give Moses the Ten Commandments? No. Can I prove it? No. Can believers prove he did? No. Just like every myth from antiquity, it's a simple matter of belief.

But we must always keep in mind that it's up to *believers* to prove it really happened and not up to *non-believers* to disprove it. It's also a good thing to keep in mind that extraordinary claims require extraordinary evidence. And I would also like to point out that there's not a single shred of evidence outside of the Bible that "Moses" even existed. Although I think he probably did, there's absolutely no doubt in my mind that he was mythologized after his death. He was a perfect example of a leader in life turned legend in death.

I'm sure some of what the Bible say's about his life story is probably true, but there's also no doubt that much was also made up. For example, 1300 years before the supposed time of Moses was a Mesopotamian king named Sargon the great. Although much of the discovered text about Sargon is lost, we do know that his mother was so afraid for her son's life that she put him in a basket of rushes and sent him down the Euphrates River. After which, he was drawn out of the river by Oki the drawer of water. And while in the care of Oki, Ishtar (the princess) granted him her love and he eventually became king. Sound familiar? I think it's pretty obvious that the followers of Moses simply appropriated this myth and applied it to Moses. It's also my opinion that Moses, or his followers, appropriated the basic idea for the Ten Commandments from the ancient Egyptian 'Book of the Dead' and maybe even the ancient Babylonian 'Code of Hammurabi' as well. But the appropriation of myth was nothing new though. The story of Noah in the Bible looks like it was taken from the epic of Gilgamesh. Referred to by scholars as the "Babylonian Noah," the hero is told by a God to build an ark, load it with animals, prepare for a rain storm…etc. And this story goes back approximately 2600 B.C.—long before the Noah of the Bible. And what gives even more credence to the idea that these things were appropriated is that most scholars think that the Jews actually began writing the Old Testament while in captivity in Babylon—exactly where Hammurabi and Gilgamesh came from. There's also another story from antiquity that looks like it's the precursor to Job. And yet another called 'The tale of two brothers' that seems to be the precursor to the Biblical story of Joseph and Potiphar's wife.

In essence, *all* religions are based on appropriation. In fact, Christianity is *the* religion of appropriation. Christianity appropriated the Jewish messiah or "Christ." Christianity appropriated the Jewish Sabbath, and put it on the wrong day by the way. Christianity appropriated the December 25th feast of Mithra (the Roman God of war) and turned it into Jesus' birthday. Christianity appropriated the idea of a virgin birth. The Halo was appropriated. Gift giving was appropriated. The "Christmas" tree is of Pagan origins. Easter is of Pagan origins. The mistletoe is of Pagan origins…etc. Fact is, religion and appropriation go hand and hand. And this is just one of the reasons we know all religions are manmade.

Getting back to Moses, I'd say he thought up the Commandments and then used the concept of God to fortify their correctness with his people. I would also like to point out the obvious here. If Moses really was on the mountain for forty days, it was probably because it took him that long to chip the commandments out of the rocks. And come on, does anyone really believe that story anyway? Just think about it for a moment. God commits all those miracles in order to free the slaves; the slaves see all those miracles *with their own eyes*; but when Moses takes too long to come down from the mountain, they start worshiping a golden calf? Give me a break! Nobody could possibly be that stupid. It's a silly, ridiculous, and unbelievable myth—period!

I think Moses, like all religious leaders (past and present), use the idea of God to scare people into acting moral. Just think about it. There was no DNA testing, fingerprinting, lie detector tests, truth serum, the use of forensic evidence, or any other way to prove someone committed a crime. It almost always came down to one man's word against another's. And as you can probably guess, this wasn't a very good system for conducting the business of justice. So convincing people that an *all-powerful, all-knowing* God was *always* watching them, would've been an excellent deterrent for crime and a great way to keep people in line. Does this mean that Moses (or anyone else for that matter) simply lied about speaking to God? Sure, why not? Human beings lie all the time if they believe it's for a good (or just) cause. Lying, under the right circumstances of course, is a perfectly moral action to take (we'll get into that in a later chapter). Or perhaps Moses simply *believed* he was talking to God when it was his own conscience he was "talking" to? Remember, at that time in history, humans knew very little about how the mind worked, but we'll also get into that later as well.

Once again, it all comes down to *faith* and people *believing* who they choose to believe. Do Jews believe God spoke to, or revealed knowledge to Mohammad? No. Do Buddhists believe God spoke to, or revealed knowledge to Jesus? No. Do Christians believe God spoke to, or revealed knowledge to Joseph Smith? No. Do Muslims believe God spoke to, or revealed knowledge to the Buddha? No. Do Confucians believe God spoke to, or revealed knowledge to Zoroaster? No. Do the Amish believe God spoke to, or revealed knowledge to Lao-tzu? No. Do Taoists believe God spoke to, or revealed knowledge to Abraham? No. As you can see, I could spend an entire page on this list and we would always come to the same conclusion: people choose to believe who they choose to believe—period! Fact is, people cannot even agree on God's identity, let alone his opinions. And we're supposed to let these people tell us what God *wants* when they can't even tell us who (or what) God *is*? It's ridiculous!

Once again, it *always* comes down to an individual mind determining what it's going to think or believe to be moral or immoral, not God. All we can do is use our own mind to figure out what truly is right or wrong, good or bad, moral or immoral, just or unjust…etc. And if you default on this personal responsibility, all you're doing is putting blind faith in another human, community, society, or religion to do it for you. And in every one of those cases you're putting your faith in men, not God. So in essence, only human beings who believe in God, but don't follow any particular religion, have faith in God because they're the only ones who don't get their core beliefs from the man (or men) who made up the religion they believe in. The former has faith in men, while the latter has faith in God.

So at this point I would like to make a crucial distinction between having *faith* in someone and putting *trust* in someone. When you have faith in someone, such as a religious leader, you're taking their word for something when absolutely no observable or verifiable proof is available. Believing the Pope's opinions on various subjects is fine if you're a Catholic, but if you believe the Pope is giving *God's* opinions, you're putting your *faith* in him. Of course, you may argue that you're putting your *trust* in him as well, but the trust you're putting in him is only in relation to giving correct *Catholic* doctrine, not God's opinions. Once he, or any other mystic, starts giving "God's" opinions, it becomes a matter of faith because he (or they) cannot prove he (or they) knows God's opinions. They all fall back on their own religions doctrines, dogmas, or their own personal experiences—that's why it's called *faith*.

Trust on the other hand, is based on knowledge of someone and on observable, verifiable evidence. For example: I put my *trust* in my mechanic because he can prove to me that he knows how my automobile works. And if I wanted to take the time, he could prove to me *why* and *how* he knows *what* he knows. It's not a matter of faith because he can simply show me, or take out a manual on the make and model of my car and say: "Here's my proof. Here's *how* I know *what* I know." And every other mechanic in the world could do the same. I can take my Ford to *any* Ford dealership in the entire world and I'll get basically the same answers to the same questions.

But is this true when asking questions of God? Not even close. If I'm in China, am I going to get the same answers as in Iran? If I'm in India, am I going to get the same answers as in Japan? If I'm in France, am I going to get the same answers as in Brazil? If I'm in Russia, am I going to get the same answers as in Mozambique? If I'm in the United States, am I going to get the same answers as in Bangladesh? Once again, not even close. Even in the same country, the answers won't be completely the same. Jews put their *faith* in Moses because it cannot be proven Moses *spoke* to God, *knew* God, or knew *any* of God's opinions—that's why it's called faith. Christians put their *faith* in Jesus because it cannot be proven Jesus *was* God, was *the son* of God, *knew* God, or knew *any* of God's opinions—that's why it's called faith. Muslims put their *faith* in Mohammad because it cannot be proven Allah revealed knowledge to him through the angel Gabrielle, or that there *is* an angel named Gabrielle, or that there are even angels, or that the revelation was from God, or even that there *is* a God—that's why it's called *faith*. Mormons put their *faith* in Joseph Smith because…etc. And the same goes for all other religions as well—that's why there *all* called *faiths*. And for you people of faith, think about this: If faith is all that's needed, then all religions must be "true" right? So obviously, simply having faith is not enough.

I put my *trust* in a scientist because he can show me the evidence that led him to his conclusion or theory. This doesn't mean he must always be right, only that he *first* looks at the evidence, and then *secondly* draws a conclusion. The *evidence* is primary, the *conclusion* is secondary. For religions, the *conclusion* (their sacred text) is primary, while the *evidence* is secondary. All religions start with the conclusion (their sacred text), then search for evidence that will conform to their foregone conclusion. If they find evidence that's contrary to their conclusion, it's the evidence that must be faulty, not their sacred text. Or as Socrates put it when trying to describe the difference between religion and philosophy: "religion is truth possessed, while philosophy is truth pursued." Of course in reality though, philosophy *is* truth pursued, but religion is only the dogmatic *belief* of truth possessed, but he was close.

Maybe a better way to compare putting your trust in someone rather than having faith in them is to compare Evolution and Creationism. Creationism is based on faith while evolution is based on trust. There are hundreds, if not thousands, of mythical stories of creation from around the world. In fact, we couldn't even begin to count the number of creation stories that have been lost forever through the passing of time. But they all have one thing in common: *Not one* of these countless stories can put forth any objective evidence to prove their myth of creation is any more valid than anyone else's. In fact, if it wasn't for their religions sacred text, they wouldn't even be able to argue the issue. Their entire argument is wrapped up in a story (or stories) that were written thousands of years ago by scientifically ignorant men. If it wasn't for their ancestor's myth story, there would be no debate at all.

However, this isn't the case with evolution. The theory of evolution could only be formed *after* actual physical evidence was observed. Scientists (Archeologists, Anthropologists, Biologists, Botanists, Genealogists, Geneticists, Geologists, Paleontologists…etc.) can put evidence right in front of my face and say: "Here you go. Here's my evidence, and here's my theory *based* on the evidence." Like Darwin before them, they came up with a theory only *after* making observations, *never* before. This is why we put *trust* in scientists and not *faith*—although we must always be on guard for scientists who take leaps of faith. *Trust* is based on knowledge of observable, verifiable, and natural facts of reality; *Faith* is based on nothing more than someone's unprovable words, dreams, revelations, fantasies, or unverifiable supernatural beliefs. This is why trust is a *real* value and faith is not. This is also why anything that anyone says about "God" is based on nothing more than mere faith.

At this point I would like to make another important distinction concerning Faith. I once heard a highly respected Professor of the History of Science say: "to be an atheist requires a great leap of faith; that is, to ascent to the unprovable premise that no God exists. Both the theist and atheist have faith; only one is *positive* faith while the other is *negative* faith." If this is what's being taught in our best Universities, it's no wonder why we're so confused when it comes to the difference between knowing and believing, faith and trust, or religion and science. What complete and absolute nonsense! The problem in this particular instance lies in not distinguishing between taking a "leap of faith" and making an "assumption." Taking a "leap of faith" may be considered making an assumption, but it's an assumption that has no proof or evidence to back it up.

For example: If you believe in God, it's a leap of faith. If you believe your religion is God's religion, it's a leap of faith. If you believe in life after death, it's a leap of faith…etc. But an *assumption* is much more than just a leap of faith. All science is based on assumption; the assumption that things will be the same tomorrow as they are today; that gravity will function tomorrow as it does today; that the sun will rise tomorrow as it did today; that when we mix chemicals together, they will react together the same tomorrow as they do today; that when a doctor washes his hands before surgery, it will kill germs tomorrow as it does today…etc. *Assumptions* are based on things that have already been *proven* in reality, while leaps of faith are based on things that *have not been proven* in reality—and that's about as different as you can get. So in reality, there is no such thing as "negative" faith, only positive faith. Let me give an example that makes the point even clearer.

I was once involved in a theological debate when one of my opponents asked one of the people who was on my side one of the most convoluted questions I have ever heard: "If you don't believe there's a Devil, then on what basis is your faith that denies his existence." Let me repeat that: "If you don't believe there's a Devil, then on what basis is your faith that denies his existence." Do you see how utterly impossible it is to answer that ridiculous question? So I responded: "There's no such thing as faith that *denies*, only faith that *affirms*. The person who *has* faith, *has* faith *in* something. The person who denies, has *no* faith in that which they are denying—that's called *lack* of faith." With that, my opponent said: "Faith that denies something is faith that *affirms* the denial of something." Once again: "Faith that denies something is faith that *affirms* the denial of something." Do you see the verbal gymnastics this person must go through to attempt to prove their point? It was like something straight out of George Orwell's '1984'. When a person says "I have faith in…etc., they *have* faith. When a person says "I don't have faith in…etc., they *don't have* faith, i.e., they are faithless. To "have" something is to *possess* it. To *not have* something is to *not* possess it. In other words, the *lack* of faith is *not* faith. And to not believe is to *not* believe. Not believing *is not* a belief, but the *lack* of belief. It really is that simple.

The reason people of faith want to confuse the issue is because they know when a person *has* faith, that faith is *always* baseless and completely unprovable—that's why it's called faith in the first place. And if *their* position is unprovable, they want to make sure that the person they're arguing against also has an unprovable position. Thus, they say something amazing like: "your lack of faith *is* your faith," either not understanding that the lack of faith is not faith, or deliberately confusing the issue in order not to lose the argument. Either way, they're just plain wrong.

Another thing I would like to point out about people from the Bible supposedly having faith in God is the *fact* that many didn't. That's right, many of the "hero's" from the Bible didn't have faith in God. Why? Simple;

because they (supposedly) had *proof* in God. For example: Moses didn't have faith in God because God (supposedly) proved his existence to him. Noah didn't have faith in God because God (supposedly) proved his existence to him…etc. If God proves his existence to you (like he supposedly did with many people from the Bible), then "faith" and "belief" are not necessary. Faith and belief are only necessary when proof is not available. So all these so-called hero's from the Bible really aren't so heroic are they? I mean, if a being has complete and absolute power over you, and he could do anything he wanted to you, wouldn't you do as he says? In most cases, of course! In fact, it would've been more of a heroic deed if someone went *against* what "God" said to do, would it not? When God struck Esau dead on the spot for touching the Ark of the Convenant, it would've been an extremely heroic act if someone would've stood up and said "Hey! Come on God, that was just plain wrong. He didn't deserve to die. What you just did was immoral and unjust." Now *that* would've been a heroic act! Of course the whole thing is just a fable anyway, but I'm just making a point.

When it comes to trust and faith I like putting people into two distinct camps. On one side you have mathematicians (when I say "mathematician" I don't literally mean a person who studies math, I mean people who use reason, logic, and common sense in problem solving), and on the other side you have mythematicians (people who use faith, beliefs, mysticism, revelations, i.e., 'non-sense' in problem solving. I could also use the term 'Mythstorian' as applied to historians who have a religious bias, but I'll just stick with mythematician for now).

A mathematician starts with a problem and works his way to the solution; a mythematician starts with the conclusion (his sacred text) and works his way though the problem. A mathematician starts with a question and works his way to the answer; a mythematician starts with the answer (his sacred text) and works his way through the questions. A mathematician starts with the evidence and works his way to a theory; a mythematician starts with a "theory" (his sacred text) and works his way through the evidence…etc. A quick example of a modern scientist who became a mythematician and took a leap of faith is a current physicist who calculates the probable existence of God at 67%. To even believe such a thing is numerically calculable to begin with is ridiculous; but even worse is him believing he's taking a "scientific" approach to doing so.

Of course I knew immediately that this guy had a belief in God, and I was right. Just how can a man who "calculates" the probable existence of God at 67%, while he says his own belief is 95% certain, be expected to come up with any objective premises to begin with is beyond me. I would calculate maybe a 5% chance. But alas, he calls himself a scientist. Whenever a person takes a leap of faith, he makes himself a mythematician. This is why *all* founders of religions, or apologists of religions, are mythematicians. Arguing from a premise of faith *automatically* makes you a mythematician, there's simply no way of getting around that fact.

The examples I just gave are just a small sample of why Science and Religion are so different. *Science* is about learning the truth about existence; it's about accepting facts no matter where they lead you—*even if those facts lead you to a conclusion you do not like*! *Religion* is about having faith and ignoring facts that go against your foregone conclusion; it's about maintaining a mental paradigm of the world that you wish were true, *regardless of how many facts tell you it's false*! *Science* is about accepting true paradigms, *even if* they don't feel good. *Religion* is about maintaining false paradigms, *because* they feel good. These are just a couple of reasons why science and religion *can never*, and *will never*, be reconcilable.

Before I go on to the topic of religion, I would like to make a few more points concerning the God of the Bible. Hopefully I can make this first point understandable, but for some reason I've had a hard time convincing many people of the validity of my following argument. Biblically speaking, it doesn't matter if you believe in God, only if God believes in you. Over and over throughout the Bible, God hardens the hearts of human beings; but if God hardens your heart, he has taken away your choice; and if he has taken away your choice, does he have the moral right to condemn you? Some people in the Bible are simply never even given the choice of whether or not to believe in him. They're simply pawns in a game created by the God of the Bible. Of course, they're *really* created by men, but hopefully you get my point.

This is just one of the reasons why I don't believe in the God of the Bible. The God of the Bible simply does not give some individuals the freewill needed to make choices, and then he goes on to condemn them. A moral God would not commit such an immoral act. Which brings me to my next point: Would a moral God *even care* if you believed in him, her, it, or them? I think it's obvious just by asking the question what the answer is. Since we cannot *know* what to believe in (him, her, it, or them), how can he, she, it, or them, expect us to believe in the right one(s). This would be holding us accountable for something we're completely ignorant of, i.e., something that cannot be *proven* one way or the other.

But just for the fun of it, put yourself in the place of God, but on a smaller scale. Let's say you write the most perfect moral text ever written. If people would just follow the advice in this book, we would have heaven on earth. But after this book gets published, some type of catastrophe takes place that destroys every copy but one. The one copy that survives is complete except for one thing, all references as to who the author was are gone; you, the writer of this great book, lose credit forever. The book is then translated into all the languages of the earth, and becomes responsible for a new paradigm of morality. We finally have peace on the entire earth, freedom on the entire earth, justice on the entire earth…etc. So my question is: Do you, the author, care if people know *you* wrote the book? In essence, do you care if people *believe* in you? Or do you care if they think you ever even existed? I know I wouldn't. It would be much more important to me that *human* beings finally became *moral* beings. *Beliefs* mean absolutely nothing to morality, while *actions* mean everything to morality. If my tiny human brain can figure this out, an omniscient brain (God) would *already* know it. Which brings me to my next point.

Would a God who needs (or even wants) to be worshipped be moral? Well, lets begin by, once again, applying this to a human being. Throughout history many human beings in power have demanded that they be worshipped by "their" people, but across the board it's not considered a moral thing. Not even considering the gargantuan size of their egos, any human being who wants to be worshipped is infected with powerlust; and any person who lusts for power over others is simply not a moral person. This is why I say that only the man who doesn't want power is worthy of yielding it.

And just ask yourself this: Would *I* want to be worshipped by others? If you answered no, then why do you believe a being who's so much more enlightened than you would want to be? If *you're* above being worshipped, don't you think *God* would be as well? Holding God to a different moral standard has been one of the problems that comes out of most religions, but we'll get to that later.

With God out of the way, let's talk religion. As you'll notice, I have a lot of problems with religion in general. One of my biggest problems can be summed up in a short story. I was once discussing religion with a group of people when one of them asked me what I had against God. Well the answer hit me like a revelation (hey, you can't *prove* it wasn't a revelation). And I answered: "I have nothing against God, I have everything against people who claim to *speak* for God." The foundations of religions that claim to speak for

God are built on nothing more than lies, falsehoods, myths, legends, fairytales, or whatever else you want to call them. Contrary to popular belief, religions have *nothing* to do with God.

All religions come from the minds of *men,* not *God.* Anyone who believes in *any* religion puts his faith in *men,* not God. If you're a Jew, you don't have faith in God, but in Moses and the *men* who wrote, interpreted, translated, and compiled the "Old" Testament. If you're a Christian, you don't have faith in God, but in Jesus and the *men* who wrote, interpreted, translated and compiled the "New" Testament. If you're a Muslim, you don't have faith in Allah, but in Mohammed and the *men* who wrote, interpreted…etc. If you believe in *any* religion, your faith has been placed in the man or men that founded that particular religion, *not* God. To put it even more bluntly, the one thing that *all* religious believers have in common is their complete, absolute, and unadulterated faith in the ideas of *men,* not God. They may *believe* in God, but their *faith* has been placed in *men.*

And I don't mean this just in general, I mean it across the board. For example: The New Testament wasn't even canonized until the 4th century. There where many different books about Jesus in circulation at the time and *men,* not *God,* decided which would be put in the Bible. As a matter of fact, we don't even know who wrote Matthew, Mark, Luke and John, the early church simply attributed those names to those books decades after the fact. We also know that many of "Paul's" writings weren't even written by Paul, but by men who came after Paul who simply attributed their books to Paul as well. And these examples are just the beginning. My point being that *all* religious ideas come from the minds of human beings, not God. And when you put your faith in them, you're putting your faith in *men,* not God.

Getting a little off track for a moment, although it's a related point, this is one thing that's always bothered me about the term 'Secular Humanism'. Secular humanism is defined as any system of thought based on the interest and ideas of men, and having to relate only to the "physical" world. But in reality, *all* systems of thought, philosophical or religious, are based on the interest and ideas of men and to the physical world. Just because theists want you to *believe* what they preach comes from God, doesn't make it so. One is said to be "God" based, while the other is said to be "man" based, but in reality, *both* are man based.

Anyone who has taken the time to study the world's major religions *objectively* can see the inconsistencies, discreprencies, falsehoods and contradictions throughout their sacred texts. If God had a hand in writing these books, he sure isn't a God of omniscience. The term 'secular' is used as a way to separate the so-called "worldly" from the so-called "divine," but in reality, no such separation exists. *Every single* thought, word or action ever attributed to "God" came from the *fallible* mind of a human, not from the *infallible* mind of a God. This is why *all* humans are humanists. When a religionist says secular humanists put their faith in men while he puts his faith in God, he's simply fooling himself. Fact is, the secular humanist, if he is rational, is putting his *trust* in men, while the religionist is putting his *faith* in men. But worst of all, the religionist is not only putting his faith in men, he's putting his faith in ignorant men who lived hundreds or even thousands of years ago. Any person who puts their faith in one of the worlds religions has put their faith in the *men* who wrote, compiled, translated…etc, the sacred book they believe in, not God.

This is easily proven because *every single one* of their major premises come from that book, *and* it can also been shown that many of those texts have changed over time (such as King James adding the story in John about Jesus' teaching "let he who is without sin cast the first stone." This story was circulating as early as the 10th century, but it wasn't canonized in John until the King James Version of the Bible came out. It's also a fact that the last 12 verses of Mark were added later as well. None of the oldest New Testaments that exist have the last 12 verses). Which also proves that if their sacred text had been written a little differently, or if different books would've been canonized, their beliefs would also be a little different. If the epistle of Barnabus, or the gospel of Thomas, or any of the other multiple books that *men* decided would not go into the Bible would've made it into the Bible, the beliefs of Christians would be different today. And of course that goes for every other religion as well.

Another thing I don't like about the terms 'secular' or 'secular humanism' is the fact that, if you use them, you're implying that there's an alternative when there's absolutely no proof that there is. Anything that's outside the realm of the "secular" is outside the realm of existence; which means outside the realm of reality. There's only one true alternative to the so-called 'secular', and that's the world of the imagined. So the debate is truly not between the secular and the divine, but between the secular and the imagined. The world of the divine *is* the world of the imagined. It has no more validity than any other belief conceived through the power of imagination. Just because the overwhelming majority of humans around the world *believe* it does (in one way or another), doesn't make it so. It has no more validity than

Santa Clause, the Easter Bunny, the Tooth Fairy, leprechauns, or a million other things created through the power of imagination. So if we're going to use a term like 'secular humanism' we need to make up a term for its only true alternative. Maybe something like 'imaginative humanism', or 'make-believe humanism', or 'fantasy-based humanism'…etc. Any such term would work as long as it's understood that *both* sides are "humanists"; the only difference being that one side (secular humanism) deals with reality *as it is*, while the other side (theism) deals with reality *as they wish it were.*

One last thing I would like to point out before I move on is the fact that "Secular Humanism" *is not* a religion—regardless of what the Supreme Court has declared. At best it may be referred to as a philosophy; and even then it's not a whole philosophy, but only a small part of any individuals overall philosophy. I think the whole legal battle was simply over secular humanists wanting the same Rights as religionists and getting tax-exempt status for their organizations as well. But no matter how you slice it, it's simply not a religion. If you don't believe me, just look up the terms 'Religion', 'Secular', and 'Humanism' separately in your dictionary and you'll see that 'Religion' and 'Secular' are nearly exact opposites. Anyway, let's move on.

Usually, religions are classified into two schools of thought: Eastern religions and Western religions. The major *eastern* religions are Hinduism, Buddhism, Taoism, Confucianism (if you consider it a religion), Shintoism, and their variations. The major *western* religions are Judaism, Christianity, Islam, and their variations. I'm really not sure how Sikhism is defined because it's a mixture of Hinduism and Islam, but I think it's defined as an eastern religion. Besides these major religions, there are also many minor religions most people have never heard of, and because they're minor religions, I'm not going to delve into them. The thing to remember is that my basic premises on various religions apply to *all* religions, not just the most popular ones.

Another thing all religions have in common is the belief that *their* religion *is* God's religion, otherwise, they wouldn't believe in that particular religion, would they? But implicit in this belief is the fact that, if true, then *all other* religions must be false. Even though some people wouldn't agree with this fact, logically, it *must* be true. If God exists, he *must* come from some point of view. He must hold some values higher than other values, right? Of course he must. But some people don't believe so. For example, Mahatma Gandhi believed that all religions are true. But if this is true, then God must give different codes of values to different people, and would God do that? Not if he's omniscient. If he's omniscient, he knows that some values are higher than other values. He, as an omniscient God, simply wouldn't contradict himself or give differing value systems. As much as I agree with Gandhi in some areas, in fact, *all* religions are false (at least when it comes to knowing God's point of view). Sure there are elements of truth in every religion, otherwise they would've never became popular systems of belief. Although *no* religion is true, *all* religions contain truth. Most religions have solid codes of conduct (if actually followed), but *none* can lay claim to represent God's opinions because none come from God, but from the minds of men.

OK, calm down. I know every person who believes in a particular religion is having fits about now, but please hear me out. I know you believe *your* religion is the only *true* religion, but everybody else does too. I ask you this: If you were born in another place or time, would you hold you're current religious views? Doubtful. If you're Jewish, do you think you would be Jewish if you were born in China? If you're a Buddhist, do you think you would be a Buddhist if you were born in Australia? If you're an American Christian, do you think you'd be one if you were born in America *before* the arrival of the European's? Not a chance. In most cases people accept the religion of their society, community, family...etc. That's right, the overwhelming majority of people the world over "choose" their religion by geographical default. Does this means that if you plucked an evangelical fundamentalist Christian newborn out of Savannah Georgia and plopped him down in Tehran Iran, that a decade and a half later he would be chanting for the annihilation of America? Yep, in essence, that's exactly what I mean.

Getting a little off the topic for a moment, this is also how most people choose their morality as well. A great example of the proof of this would be a study done by Israeli psychologist George Tamarin. He presented the account of the battle of Jericho from the book of Joshua to 1000 Israeli children between the ages of 8 and 14. He then asked them if it was moral of the Israelites to destroy Jericho and kill all the men, women and children living there. 66% said it was, and 26% said it wasn't. He then asked another group of Israeli children the same question. Except this time he replaced "Joshua" with "General Lin" and "Israel" with "a Chinese kingdom 3000 years ago." This time only 7% said it was moral, while 75% said it wasn't. So in essence, if loyalty to Judaism was removed from the equation, the overwhelming majority were suddenly able to distinguish the truly moral from the truly immoral. My point being that the religion of a particular geographical area sets a moral paradigm that's difficult for the inhabitants to overcome—no matter how immoral it is.

Of course there's always going to be exceptions to the rule, but in general, *geography* determines religious points of view more than any other factor. Of course some people in India may become Christian instead of Hindu. Some people in Israel may become Christian instead of Jewish. Some people in China may become a Hindu instead of Confusion or Taoist…etc. But even in these cases, in order for a person to change their religious affiliation, they must first be exposed to another religion. A Shinto can never become a Buddhist unless he's been exposed to Buddhism. A Christian can never become a Taoist unless he's exposed to Taoism. A Hindu can never convert to Judaism unless he's exposed to Judaism…etc. *Geography* is the primary factor for a human beings religious point of view, and *exposure* is the secondary factor for a human beings religious point of view.

And of course another element of the exposure factor is that it must be a *positive* exposure and not a *negative* exposure. If a person is introduced to a religion that seems to make more sense to them, and seems to be better than the one he grew up with, it's only natural for some to convert to the new religion. If a person comes from a dysfunctional family that happens to be religious, it really should be no surprise if he finds another religion more comforting than the religion that apparently didn't help his own family. In most cases, it's the type of exposure a person has (positive or negative) that will help determine his future course when choosing a religion for himself.

Since geography is the primary factor by which most people become a certain religion, wouldn't that mean that salvation is based mostly on where you are born (that is if you believe in such nonsense)? If indeed only the people who've accepted Jesus as their savior are to be saved, then absolutely. This is why the fundamentalist Christian belief that only Christians will go to heaven is so absurd (and of course this also applies to Muslim fundamentalists, Jewish fundamentalists…etc.). A God who bases "salvation" on geography, and not merit, simply wouldn't be a just God. This is easily proven if people would just take the time to put themselves in another's shoes for a moment. Imagine you're born and raised as a Hindu in India. You've heard of the Bible (maybe), but you've never gotten a chance to read it for yourself (or maybe you have). Why in the world would you believe the religion that you, your parents, your grandparents, your great grandparents…etc, believe in is false, but a more modern religion from far away is true? Especially if you're a semi-educated Hindu and know your religion is, in fact, much older? Would this make any sense? If anything, Hindu's probably wonder how Christians can be so adamant about their religion when even scholars from predominantly Christian nations say Hinduism is older.

If that's not good enough, then just asking yourself why you don't change *your* religion. I'd bet nothing a Hindu, Buddhist, Muslim…etc, ever said to you could convince you to change *your* religion, so why would it be any different for them? Of course that's because *your* religion *is* God's religion, right? My whole point being that thinking other human beings are going to hell just because they don't belong to your religion is so arrogant and such an abomination of justice, I simply cannot understand how *anyone* doesn't realize that any *just* God would dismiss it out of hand.

If fact, I've always wondered how believers of monotheistic religions could possibly think their God could be so evil. Seriously, just think about it for a moment. They believe if a person doesn't believe in *their* God, their God will send them to be tortured *for all eternity* in a place that's so bad it can't even be described. So even if a Buddhist (or anyone else who doesn't believe in their God) never lied, cheated, stole, murdered, gave everything he had to the poor, was always nice, loved his neighbor, loved his enemy…etc, SORRY, he's still going to HELL! Could a God have a rule more *evil* than that? What kind of a "Supreme Being" would send the *overwhelming majority* of human beings off to be tortured for all eternity without making it *perfectly clear* to them that's what will happen if they don't believe in the right religion? Doesn't that sound more like something their make-believe devil would do? The whole thing is simply unbelievable.

This leads me to the problem with proselytizing. The problem with Christian proselytizing (or any other for that matter) is that it's an all-or-nothing proposition. For example: In order for the civilizations of Asia to accept the validity of Christianity, they must first accept the validity of the Bible; and in order to accept the validity of the Bible, they must ignore the *fact* that people have been living in Asia for, according to most experts, over two million years—much longer than the 6000 or so years covered in the Bible. When the earth was being "created" in Genesis, human beings had already been living in Asia for eons. So would it make any sense for a culture to ignore their *true* history and replace it with a *false* history? Of course not, it would be ridiculous!

Yes, people have the right to *believe* whatever they want, but to deny their own history would be beyond the scope of rationality. Human being's who come from a specific geographical location, come from a specific geographical location—period! Of course, their ancestors may have come from somewhere else, but that certainly cannot, and should not, be used to deny the history of generation upon generation upon generation...etc. That would simply be a lie and bordering on immoral. Human beings should be proud of who they are and where they come from. After all, you're here! You made it! You're part of group that succeeded. Now, I'm not saying you should get your self-esteem from your race, culture, genealogy...etc; only that you should accept *who* you are and *where* you came from. You can appropriate the history of any group of people you want, but it will never be *your* history. Accept who you are, and attempt to find out more about your own actual history. Of course much of your *actual* history is lost forever, but it's still your *true* history. Embrace it!

Another problem I have with proselytizing is in the way it's usually done. In most cases, when a Christian goes to another country to "preach the gospel" and "convert," it's more like bribery than proselytizing. If Christians are so sure that their religion is true, why do they resort to *buying* converts? Why do they base converting others on giving them worldly offerings? Of course they'll say they're just giving food, clothing, and other material goods in order to help the poor, but couldn't it be argued that it's being used as a tool to *bribe* converts? If you lived in a poor nation (most likely made poor by your governments policies by the way), and if your children needed water, food, clothing...etc., wouldn't you "convert" just for the sake of your children's survival? I probably would. Why don't Christians convert with *words* like Jesus did instead of giving poor people material goods in order to convert them? I think it's extremely ironic that a religion that tells people to live for the spiritual and not the material, uses the material as a tool of recruitment. Once again, actions speak much louder than words.

Anyway, it should be pretty obvious by now that geography and exposure are the basic causes of an individual's religious beliefs, but I would like to expand upon that premise a little further with a question: If God supports a particular religion, why has it never happened that a person born in a community of *one religion* wakes up from a dream or has a revelation about the truth of *another* religion he's never been exposed too?

For example: Why hasn't a Taoist from China who has never been exposed to Christianity, ever come forward and said something like "God told me in a dream last night that Taoism is not the true religion. God told me about his son Jesus, and that Christianity is the *one and only* true religion.

Now, even though I've never even heard of this man named Jesus, I've become born again. I've accepted Jesus as my savior, and now I must find a Bible so I can study Gods true religion." Wouldn't this have happened *at least once* in all of history? Or maybe a Christian who has never been exposed to Shintoism has a revelation from God telling him Shintoism is the true religion? Or maybe it happens to a Buddhist concerning Islam. Mix and match *any* of the world's religions in *any* combination you want, and guess what? IT'S NEVER HAPPENED!

If "God" is the God of any particular religion, wouldn't it have happened at least one time in all of history? Wouldn't God have let at least one person *in all of history* know he was following a false religion? And then told him about the *true* religion? To me, it just doesn't seem possible for him not to have. That is of course if he's truly a *just* God (Remember also that examples like Paul's conversion from Judaism to Christianity doesn't apply here because he had already been exposed to Christianity. It would only apply if he had never been previously exposed).

It's painfully obvious to any objective thinker why none of those scenarios has ever happened: The mind, whether the conscious or the subconscious, can only deliberate on things it's been exposed too. In other words, in order to "think" it must have something to think about. There's simply no way for a mind to deliberate the merits of Zoroastrianism, when it has no idea what Zoroastrianism is. This is one of the reasons why we know the human mind is responsible for religious ideas and not God (I guess before I go on here I need to point out that, although I've spent years looking for examples that would apply above, and have never found any, doesn't necessarily mean they don't exist. Maybe I simply haven't heard of them. I leave it up to you to look out for such examples for yourself, and if you find them, please make them known. But remember, if you here of a case, don't just accept it on faith—investigate it. I also have to say that, now that this idea is known, I worry that religionists are going to set-up the entire scenario and attempt to use it as proof that *their* religion is true, but there's nothing I can do about that. If they're willing to lie, manipulate, and deceive in order to perpetuate their religion, I guess that means they don't *truly* believe in their God, do they? I just know that if each case that comes forward from this time on is thoroughly investigated, they will be proven to be nothing more than shams).

The mind is also responsible for the utterly ridiculous phenomena of religious people seeing their deity in physical objects. For example: In

Christian nations, religious people tend to see the form of Jesus in clouds, in shadows from trees, in a stain on their wall, in mud puddles…etc. There was even one person who had a potato chip that looked like Jesus (at least what Americans believe Jesus looked like). And in the paper the other day, a grilled cheese sandwich with the image of the "Virgin" Mary (How do they even know what she looked like?) sold on e-bay for something like eighteen thousand dollars—unbelievable! In Buddhist nations, people see the Buddha. In Hindu nations people may see many different Gods because Hindus believe in many Gods. In Israel, Jewish people tend not to see such things because they don't identify "God" as having *any* type of physical form.

You can even take this to the next level. For example: Catholics not only see *Jesus,* but they see the "Virgin" Mary as well; while Protestant Christians only tend to see Jesus. This is because the importance Catholics place on Mary is much higher than the importance Protestants place on Mary. Isn't it obvious? Why don't Buddhists ever see Jesus? Why don't Christians ever see Mohammad? Why don't Jews ever see Mary? Why don't Taoists ever see Zoroaster…etc? Simple, because people only see what they have been psychologically conditioned to see. How could it be any different? "God" is as people want him, her, it or them to be. And when you have 6 billion human beings constantly looking for their deity, or for a "sign," they're going to see him, her, it or them every now and then. That's just simply the law of odds. As a matter of fact, let me make this point more clear with an amusing example from my own life.

As I wrote at the beginning of this book, when I can, I get my definitions and axioms from the philosopher Ayn Rand; but there's also another book I'm deeply indebted to by Dr. Leonard Peikoff entitled 'Objectivism: The Philosophy of Ayn Rand'. Anyway, when speaking of this book, most Objectivists simply refer to it as OPAR. So one night I was thinking to myself "Why should I keep writing out 'Glossary Of Objectivists Definitions'? Why not use the same tactic used for OPAR? In essence, just use the beginning letter of each word." So I looked at the cover of the book and was shocked to see the word G-O-O-D. I thought "perfect"! Laughing to myself, I decided to refer to it as 'The Good Book'—very ironic considering the fact that Christians call the Bible 'The Good Book'. It's also ironic considering Christians find meaning in their "Good Book" just like Objectivists find meaning (the meaning of words) in our "Good Book." And then I looked at it again, and to my astonishment, the word GOD leaped out at me. You see, the title on the book has the first two words "Glossary Of" next to each other;

underneath them it has the word "Objectivist"; and underneath that it has the word "Definitions." So going from the top down it says GOD. I was stunned and amused at the coincidence. I mean, what are the odds? To call something the "Good Book" and then a second later see the word "GOD"? Jeeze! So then it hit me: If I were a religious person I would definitely see this as a "sign" from you know who (or maybe it really is? Maybe God wants me to be an Objectivist? Hey, you can't *prove* he doesn't). It's just part of human nature to look for coincidences, connect the dots, see signs…etc; but those "signs" are, in fact, nothing more than coincidences. Or as I always tell my kids: "If it wasn't a coincidence, you wouldn't have noticed it."

My whole point being that *your* religious views, or perceived "signs," are no more valid than anyone else's—it's all a matter of belief. And what are beliefs? They're simply concepts formed in the imagination that have no basis in reality or enough evidence to prove them to be true. Obviously, if proof was available, you wouldn't need to believe—the facts would be right before your eyes. This is the difference between *knowing* something, and *believing* something. When you *believe* something, you're taking something for granted that *cannot* be proven to be true. When you *know* something, it *can* be proven to be true. Here are a few examples:

We *know* 2 + 2 = 4. Know matter what language the question is asked in, as long as the concept of two is understood correctly, the answer will *always* be four—it can never be anything else. We *know* when water gets cold enough it freezes, and when it gets hot enough it boils. We *know* humans will die without oxygen and they'll die without water. We *know* when two dogs mate the female *will not* give birth to a platypus. We *know* these things to be true because we can *prove* them to be true, there's absolutely no evidence to the contrary.

However, when someone *believes* something, especially concerning religious affairs, there's *tons* of evidence to the contrary. Just ask the people who believe in another religion. There are laws of nature, and the law of cause and effect. Some of these we know, and some of these we don't—that's what *science* is all about. This is why Francis Bacon said "In order to command nature, we must first obey it." When we *know* something, it's an absolute. When we *believe* something, we do not *know* it. It's a *belief* because it's either not true, or we simply do not have the evidence to *know* it. Making the distinction between knowing and believing is what true wisdom is all about. It can be a very difficult thing to do, and we all make mistakes, but it's impossible to do if you let others do your thinking for you. Most people only make the distinction between knowing and believing when their backs are against the wall and they're intellectually forced too, but it's a distinction that must be made in order to gain true wisdom.

Another harsher way to look at beliefs is to see them as pure and simple nonsense. After all, what is nonsense? Nonsense is the word we use to describe that which is nonsensical. And what are things that are nonsensical? Simple, things that cannot be identified or proven by using our senses, i.e., things that are outside of the realm of seeing, hearing, touching, smelling and tasting. If what you're talking about is outside the realm of our senses, or cannot be proven using the senses, it's nonsensical—no matter how much you want to believe in it. And that's also why the belief in God or Gods is nonsensical as well. If a theist claims to *know* God exists, it gives an atheist permission to claim to *know* God does not exist. Why? Simple, because the theist has rendered the term "to know" to be meaningless. Anyone could claim to know anything because there would no longer be a standard for knowing as opposed to believing.

I would also like to point out that, although most human beings seem to have an innate need to believe in something, it's the *belief* that's important, not *what's* believed in. In other words, when talking about religious beliefs, if it wasn't for Jesus, Christians would've believed in someone else. If it wasn't for Mohammad, Muslims it would've believed in someone else. If it wasn't for Lao-tza, Taoists would've believed in someone else. If it wasn't for the Buddha, Buddhists would've believed in someone else...etc. Of course if you ask a believer about this they will disagree, but that's only because they believe *theirs* is the *true* belief and everybody else's is false. The problem is *they all believe that!* And because they all believe it, it proves my point perfectly. So let's look at some specific beliefs to make things more clear.

Some examples of beliefs are: The belief in God or Gods, the belief in the devil, angels, demons, miracles, heaven and hell, purgatory, reincarnation, karma, life after death, the soul, spirits, glossolalia (speaking in tongues), ghosts, goblins, witches, warlocks, psychics, horoscopes, magic, voodoo, numerology, tarot cards, Santa Claus, the Easter bunny, the tooth fairy, unicorns (Believe it or not, the Bible "confirms" the existence of unicorns), or a myriad of other silly unprovable, nonsensical, man-made things (or should I say non-things?). For some reason, the majority of human beings around the world seem to have a problem wanting to distinguish between imagination and reality (or they simply choose not to do so). And I think this is probably because every culture in the world has part of its history based in myth, legend and folklore. And because of this, nobody's willing to admit that much of their history is made-up because they believe it would take away important elements from their culture.

But what people need to understand is that *truth* and *reality* are always much more important than myth and legend. And not only that, but they can also be much more interesting and powerful as well. Yes, the power of imagination is an incredible tool of survival. In fact, it's one of mankind's most important tools; but like all tools, it must be used in accordance with the facts of reality. Just because the human mind can conceive of things that have no basis in reality, doesn't give them a basis in reality, i.e., it doesn't make them real. There's an objective reality out there, but it can only be discovered by those who do their best to have as little beliefs as possible. Those who choose to hamper their minds with beliefs may be able to identify reality in many cases, but they automatically handicap themselves from the start. *Beliefs* make all things possible, that's why they're so powerful for most people. But *reality itself* dictates that all things *are not* possible. *Beliefs* negate the concept of identity. If everything is possible, then nothing is impossible; and if nothing is impossible, then identity *itself* is not possible. I really don't want to spend too much time on beliefs because I could easily fill an entire book, but I would like to quickly touch upon a few before we move on. So let's start with miracles.

To begin with, there is no such thing. The belief in Miracles is simply the psychological phenomenon caused by the human minds attempt to prove to itself that events take place for a reason, i.e., they're based on nothing more than a human beings need for purpose and to make sense out of existence. People see something happen that they don't believe would happen in a normal state of nature and say something like: "See, what are the chances of *that* happening without divine intervention"? They evaluate an experience by looking at a specific statistical improbability and turn it into a "it happened for a reason" scenario. If a man falls out of a ten story window and lives, it's a miracle! If a man is shot five times and lives, it's a miracle! If a man survives the collapse of the World Trade Center, it's a miracle! But a "miracle" by definition, must be something that is *outside* of natural reality; it must be in the realm of the supernatural. And since nothing "supernatural" has ever been proven to exist, miracles fall into the category of human beliefs. In essence, you cannot call something a miracle simply because it falls into the realm of a statistical improbability.

As a matter of fact, having survivors after a catastrophe is a statistical probability, *not* a statistical improbability. The person who lives through it may *believe* it to be divine intervention and say something like: "It had to be a miracle, because what were the chances of me surviving through it *without* a miracle"? Well, the chances may have been slim that *you* survived, but the chances were overwhelming that *someone* would have survived. And if you're talking about someone surviving an incident against the odds, it's simply not a miracle. Once again, a miracle must be outside of natural reality or it's not a miracle—it cannot just be a statistical improbability. And we also need to keep in mind that just because something cannot be explained at the time, doesn't make it a miracle either. A true miracle would not just be the unexplained, but the unexplainable.

But let's look at what I consider the opposite of miracles. Let's look at what we call 'freak accidents'. When someone dies from a freak accident, why isn't it called a miracle? After all, the odds of a freak accident happening to someone are just as great as the odds of a so-called miracle happening to someone; the only difference being that miracles are viewed as positive, and freak accidents are viewed as negative, i.e., the only difference being one of perception. Sorry to disappoint you believers out there, but if God is able to control one, then by definition, he must be able to control the other. And for every person who *survives* because of a "miracle," there's a person who *dies* because of a freak accident. So why doesn't God ever get credit when someone dies in a freak accident? Simple, because in most cases human beings are psychologically conditioned to give God credit when *good* things happen, but blame something else when *bad* things happen. It's simply a human paradigm. But the point I would like to stress here is that you cannot have it both ways. If God is All-Powerful then he must be in control of freak accidents as well as miracles.

Another fact I would like to point out is the fact that the so-called miracles of today are a far cry from the so-called miracles of the past. In ancient times, supposed miracles were not only unexplainable, but unambiguous as well. Today, miracles are just the opposite—they're usually explainable and they're *completely* ambiguous. In other words, in the past, when a miracle supposedly took place, there was absolutely no doubt that a miracle took place. And this isn't just true in regards to the Bible, it was true all over the ancient world. But today's miracles are *always* completely unprovable, undocumentable, and ambiguous assertions. Why is this? I think the answer is obvious. In the past, proof wasn't necessary. In the past, the overwhelming human paradigm was one of ignorance that allowed for the existence of miracles. Today, the paradigm is the opposite. In today's world, intelligent people want proof. Of course *some* people today don't need proof, but most people do (at least when it comes to *true* miracles, that is. Although many people simply accept today's watered-down standard for miracles).

In the past, humans knew very little about how the physical universe worked. When it came to "the big picture" our ancestors were extremely ignorant; just like we're extremely ignorant compared to people who'll be living thousands of years into the future. That's just how the accumulation of knowledge works. But when it came to everyday survival in the natural world, our ancestors knew much more about their natural surroundings than we do. And that's simply because the type of knowledge our ancestors valued (how to find water, what types of plants were edible, how to catch, kill, and prepare food, how to watch the sun, stars and planets in order to keep track of the passing seasons…etc.), is no longer valued by us (at least in industrialized nations) because that type of knowledge is no longer necessary for everyday survival. But once again I'm getting a little off track here so let's get back to miracles.

So why don't we see the types of miracles from antiquity (such as the parting of the "Red" Sea, raising of the dead, turning staffs into snakes…etc) that we see today (surviving a fall, surviving an accident, giving birth…etc)? Simple, because miracles from antiquity are nothing more than mere myths. Doesn't anyone find it amazing that no miracles are ever caught on tape? I mean, come on people. We've had cameras, televisions, and video recorders for decades now, and not one time has a miracle ever been recorded—what are the chances? The odds are so great that it could almost be considered a miracle that a miracle has never been captured on tape. I do think though that it's only a matter of time before believers attempt to make forgeries using modern technologies. After all, throughout history believers have been more than willing to produce fake artifacts and such in order to push their religious agendas. I've always considered it ironic that people who believe in the Ten Commandments (Don't lie, cheat, or bear false witness) would break them to further their cause, but it happens, and happened, all the time.

As a matter of fact, as I was watching television the other day I thought of a perfect example of how a religious zealot using modern technology could use it to further his cause. I saw a television show about how a man invented a device that allowed him to actually aim the sound waves from his voice in one limited direction. It kind of works like a laser pointer, only instead of light, it sends sound waves. For example: If you had ten people in your front yard, you could use this device to speak to one person without anyone else hearing your voice. At first I thought of the military applications of such technology, but then it hit me. Just imagine this device in the hands of a fundamentalist zealot; a zealot who believes the end justifies the means. Just imagine it's Sunday morning and the normal church service has begun. Only for one unsuspecting individual, this service is going to be far from normal. As he's sitting there, a commanding voice out of nowhere says: "Bob, I love you, but don't you think your drinking is getting the best of you? Bob, your family loves you, don't you think they deserve more from you…etc.." Or perhaps more likely: "Bob, I love you, but don't you think you could do better things with the wealth you've earned? Perhaps, give more to the church…etc.." As Bob hears this, he looks around to see if anyone else hears it, but obviously nobody does. Finally, he simply asks the guy sitting a few feet away: "Excuse me, but did you just hear that?" And of course the man says "no." So Bob's now wondering: Did God just speak to me? Did I just receive a revelation?…etc. You get the picture. This new technology can easily be used to manipulate the ignorant or unaware, just like technology in the past was used to manipulate the ignorant and unaware in order to fleece them. It's yet another thing people need to be on guard against.

Another thing about the whole idea of miracles that's always confounded me is this: Don't people find it just a little too suspicious that in the past, these supposed miracles were going on all over the place, but now, they're not going on anywhere? Why is it that, in the past, people were being born of virgins, raising the dead, walking on water, healing the sick, turning water into wine, levitating or flying around…etc, but now, none of these things are happening anywhere? Of course most people don't know this because the overwhelming majority have never even heard of the ancient texts that tell these stories (except of course for one ancient sacred text *they* believe in), but they do, in fact, exist. The only *rational* explanation that makes any sense at all is that these "miracles" weren't taking place anywhere in the world, people only *believed* they were because of a paradigm of ignorance that allowed for there existence. Anyway, let's get back to modern day "miracles" with a few examples.

A few years ago nine men were stuck in the bottom of a mineshaft in Pennsylvania and were unable to get out. As I watched the events unfold on television, I was simply flabbergasted at the amount of times the terms "miracle" and "divine intervention" were used to describe the events. This was a perfect example of human beings giving credit to a miracle when absolutely no miracle took place. The rescue was truly a triumph of human will, determination, and technological know how—*not* divine intervention. As I watched, I kept thinking to myself: "Do Americans no longer believe human beings have the ability to be benevolent, ingenious, or heroic? Come on people"!

Anyway, at roughly the same time this so-called "miracle" was taking place, a jet on the other side of the world crashed killing 83 people and injuring another 200 or so. If "God" reached out to save the 9 miners, then he must have also decided to ignore the horrible fate of the nearly 300 people who were either burnt, battered, or crushed to death in the plane accident. You simply cannot have it both ways. If God has power over one, he must have power over the other as well. According to many, and for some incomprehensible reason (as always), "God" decided that the nine miners were of a higher value than the 83 passengers who died in that crash. Do you actually believe God would do such a thing? Do you actually believe God valued the lives of those nine men more than he valued the lives of the men, women, and children on that jet? If you believe this nonsense, how would you feel if *your* loved ones died a terrible death because, well obviously, they weren't worthy of Gods divine intervention?

And to those of you who believe God intervened to save *your* loved ones, I ask you this: Just how gigantic is your ego? And this: How do you think others who've lost loved ones in accidents feel when you claim a miracle took place, and then thank God after *your* loved one lived through an accident, but *their* loved one died? Are you not implying that *your* loved one was sooooo special that God himself saw it necessary to save him, but *their* loved one wasn't special enough for God to save? You may not have realized it, but yes, that's exactly what you're implying. Utter arrogance! Utter hubris! Utter nonsense!

Now, how about the "miracle" of spontaneous healing? Once again, there's no proof of a miracle. Now don't get me wrong here, I'm not saying people never heal without any *verifiable* reason (and when I say *verifiable*, I mean not verifiable at present). I'm saying these healings are not miraculous. I'm saying when these things happen it's most likely caused by some type of psychological phenomenon such as a positive attitude, a placebo effect...etc. Studies have shown that people who pray and people who have a positive attitude *both* heal quicker than those who don't, but there's no proof that it's God answering those prayers. It's much more likely that praying relieves stress, which in return, helps people heal faster (or something like that). And remember, just because we don't completely understand something at this point in time, doesn't mean it's miraculous or supernatural either. The mind is still a very mysterious thing.

There's also another important point I would like to make about "miraculous" spontaneous healings. Why is it that when these things take place it's never something that can be shown to be truly, absolutely, and incontrovertibly miraculous? Now, if someone grew an arm back, *that* would be quite an argument would it not? Or how about a hand? Or a finger? How about just a fingertip? At least if one of these things took place we couldn't just attribute it to the placebo effect or a positive attitude, could we? That would take something really special, would it not? But of course those things never happen do they? Does God have something against people who lose limbs? Anyway, it's just more proof that spontaneous healings are not miraculous.

Another example that modern-day religionists give for the existence of miracles is the "miracle" of birth. But this is utterly ridiculous if you look at it from a historical point of view. Nowhere in the Bible (or any other sacred text as far as I know) does it state that the birth of a new life is miraculous. As a matter of fact, the exact opposite is implied. The reason the birth of Jesus is considered miraculous is because *it wasn't* normal; just like the birth of the Buddha is considered miraculous because *it wasn't* normal; just like the birth of Lao-tzu is considered miraculous because *it wasn't* normal....etc. Birth, like life, is only considered miraculous by today's watered-down standard for miracles. And why is this? Because *real* miracles do not exist; and because real miracles do not exist, modern mystics had to replace them with *natural* miracles, which of course, are not miracles at all.

It may seem a little strange, but I like drawing an analogy between miracles and cannibalism. In ancient times people believed *both* were going on all over the place, when in fact, neither really was. However, because of ignorance, this was the paradigm of the majority of the world's population. Yes, there was *some* cannibalism going on, but very little (of course here I'm referring to *historic* and not *pre*-historic man. In prehistoric times there may have been much more cannibalism going on than we would like to admit). But if you asked one group of people if *they* were cannibals, they would've responded with outrage: "What, us? Of course not! But *those* people are." And then if you asked *those* people if *they* were cannibals, they would've said: "Are you kidding? Of course not! But *those* people over there are"...etc.

Organized cannibalism seemed to be going on all over the world, when in actuality, it really wasn't going on very much at all during historic times. In essence, this was the same with miracles except to the extreme. Everyone *believed* miracles were happening all over the world, when in fact, they weren't happening anywhere. People just *believed* they were.

Before I go on, allow me to give some examples of ancient miracles compared with modern miracles. My ancient examples are from the Bible, while my modern examples are from my local paper.

The parting of the "Red" sea vs. "Sometimes I've been feeling bad and I got a good phone call or letter." Raising the dead vs. "My dad had his leg amputated and doctors said he wouldn't make it but he did." Calming a thunderstorm with a few words vs. "My friends brother-in-law survived a gallbladder removal with a liver that was in poor condition." Feeding thousands with only a couple of fish and a few loafs of bread vs. "My kitten was poisoned and we were able to make him better." Changing staffs into snakes vs. "My husband was supposed to die two years ago, but he's still alive." Turning the Nile into blood vs. "I should've been killed in a car accident, but I wasn't." Do I have to go on? If you refuse to see the difference between ancient miracles and modern miracles, then there's really no point in me giving more examples. But if you want some more examples of miracles that are not miracles, I suggest you go to the December 2002 issue of readers digest. It illustrates perfectly the difference between modern so-called miracles and history's so-called miracles.

So, how about prayer? Does praying work? I guess this would depend on what you mean by "work." If you mean that when people pray it can cause less stress and good things to happen, then yes, maybe it does work. But is it the praying that works, or is it the fact that it gives people a positive attitude that can bring about positive results that makes it work? I would say the latter. Once again, I would say that a positive attitude can work miracles.

Now, if you mean prayer works in the sense that when you pray to God he may personally answer your prayers, then no, I don't believe in prayer. There's simply no proof that God answers prayers. This is why praying falls into the category of beliefs. It doesn't matter how many people give testimonies of prayer working for them, because you can also get testimonies supporting everything from astrology to palm reading to voodoo to witchcraft to alien abductions…etc. If personal experience equates as proof, then these beliefs are as valid and as true as prayer. An individual's personal experience may prove to *them* that God is involved in their life, but it proves *nothing* to anyone else.

I would also like to point out that when it comes to prayer, the overwhelming majority of the time we only hear from one side of the argument. For example: Let's say a plane is about to crash and the people on board begin to pray. If they live, they say their prayers were answered; thus supplying the "proof" that prayer works. But what if they die? I recently heard of another plane crash where *all* 200 people on board were killed. Are you going to tell me that *not one* of these people prayed while the plane was going down? Although I can't prove it, I think it's much more likely that the *overwhelming majority* of people on board probably prayed. But since they're all dead, we don't hear about how their prayers *weren't* answered, do we?

I like drawing an analogy between those who lose in war, and those who "lose" in prayer. As the saying goes: "Those who win the war, write the history." Well, this holds true with prayer as well. Those who "win" in prayer also write the history. The reason *both* sayings are true is because the "loser" never gets a hearing because obviously, he's dead! Yes, prayer may have possible psychological benefits for some, and those psychological benefits may even turn into physical benefits, but that doesn't mean a Supreme Being had anything to do with it.

There's also another problem with prayer. Exactly which God are we supposed to pray too? Don't Christian's find it unnerving that Hindu's, Muslims, Shinto's, Sikhs…etc., also claim God(s) answers their prayers as well? If the only way to God is through Jesus, then why is God answering prayers made to "false" Gods? Of course Christians may use the "Their prayers are being answered by the Devil, not God" argument, but to any objective thinker, this argument is utterly ridiculous. This is simply just another thing they *believe* and do not *know*.

I was going to go on from prayer to life after death, but as I was writing this section an interesting news story came out of Texas that I just had to add. Apparently, four students from a high school cross-country team decided to stop and say a prayer before they arrived at a track meet. So they pulled the car over to the side of the road, got out, and began to pray. As they were praying, a passing car went off the road and struck the four, killing one and sending the rest to the hospital. How ironic is that? What more really needs to be said? Apparently, sometimes praying can actually be bad for you health, *and* it can even be deadly! Or as far as we know, maybe God *did* answer someone's prayer? Couldn't it be argued that maybe he answered the prayers of someone on the opposing team? My point being that you can never *know* one way or the other. This is why prayer is nothing more than a *belief.*

The last belief I'm going to touch upon is life after death. So, is there life after death? Is there a heaven and hell? Is there a purgatory? Is there reincarnation? Is there Nirvana? Is there…etc? Anyone who answers *any one* of these questions is answering the un-answerable. We, as *living* beings, will simply never know what will happen *after* we die *until* we die—and probably not even then. Anyone who says they *know* is either lying or fooling themselves. Personally, of course I hope there is life after death. Who wouldn't? But just because I hope there's life after death, doesn't mean there *is* life after death. I know this may sound strange coming from an atheist, but I also hope there's a cosmic judge (God?) holding people accountable for what they did while they were alive. I would love to see murderers, rapists, child molesters…etc, get their just due. As a matter of fact, nothing would make me happier. I would especially love to see God (or the Gods) confront people who had the audacity to speak for him, her, it, or them. Nothing would give me more satisfaction than to see the look on some fundamentalist zealot's face when God called him on it.

Anyway, getting back to life after death, people have the right to believe whatever they want to believe. But they need to remember that it's just a belief and not something that they know one way or the other. This reminds me of a conversation I once had with my mother. We were talking one day and out of nowhere she told me she might be an atheist. When I asked her why, she said because she didn't believe in life after death. Well, I thought about it for a moment, and it hit me: What does one have to do with the other? Just because you don't believe in life after death doesn't mean you can't believe in God. Just because in *our* society the two are *believed to be* inextricably connected, doesn't mean they are. Just because the paradigm of the majority (Christians) is dominate, doesn't mean it's true. Maybe, just maybe, Gods gift to us is the gift of life itself and not some form of life after death. And maybe, just maybe, God wishes human beings would quit squandering this precious gift of life. Who's to say? Nobody can ever know one way or the other, it's all a matter of guess work. Maybe God meant for life on earth to be heaven, but human beings came up with their own screwed-up paradigms instead of using Gods? This belief, although a minority belief, and although I don't believe it myself, may be the correct belief. My point is, once again, that when we're talking about *beliefs,* we'll never *know* one way or the other, that's why they're called *beliefs.*

There's also another big problem with many beliefs. How can we ever objectively apply justice if some of these beliefs are even partially true? If there's a devil, if there are demons, if there are witches, warlocks…etc, and if they have power over us, or ways of manipulating us, how can we hold human beings accountable for anything they do? If the devil made me do it, how can you hold *me* accountable? If demons were in control of my actions, how can you hold *me* accountable? If a witch cast a spell on me, how can you hold *me* accountable? If a Voodoo priest slipped me a magic potion, how can you hold *me* accountable?…etc. Human beings cannot be held morally (or even legally) accountable for things they're made to do. So once again, if there's a devil, demons, witches, warlocks, magic potions…etc, nobody can ever be judged *objectively* because we can never know if some type of a "secret force" made them do it.

Another point I would like to make here (since we're talking make-believe), is that, although I'm an Atheist, I may actually be doing Gods work, right? If people of all religions can use the "I'm doing Gods work" argument, why can't I? There's no proof that a human being must believe in God in order for God to work thru them. So using the theists own way of thinking, why can't I say I'm doing Gods work? After all, "God works in mysterious ways" right? Do I believe it? Of course not, but who knows? Maybe God hates yes men. Maybe God wants human beings to use the brain he gave them to question and think for themselves? Why would God give us the gifts of humanity (reason, rationality…etc) and then want us to ignore them? Or as a man named John Hutchinson once put it "Unthinking faith is a curious offering to be made to the creator of the human mind."

Instead of following religious authority figures around like sheeple, maybe God wants us to be our own man (or woman of course)? Maybe, just maybe, God wants us to spend our lives creating and perfecting our own moral character and helping others do the same? Who knows? I'll tell you who *doesn't* know: Fundamentalist Christians, Fundamentalist Muslims, Fundamentalist Jews, Fundamentalist Sikhs…etc. They can *believe* whatever dogmas they want, but they certainly don't *know* if they're true. What I wrote in the last couple of paragraphs has just as much validity as any belief system ever written.

What most people don't seem to realize is that the number of proponents of a certain belief has absolutely nothing to do with whether or not it's true. For example, what's the best hamburger you've ever eaten? Was it at a large chain restaurant? Was it at a small family owned restaurant? Was it from your own barbeque?…etc. My favorite is called the Bowserburger from a local bar/restaurant near my home. Anyway, just for the fun of it, I asked a number of people this question and did my own little unscientific survey. And what were the results? *Not one person* said McDonalds made the best hamburgers! But how can this be? After all, when it comes to *numbers* nobody even comes close to selling as many hamburgers as McDonalds, so they *must* be the best, right? It would seem that way, but it's obviously not true. McDonalds knows how to market, sell, and replicate hamburgers much better than it can actually make hamburgers taste good. My point being, once again, that what may be the majority opinion or belief is not necessarily the *true* opinion or belief.

Now, when looking at particular beliefs, just look at how the concept of heaven has changed over time. In modern times, heaven is defined as the dwelling place of God, angels, and where the chosen few go after they die. But it's never explained exactly *where* heaven is located. In the past, whether we're talking about the Bible, Quran, or other sacred texts, "heaven" was located just above the earth somewhere. Up in the sky, up in the clouds…etc. "It rained from heaven," or Jesus "ascended to heaven," or better yet, the Tower of Babel was evil because, as the Bible puts it, the Babylonians built it to "ascend to heaven." Or, the stone that "fell from heaven" (a meteorite I believe) that's worshipped by Muslims in Saudi Arabia (Mecca), are just a few quick examples. And of course this is also why the some mountains tops are sacred places when it comes to many religions. Obviously, people thought if they went to the top of mountains they would be closer to God.

And then of course, multiple times in the Old Testament human beings sacrificed animals and cooked them for "a soothing aroma to the Lord." Although primitive, these people weren't stupid. They assumed correctly that if smoke went up, so would smell. They believed God would smell the "soothing aroma" up in heaven just above them. Being ignorant, they simply had no idea how vast the universe actually was. By all accounts in historical times, heaven was just above us. It was an actual place just above us in the physical universe—not in some un-definable, un-locatable, unknowable place in another dimension or some other far away universe. As a mater of fact, the concept of other dimensions or other universes hadn't even been thought-up yet. The reason Heaven's location was changed over time is because of the growth of human knowledge. Once mankind started to better understand the planet, sky, sun, solar system, galaxy, universe…etc, the belief that heaven was "up there just above us" became absurd. It was yet another notch in the belt for human reason, and yet another blow against human beliefs. Every time science increases human knowledge and understanding, religious beliefs lose credibility. And because of the reasons given above, *anything* and *everything* mankind has to say about heaven (or life after death) is based on nothing more than mere belief; just like *anything* and *everything* having to do with God, as defined by man, is based on nothing more than a man-made belief. Whether we like it or not, this is an irrefutable fact of reality

This is why all religions are based on faith and belief. People *must* have faith because facts and evidence are not available (at least not when it comes to God, or the Gods, point of view). This is one of the differences between religion and philosophy. Religions make the claim that they *know* God's point of view, while philosophy does not (although some philosophers do). Both are systems of thought, but philosophy makes no absurd claims to the divine. Philosophy must prove its assertions, religion doesn't have to. Philosophy *knows and accepts* that ideas come from the minds of men, religion does not (with some exceptions). As I mentioned earlier in reference to secular humanism, *all* systems of thought are *man* based. Just because religious believers *believe* they possess God opinions doesn't mean they do.

This is one of the reasons why leaders of different religions never get together to debate God, God's history, God's opinions…etc, with each other. If they did, average people listening to the debate could only come to one conclusion: Nobody really *knows* anything about "God," it's all a matter of belief and faith. They *will* get together to find common values and principles, but they *will not* get together to debate God, Gods history, Gods opinions…etc. They *will* get together to find common ground, but they *will not* get together to debate uncommon ground. Why? Because they know when their religious text speaks for God, they're truly *not* speaking for God. They're just giving their own religions *belief* of God, Gods history, Gods opinions…etc. All religions *believe* their sacred texts were inspired by God, but *none* can prove it—that's why they're called systems of *belief.* Most religionists have an unwritten code of conduct: If you don't question, criticize, or challenge *my* beliefs on God in public, I won't question, criticize, or challenge *your* beliefs on God in public. Equating this with the Wizard of Oz, modern religious leaders choose to "ignore the man behind the curtain" as long as the other leaders ignore the man behind *their* curtain.

But just for the fun of it, let's just take one example and imagine what a conference on say, Creationism, would be like. You would have religious leaders from around the globe debating which one of the world's myths of creation is true. Jew vs. Hindu, Christian vs. Taoist, Muslim vs. Shinto…etc.

Although some religions share their myth of creation with other religions (such as Judaism and Christianity), most do not. Most religions have their own myth of creation. And although some may share the same *basic* myth of creation (such as Islam and Christianity), the myth has variations.

For example: According to Jews and Christians, God created the world in six days and then rests on the seventh; but according to Islam, God created the world in six days but did not rest, he continued to work. Obviously, both cannot be true. I think if a conference like this ever did take place, it would be one of the most enlightening and educational conferences ever. After watching it, the average person could only come to one conclusion: These "experts" have *no idea* how the world was created—they're just guessing. They would also realize that they aren't even *educated* guesses, but guesses based on stories written by ignorant men thousands of years ago. And this is why leaders from different religions will not have this type of conference. It would be a no-win proposition for everyone involved. Since they could never come to an agreement on even a simple thing such as "Creation," it would make them all look like a bunch of dogmatic zealots hell-bent on maintaining their own ego and religions power base. In other words, it would unmask them for what they truly are. Once and for all, it would show people the world over that, contrary to what they want you to believe, nobody can speak for God, and no religious text can speak for God either.

While I'm on the topic of people who claim to speak for God, I would like to address "spiritual" experiences and so-called "personal relationships" with God. As mentioned earlier, the thing about spiritual experiences is the fact that although they are sometimes at the heart of an individual's belief system, they truly mean very little to others who haven't gone through the same experience. People from every culture on earth claim to have (or had) spiritual experiences, but the question is: Were they created *internally* or *externally*? In other words, is the person experiencing something supernatural, or is it an experience of their own making? I would say all evidence points to the fact that it was an experience of their own making. I say the experience comes from their own mind, i.e., people choose to see things the way they want to see things, and they deliberately search out coincidences, or have "experiences" in order to substantiate their beliefs. Allow me to explain by telling you about my own "spiritual" experience.

To begin with, there's simply no way I can possibly describe my experience in words adequate enough to live up to the task. Now, I realize this may sound like a cop-out, but I can only say that I'll do the best I can. I would also like to point out that most people who've had such an experience also say the same thing. This is probably because these types of experiences are so individualized that they only really make sense to the mind that created them. Once again, I do think these types of experience come from the mind of the person and not God. With that said, here goes.

On the morning of May 1, 2003, I woke up from a dream around 3:45 AM that can only be explained as an extremely unique, or as others would put it "spiritual" experience. To begin with, there was absolutely no middle ground between being deeply asleep and being completely awake. One second I was dreaming, the next second I was wide-awake and deep in thought. As far as I can remember, this had never happened to me in my entire life. Anyway, I awoke with so many thoughts going through my mind, I felt like a multi-tasking super computer. I knew exactly *why* I was here, and exactly *what* I had to do. It wasn't what I would call a life *changing* experience, it was more like a life *affirming* experience—coincidently enough, exactly what I needed at the time.

Although I could only remember a few moments of the dream, I couldn't stop processing it for the next 2 hours. All my life experiences seemed to come together as a chain of unbroken purposeful events reaching toward undeniable goals and objectives. Obviously, this dream was much longer than what I remembered because of the effects it had on me both physically and psychologically. Physically, I felt refreshed and rejuvenated, but when I got up to wash my face and looked in the mirror, my eyes were completely bloodshot and nearly swollen shut because of the amount of crying I must have done. I know it sounds paradoxical, but this dream was *both* the apex of absolute joy and of absolute sorrow. It was, without a doubt, the most emotional experience of my entire life. How it's possible to feel total euphoria and total sorrow in a single all-encompassing experience I have no idea, but that's exactly what happened. I can only say that the mind works in mysterious ways.

Now I suppose you want to know exactly what I remember of this dream right? Sorry, but there's no point in saying what happened because it simply wouldn't make much sense to anyone else. As a matter of fact, if I told you, you would probably say something like: "That's it! That's your amazing dream? Big deal"! And guess what? I wouldn't blame you. As I mentioned earlier, these types of experiences never seem to really make sense to anyone but the person who has it. All I know is that this dream made it perfectly clear to me that I was going in the right direction with my life, which bring me to my next point.

Why don't I consider this dream a religious or divinely inspired experience? Simple, because it was *exactly* the type of dream my mind would have created itself. I've been an atheist my entire life and this dream only confirmed my convictions. If there's a God, why would he let that happen? Why would God allow such a special, life affirming experience happen to an atheist? It makes absolutely no sense. I had this experience because, subconsciously, *I wanted* to have this type of experience. Just like when a religious person has a spiritual experience; they have it because, deep down, they want or need to have it.

Doesn't anyone find it just a little too coincidental that when people have an experience of this sort, it's always the exact type of experience you would expect that person to have? For example: When a Christian, or a person living in a Christian community, has a spiritual experience, it's always a "Christian" type of experience. When a Buddhist, or a person living in a Buddhist community, has a spiritual experience, it's always a "Buddhist" type of experience. When a Muslim, or a person living in a Muslim community, has a spiritual experience, it's always the exact type of experience you would expect them to have…etc. Why don't Buddhist's, or people living in Buddhist communities, have Christian experiences? Why don't Christians, or people living in Christian communities, have Buddhist experiences? Why don't Muslims, or people living in Muslim communities, have Taoist experiences?…etc. Simple, because their minds simply cannot create, or relate to, a type of spiritual experience it's never been exposed too. This is why *my* experience was exactly like the type of experience I would have— because it's the only type of experience that would make any sense to me, or mean anything to me.

Getting a little of topic for a moment, this phenomenon also goes for Near Death experiences as well. Although I haven't done much research concerning Near Death experiences, I've noticed they seem to work in the same way as spiritual experiences. People who live in places that are dominated by Christian paradigms, usually have Christian types of Near Death experiences. For example: Many Christians talk about seeing the "Pearly Gates" during their experience, but Buddhists certainly don't. Isn't it just a little too coincidental that people have the exact type of experience you would expect a person living in that time and place to have? Of course there are some similarities around the world (such as most people seeing a bright light), but those similarities could easily be attributed to physical phenomenon and not supernatural phenomenon. I suppose if a person is losing consciousness, a side effect probably would be seeing light in one way or another, wouldn't it? But as I said, since I haven't done enough research into this subject, I really can't give a truly informed opinion at this point in time. However, I do think the phenomenon is psychological and not supernatural.

Another thing that shows me that these types of experiences are created in the mind of the individual, and are not from God, is the timing of the dream. It was at a time in my life when I was having to make a very important decision. The place I work was in financial shambles and I wasn't sure if I would have a long-term position with the company. I loved my job because I was able to listen too books on tape while I worked, but I wasn't sure how much longer it was going to last. So my choice was to either go back to school and get a formal education, or to continue what I was doing and hope to get my book finished before I lost my job. The first choice was much more practical, while the second choice was geared more toward long-term happiness, but less toward economic security. In the end, my choice really came down to the fact that this book was, professionally speaking, the most important thing in my life—I had to finish it at any cost. Thus, my mind created the supporting experience it wanted.

Another reason why I think these types of experiences are created in the individuals mind, is because at the time I had this dream, I was in the process of working on this chapter on religion; and while doing so, many months were devoted to the study of religious experiences and why people have them. I was completely wrapped up in the experience of religion, and religious experiences. I think my mind wanted me to feel what the experience would be like, so it created a scenario that would conform perfectly to my individuality, i.e., it created the experience it wanted. I think this is precisely what happens in every type of spiritual experience. Why else would people always have the *exact type* of religious experience you would expect the person living in that time, place, and community to have? Obviously, they have it because their mind created it. I think it really is that simple.

Now I'd like to get back to the phenomena of human beings who claim to have a so-called "personal relationship" with God, or more precisely, personal relationships with Jesus. Yes, once again I choose to pick on Christians, but that's only because I know their religion best. But please keep in mind what I'm about to say applies to all religions who believe in a Deity, not just Christians.

When a Christian tells me he's having a "personal relationship" with

Jesus, is he? No, he's simply fooling himself. The only personal relationship he's having is with his own imagination. Can I absolutely prove this? Of course not. Once again, I cannot prove a negative. But I can give an example of proof that I think is adequate enough to prove it to any rational mind.

To begin with, it's one thing to say you *believe* in Jesus or follow the teachings of Jesus, it's quite another to say you're having a *personal relationship* with him. Having a "personal relationship" with another implies a dialog; it means you're actually communicating on a regular base's with the other. And as I have said, I cannot prove *absolutely* that it doesn't occur, but I *can* prove that at least 99% of the people who claim to have this relationship with Jesus are simply fooling themselves. How? By doing a simple experiment. Let's take a survey of 100 Christians (the number's not important, but the more the better) who claim to have a personal relationship with Jesus, and then give them a list of 25 questions to ask Jesus during their next encounter (of course these people cannot know who else is in the study, or what questions will be asked beforehand). Questions such as: When was the earth created? When was he born? Is he for or against the death penalty? Is it moral to charge interest? What's his favorite color? Should we always turn the other cheek, or are there times when an eye for an eye is appropriate? If there was an Adam and Eve, what color were they? Were there dinosaurs on Noah's ark? Did humans evolve into our current physical shape, or did he (or God) make us as we are from the very beginning; and if he did, what about all of the not-quite-human skeletons that have been discovered? Were they at least part human? If humans didn't evolve into their present form, why do they have tailbones? And why is it that, on rare occasions, human beings are even born with tails? Why do humans have an appendix? What's the exact percentage of DNA we share with chimpanzees? Is there life on other planets? Is there *intelligent* life on other planets? What is the meaning of life? If a tree falls in the forest and nobody's there to hear it, does it make a sound?…etc.

Make sure to have a controlled environment, and that there's no collaboration among the participants, and then collect the answers as soon as possible. If all these people are having personal relationships with Jesus, they should all come back with the same answers, right? If they don't, they're obviously not having a personal relationship with Jesus. Fact is, you won't even have *two* people who come back with the same answers. And if everyone has different answers, then *at the very most*, only *one* could have the correct answers; and if only *one* has the correct answers, then only *one* could possibly

simply. I'm also sure that many of the other ancient books from around the world are also, at least partially, based in historical fact and reality as well. I'm sure that the stories from ancient Greece, India, China, or anywhere else around the world have some historical bases too, but that doesn't mean "God" had anything to do with them either.

Getting back to geography, if you add up the square footage of this region, it's probably less than five percent of the world's entire inhabited landmass. If the Bible is a history book, it's only a history of a very small percentage of Middle Eastern people. In a way, the Bible itself even confirms this in Genesis in regards to Cain's wife (where did she come from?). When the earth was being "Created" in Genesis, human beings had been living in Africa, India, China, Europe, Australia and the Americas for thousands of years; and in some places, for tens of thousands of years; and in other places, for hundreds of thousands of years. And if you're going to include our not-quite-human ancestors, we're talking a few million years.

This is one thing that's always amazed me about groups of people like, just for a quick example, African-Americans (among many others of course). Most have blindly and ignorantly accepted a Biblical view of history. Mankind's history goes back many times further in Africa than anywhere else on earth. As far as I know, according to all physical evidence, the human race began in Africa. Just because humans weren't advanced enough to write it down at the time, doesn't mean it didn't happen. Biblical history of mankind is just the tip of the human biological iceberg. In fact, it's just the tip of *one of many* human biological icebergs.

Why people from different races and cultures accept Middle Eastern Biblical history as their own amazes me! My roots are part Scandinavian, part Cherokee, and who knows what else. As a matter of fact, I didn't learn I was part Irish until I was 40 years old. Like most Americans, I'm a mutt. My ancestors may have had Biblical history forced on them, or they may have accepted it by choice, but one thing is for sure: *my* heritage *does not* go back to the Biblical Middle East, and neither does probably 95% of all other human beings on earth.

If you don't agree, you're simply not looking at the big picture. So let me try to explain this by using a smaller picture. As an American, do you celebrate Thanksgiving? If you do, why? The overwhelming majority of current Americans aren't related to the Pilgrims in any way whatsoever. Thanksgiving has become a part of our culture only because we have accepted it as part of our collective American history. This is also true of

Christmas, Halloween and some other national holidays. Do you drink green beer on St. Patrick's day? If so, why, are you part Irish? My whole point being that the *actual* history of 99% of us will never be known (although DNA is now changing much of that). I would even argue that 100% of us will never know our *complete* history. Just because you may have accepted Biblical history as your own, does not make it *yours*.

Getting back to religion in general, I would like to make a suggestion. If you truly want to understand *your own* religion, study another's. If you're a Christian, study Taoism. If you're Jewish, study Buddhism. If you're Hindu, study Islam…etc. After all, whether you know it or not, your religion is a descendant of another. Christianity has its roots in Judaism. Islam does as well, and claims to be the true fulfillment of the Bible—as does Mormonism. Buddhism is a descendant of Hinduism, as is Jainism. Sikhism is a mixture of Hinduism and Islam. If you're a Protestant Christian, your roots are based in the Catholic Church; whose roots are based in Judaism, whose roots are partly based in ancient Egypt and ancient Babylon…etc.

This is why it's important to study other religions. I guarantee if you take the time to do this *with an open mind*, your view of your own religion will change immeasurably. Although I disagree with much of Oliver Wendell Holmes' philosophy, he did make a profound observation when he said: "A mind once expanded, can never return to its original dimensions." If your faith is as strong as you believe it is, you shouldn't be afraid to study other religious points of view. After all, that's how we truly learn. If the only people you read or talk too believe as you do, you're never really going to expand your mind. You're going to confine it to a tiny, dogmatic, cerebral birdcage-sized view of reality. Is that what you want? This is yet another gripe of mine about religion. People are so afraid their faith will come into question, they refuse to open their minds to other points of view. In other words, they refuse to think. I heard somebody once say "the essence of religion is unquestioned obedience," and I couldn't agree more. Religion *by its very nature* causes people to go into a self-imposed mental shell in order to be able to maintain the belief that *their* religion is the *true* religion.

I see this happen where I work all the time. Because of the nature of my job, I'm able to listen to books on tape throughout my workday. I've averaged at least 1000 hours worth of listening time per year for over a decade now. If fact, it's why I still hold my current job. It's great, I actually get paid to learn. And I've also been able to get some of my co-workers to do the same. It's worked out well because we trade books with each other to provide variety.

Anyway, after doing this for a while I noticed a pattern. Every time I brought in a book or lecture series on another religion, Christians didn't want to listen to it—I couldn't believe it. For example: Over the years I've purchased many University level lectures on Islam, Buddhism, Taoism…etc., and my Christian co-workers simply won't listen to them. Why wouldn't someone who supposedly values God want to listen to another religion's opinion of God? But even worse than this, I saw another pattern. Devout Christians didn't even want to listen to lectures on Christianity *itself* if it was different than their own little brand of Christianity.

For example: The man I usually worked next too didn't make it to work for a few days so a replacement was brought in. While talking to him at lunch I discovered that he was a Jehovah's Witness. So I told him I was interested in his religion and that if he had any tapes about it, I would be grateful if he would let me listen to them. He said he did, and the next day he brought in a book on tape entitled 'The greatest man who ever lived'. The book was about Jesus, and it was basically just the New Testament. After I finished it, I ask him if my other co-workers who listened to books on tape could listen to it as well. He said yes, so on the next break I told two of my Christian co-workers that the man I was working with was a Jehovah's Witness, and that they might want to listen to the book he had brought in about Jesus. To my astonishment *both* declined the offer, I couldn't believe it! Exactly what were they afraid off? I think I already answered that question earlier.

Another example would be when I purchased a lecture serious from The Teaching Company entitled 'The Historical Jesus' by Professor Bart Ehrman of the University of North Carolina, and the only people who didn't care to listen to it were my *Christian* co-workers. I suppose part of the reason they didn't want too was because I had told them that, at times, it was critical of Christianity, but so what? Here you have a professor who, arguably, knows as much about Jesus as anyone else alive—and Christians aren't interested in is opinion? Here you have a man who's spent decades studying Jesus and the New Testament—and Christians aren't interested? Here's a man who's read the Bible in many different languages *and* of different historical time periods—and Christians aren't interested? How is this possible?

As an Objectivist, I want to hear anything I can get my hands on about Objectivism. Not only stuff from other Objectivists, but sometimes more importantly, stuff from people who disagree with Objectivism. If you want to know the truth, you must be willing to listen to others who think (or believe) they possess it. And only after you've listened to their evidence can you make a determination on the validity of their claims. Now, I understand that these few examples don't prove that *all* Christians keep their heads buried in the sand, but it's a definite pattern among the Christians I've come in contact with. I also assume this phenomenon isn't exclusively Christian. I suppose if I was surrounded by Muslims, and was trying to get them to listen to books on Islam that came from a different perspective than their own, it would probably be the same. So once again, religion *by its very nature* encourages ignorance and misunderstanding among humans, and will continue to do so as long as people take it seriously.

Now, after you've spent time studying another religion, go back and study your own religion with an open mind. It never ceases to amaze me how a person from one religion can be so critical and logical about someone else's religion, but will be completely uncritical and illogical about their own. For example: When I tell Christians about the births of different religious leaders around the world they almost always chuckle. According to the religion of Taoism, Lao-tzu is said to have been born after a shooting star fell into his mother's womb; and when he finally came out of his mother, he was already a wise old man with gray hair. According to Buddhism, when Gautama Siddhartha (the original Buddha) sprung from his mother's side, he immediately took 7 steps and said: "this will be my final birth." Although I haven't spoke to any Taoists or Buddhists about this, I can almost guess what their reaction would be to the Christian claim that Jesus was born of a virgin.

What most Christians don't seem to understand is that most of the worlds religion's believe their founder was miraculously conceived, could perform miracles, could heal the sick, transcend death…etc. As a matter of fact, one ancient text said that a contemporary of Jesus (Appolonious of Tiana) could perform miracles, heal the sick, caste out demons, and raise the dead. Before his birth, an angel told his mother that he was going to be divine, his birth was accompanied by miraculous signs, and as a youth he amazed adults with his knowledge of religious affairs. As an adult, he left home to travel and preach, he told people to live for the spiritual and not the material, he had disciples who believed he was divine, and he performed miracles for them to confirm their faith. He then angered the powers that be and was handed over to the Roman authorities to be punished. After death, he ascended to heaven only to return again and be seen by his followers, who then proceeded to write books about him. The comparisons with Jesus are striking. But most Christians have never even heard of this man, and even if they had, I guarantee they wouldn't believe what was written about him. You see, inevitably, people will study another's religion (or beliefs) with a critical, reasoning mind, but they will *almost never* study their own religion (or beliefs) with a critical, reasoning mind.

Or how about this comparison: Three thousand years before Jesus (according to the ancient Egyptians), "Horus" was born on Dec. 25th, his birth was foretold, he was born of a virgin, was adorned by three kings, there was a great star in the east, he performed miracles (healed the sick, walked on water…etc.), he taught at 12, was baptized at 30, had 12 disciples, was called the "lamb of God," "the light," and "the good Shepard," was crucified, buried for 3 days, and then resurrected. Sound familiar? Many of these miracles apply to others as well (Attis, Krishna, Mithra, Dionysus…etc). So once again, why don't people believe these stories? Simple, because people will study another's religion (or beliefs) with a critical, reasoning mind, but they will *almost never* study *their own* religion (or beliefs) with a critical reasoning mind.

Which brings me to my next point: Have you ever studied your religion's history or actually *read* your religion's sacred text? I couldn't tell you how many times I've asked Christians if they've actually read the Bible and they've told me no. I've asked people *in their 60's* who say they've been Christians their entire lives and they've never read the Bible for themselves—unbelievable! If you're going to call yourself something, you really should discover *for yourself* the meaning of that which you're going to call yourself. This point really hit home when I was talking to a protestant minister and I discovered that he didn't even know who Martin Luther was! How is that possible?

Another good example comes from Professor Bart Ehrman of the University of North Carolina at Chapel Hill. At the beginning of each semester Professor Ehrman asks his new students a few questions. I can't quote him directly because I get this from memory, but it goes something like this: He begins by asking how many of them have read Dan Browns 'The Da vinci Code', and the overwhelming majority raise their hands. He then asks how many have read the Bible, and only a couple of people raise their hands. Next he asks how many believe the Bible is the word of God, and once again, the overwhelming majority raise their hands. Last but not least, he says something like: "Let me get this straight. You took the time to read a book written by a *man*, but you haven't taken the time to read a book written by *God*"? What more do I really need to say?

And of course I'm not just talking about Christians. It may seem like I'm really running Christianity through the ringer, but that's only because I live in a predominately Christian nation, and most people reading this book probably consider themselves Christian. If I knew the majority of people reading this were going to be Muslims, then they would be on the receiving end of most of my comments. But don't worry Christians, for every disparaging comment I make concerning Christianity, I could make an equally valid disparaging comment concerning Islam or any other religion. It's just that I don't think I should spend time doing it in this particular book because of who I think the audience will be.

Next I would like to make some comments about Truth. Do you value truth? If you do, you'll take the advice I've given about studying other religions. If you don't take the advice, you simply don't value truth. You're just hiding in your own little world wearing self-imposed blinders. I hate to sound harsh here, but are you so ignorant and arrogant that you believe the "Truth" can only be found in only one book or one set of books? *Religion* seems to be the only human intellectual endeavor where people believe "the truth, the whole truth, and nothing but the truth" can be found in only one source. In all aspects of human knowledge, *only religion* makes such a ridiculous claim.

Think about it. If you want to know about philosophy, do you only study the works of Plato? If you want to know about psychology, do you only study the works of Freud? If you want to know about evolution, do you only study Darwin? If you want to know about economics, do you only study Adam Smith? If you want to know about clowns, do you only study Bozo? You see, know matter what you want to learn about, your studying possibilities are almost limitless. Sure some subjects are going to be much easier to master than others, but we're talking about two of the most complex of subjects: God and Truth. If you believe you can know "God" or "Truth" by studying *one* book, you're simply fooling yourself because you will never know either by taking that simplistic approach.

In a way, this is one thing that's always made me laugh about so-called "theologians." A theologian is defined as a person who studies's God and religion. But since most western theologians throughout history have only studied the Bible and other *western* works, by definition, they cannot be called theologians. To me, a *true* theologian could only be a person who first studies *all* of the world's *major* religions, and then tries to study as many of the world's *minor* religions as possible. Since there's no way to ever know which religion is God's religion (if any), then the person searching for the truth must look anywhere and everywhere possible for the answers, not just in his own regions or religion's sacred texts.

I was quite simply amazed when I began seriously studying the world's religions to find out that the study of Comparative Religions was only a few decades old. The overwhelming majority of human beings base their lives on this stuff and its only recently been studied in a objective, comparative manner? How is this possible? In my opinion, it can only be explained by the fact that, since each religion had everything to lose and nothing to gain from such studies, they all stuck to their own religion out of fear that theirs might be proven to be false. In this aspect, I like drawing an analogy between religion and karate, so let me first lay the groundwork.

I've studied various martial arts ever sense my late teens and the first thing I discovered was the fact that they all think *their* fighting style is *the best* fighting style. Being that by this time in my life I had already been in a few dozen fights, I knew that much of what each system taught simply didn't work in the real world. They all had some techniques that would work in a real fight, but they also taught a lot of nonsense. I knew this, but how does a young punk teenager tell this fact to seasoned Black Belts who've been studying karate for years? The only way to really prove it to them would've been to start a fight with them and prove it that way. But of course this wasn't going to work because I would end up in jail. It's too bad, but without being able to prove something with actions, words sometimes seem meaningless.

Anyway, in 1993 a new type of martial arts tournament began called the Ultimate Fighting Championship (UFC). And since the only rules were you couldn't bite or eye gouge, it was basically as close to street fighting as possible. It immediately became clear that the best fighters were not the strict traditionalists, but the fighters who schooled themselves in as many forms of combat as possible. If you wanted to win, you not only had to know *your* style, but the styles of others as well. If you were a striker, you had to learn how to wrestle. If you were a wrestler, you had to learn how to grapple. If you were a grappler, you had to learn how to strike…etc. It became obvious that being a "Master" of any one style simply didn't cut it. I had known this for years, but why did it take so long for the martial arts community at large to discover this? Well, one of the reasons is because most martial artists haven't actually been in many *real* fights. The only fighting they've done is in the dojo they belong too. And since most dojo's only teach a particular traditional martial art, the student never learns what a real fight is like. The UFC changed all that. It showed that much of what is taught in traditional karate schools is useless. The courageous people who put on this tournament changed the martial arts paradigm forever. No longer could practitioners of one school of karate claim absolute superiority over the system of another. If you wanted to be a great fighter, you had to be well-rounded—period!

But the *main* reason it took so long for the martial arts community to discover much of what it taught was useless, was because karate, like religion, was stuck in a paradigm rut because nobody was willing to risk putting everything on the line. There was simply too much to lose and very little to gain by the people who's very livelihood depended on maintaining the status quo—and this is *exactly* what goes on with religion today. They have *everything* to lose and *nothing* to gain by debating other religions in public. But the fact is, while *they* have much to lose, *society at large* has much to gain. What's gained by both comparative religion and comparative karate is truth itself; which is of course, one of the highest of values.

The next observation I would like to point out concerning God, religion and morality, is the fact that religious people never judge *their* God, or their religion's founder, by the same moral standards they judge other people's God, religion's founder, or even other human beings. For example: If I had the power to save a life, stop a crime, end child abuse…etc., and chose not too, I would be judged by these people as immoral or maybe even evil—and rightfully so. But they don't consider their omnipotent God immoral for not intervening. If a toddler walked onto a busy street and I had time to save him before he was stuck by a car, but chose not too, I would be called immoral—and rightfully so. But they don't consider their omnipotent God immoral if he chooses not to intervene. If I had it in my power to stop a rape, but chose not too, I would be called immoral—and rightfully so. But they don't consider their omnipotent God immoral if he chooses not to intervene. If I had it in my power to stop a child from being tortured, but chose not too, I would be called immoral—and rightfully so. But they don't consider their omnipotent God immoral if he chooses not to intervene. Of course I could give an endless supply of examples, but just those alone should be enough to make the point. And to say, as the religious person does, "God works in mysterious ways" simply doesn't cut it. It's still judging by two different moral standards.

If you believe in the God of the Bible, allow me to give a couple of specific examples. But first I would like to point out that, in my opinion, and in the opinion of Jews (you know, the people who *wrote* the Old Testament), the God of the "Old" Testament, is certainly not the God of the "New" Testament. Anyone who reads the entire Bible *objectively* can easily see that they're of a completely different character. The God of the Old Testament is much more of an authoritarian type than the God of the New Testament. The God of the Old Testament is about absolute punishment for absolute sins or crimes. The God of the New Testament is about forgiveness and turning the other cheek. Christian apologists can use all the rationalizations they wish, but the Christian God of the "New" Testament is simply not the same as the Jewish God of the "Old" Testament.

I would also like to make an important point for Biblical literalists out there. In the next section it may seem like I'm judging God, but this couldn't be more false. I'm judging the *men* who had the temerity to write these Biblical stories as if the morality preached in them *came* from God. Just because you *believe* these stories were inspired by God, doesn't mean they were.

Now let's get back to religious people judging human beings by a different moral standard than they judge their God or their religion's founder. Let's start with Adam because that's where, according to the Bible, it all started.

As the old Christian saying goes: "In Adams fall, we sinned all." That *one* saying says it all. Holding *all* human beings responsible for the sin of a single human being is probably the biggest miscarriage of justice ever thought-up by man. Would *any* of us today ever even consider such an abomination of justice outside of a religious context? Not a chance! This is, without a doubt, one of the most immoral things we could ever consciously do to a fellow human being—*and we all know it! Every single person* I have ever talked too *knows* it's immoral to hold someone accountable for something when they had absolutely no choice in the matter. If a case were ever taken to court trying to hold someone accountable when they had absolutely no choice in the matter, it would be thrown out immediately. But even though Christians know this, they still cling to the ridiculous idea of "original sin." I submit to you that the only reason they still cling to this absurd notion is because it's one of their dogmas. I also submit to you that no *real* Christian would ever commit such an abomination of justice upon a fellow human being because they *know* it's not only immoral, but evil as well. So why don't they judge their God by the same moral standard they judge themselves or other human beings? You'll have to ask them.

How about the "fact" (according to them at least) that God is going to send people to hell for believing in other religions? Once again, would a *just* God do such a thing? All around the world human beings live by a different set of religious rules and beliefs. Why? Because *they* believe theirs *are* God's set of rules and beliefs. They believe *they* have it right and everybody else has it wrong. So how could a *just* God send billions of people to hell when he didn't make it clear to them *what* to believe and *which* set of rules to live by? This would be like setting a chess board in front of someone who doesn't know the rules of the game and then chastising them when they made an illegal move. Unless God makes it perfectly clear *to each and every one of us* which religion is his (if any), then it would be EVIL of him to condemn anyone to eternal damnation. This simply wouldn't be a just God—period! In this case, ignorance of the law is a perfectly moral and justifiable excuse.

For those of you who are parents, do you punish your children harshly for something they do out of ignorance, or do you punish them according to their culpability? Of course sometimes we must compel our children to do certain things because they're simply to young and ignorant to make some decisions for themselves, but when we do this, we try to explain to them the reasons for our actions, don't we? And we do this in order to make it perfectly clear to them *why* they're being punished. Without making it clear to them (of course being age appropriate), it truly wouldn't be moral to punish them. So if *you* don't hold children or other adults morally accountable for things they're ignorant of, why do you think God would? If he doesn't make it perfectly clear to *his* children (human beings) which is the correct path, and then he sends them off to hell anyway, then *he* is the one being immoral, not his children.

Or just ask yourself this: Is it more important that my children believe in my God and my religion, or is it more important that they are good, honest, decent, moral, caring human beings, regardless of what they believe? In my not-so-humble opinion, it's more important that they become good, honest, decent, moral, caring human beings. Of course they can do both, but I'm just asking which is *more* important. If becoming Christians is how my sons find meaning, purpose, happiness…etc; and if that's what it takes to make them decent human beings, then I hope they become Christians. If becoming Buddhists is how my sons find meaning, purpose, happiness…etc; and if that's what it takes to make them decent human beings, then I hope they become Buddhists. If becoming Taoists…etc. Of course I'll never understand it, just like I don't understand how anyone else does it, but it's a choice they'll have to make on their own. If we're all God's children, wouldn't he want the same? Because unless he makes it perfectly clear to us which beliefs are the correct beliefs (which he obviously doesn't), then that's simply what he'll have to settle for—and it would be the only *moral* position as well. Now let's get to some examples from the "Old" Testament on how people use different moral standards to judge God.

To begin with, let's look at the story of Cain and Abel. Exactly what started the whole mess? Wasn't it God's rejection of Cain's offering and his acceptance of Abel's? Please read the story and then answer this: Would you do what God did to *your* child? Not if you're moral. So was this a moral action by God? Not if you're going to be consistent. Would any good mother or father do such a mean thing to their own child? No, so why isn't this judged as an immoral act by God?

How about the story about God, Abraham and Isaac? According to the Old Testament, God told Abraham to sacrifice his only son Isaac as a burnt offering in order to prove his loyalty. So Abraham obediently ties Isaac's hands behind his back, lays him on top of a wood pile, and just as he's ready to slice Isaac up with his knife, God intervenes and saves Isaac because Abraham proved his loyalty to him. Does the term "sadistic" ring a bell? How people could possibly consider this action by "God" moral is beyond me. If anyone else were to put their own child through this type of nonsense, he would be immediately called an immoral masochistic sadist.

In Leviticus 20:13, "God" says homosexuals are to be put to death. Now, you may believe homosexuality is immoral, but do you believe it's so bad that people should be put to death because of it? I don't. And do you *really* believe God would? Really?

In Leviticus 22:16-21, "God" tells us which priests are fit to make sacrifices: And the Lord said to Moses "Tell Aaron that any of his descendants from generation to generation who have any bodily defect may not offer the sacrifices to God. For instance, if a man is blind or lame, or has a broken nose of any extra fingers or toes, or has a broken foot or hand, or has a humped back, or is a dwarf, or has a defect in his eye, or has pimples or scabby skin, or has imperfect testicles—although he is a descendant of Aaron, he is not allowed to offer the fire sacrifices to the Lord because of his physical defects." Are these the edicts of a loving, just God? If a man has a humped back, extra fingers or toes, is blind, has "imperfect" testicles, or is a dwarf, didn't God make him that way? Isn't "God" treating these people unjustly over something they had no choice over? Is a dwarf less of a man because he was simply *born* a dwarf? Only an imperfect, immoral God would have such imperfect, immoral standards for judgment (which of course, by definition, would mean he isn't God at all). It's too bad someone back then couldn't have asked God: "What would Jesus do"?

In Numbers 15:32-36, what does "God" tell Moses to do with a man who is in the forest picking up firewood on the Sabbath? "The man shall surely be put to death; all the congregation shall stone him with stones outside the camp." Doesn't sound moral to me, does it to you?

In Deuteronomy 13, "God" tells us what to do with anyone who tries talking you into believing in another God: "You shall surely kill him"—even if it's your own brother, son, daughter, wife, friend…etc. Sound moral?

In Deuteronomy 15, "God" tells us slavery is OK, but you *should* (not must) set him free in his seventh year. Sound moral?

In Deuteronomy 21: 10-14, "God" justifies rape and forced marriage: "When you go to war against your enemies and the Lord gives them into your hands, and you take them captive, and see among them a beautiful woman, and you have desire for her and want to take her for yourself as your wife…etc," "after she has mourned for a month you may go into her and make her your wife…etc." Sound like the teachings of a moral God? Would this be a moral standard if prescribed by a man? By the way, this is also one of the teachings in Numbers 31: 17-18 "Now therefore, kill every male among the little ones, and kill every woman that has known man by lying with him. But all the young girls who have not known man by lying with him, keep alive for yourselves." Sound moral?

In Deuteronomy 21: 18-23, "God" tells us what to do with a gluttonous, drunkard son: "All of the men of the city shall stone him to death." Sound moral?

In Deuteronomy 22:13-21, "God" says if a man marries a woman and then finds out she's not a virgin "the men of the city shall stone her to death."

In Deuteronomy 23: 24-25, "God" tells us: "When you enter your neighbors vineyard, you may eat grapes until you are fully satisfied, but you shall not put any in your basket." And: "When you enter your neighbor's standing grain, you may pluck the heads with your hand, but you shall not wield a sickle in your neighbor's standing grain." Don't *both* of these two actions fall into the category of stealing? Are they moral?

And then there's Jephthah from Judges 11: 30-39. This man promises God that if he lets him defeat the Ammonites, he'll sacrifice the first person he meets when he gets home as a burnt offering to the Lord. He then goes on to win the battle "with a very great slaughter" and heads home. As he's approaching home, his beloved daughter comes running out of the house to meet him…etc. Anyway, to make a long story short, he sacrifices his daughter as a burnt offering to the Lord and "the Lord" has no problem with it. Does this sound like a moral God to you? Since he intervened with Abraham and Isaac, why didn't he intervene here? My point being that if this story was in the Quran or another sacred text from around the world, Christians would be using this story as an example to show how immoral the God of Islam is; hence, the different moral standard.

How about when the God of the Bible gives "His people" the land of the Canaanites? Of course this is under the condition that they "slaughter every man, woman, and child," but hey, that's life right? But seriously, would a moral God be behind such an atrocity? This is *obviously* a story made-up by Jews in order to either justify murdering multitudes of people in order to steal their land, or to give the Israelites the courage to invade Canaan in the first place; or most likely, a little of both. It's absolutely amazing to me that, even to this day, human beings are ignorant enough to fall for the "God's on our side" argument to justify war (even Hitler said God was on his side).

Anyway, when God promised the Jewish people the land "flowing with milk and honey" it needs to be remembered that the milk and honey belonged to someone else! In my opinion, the Jews were simply sick and tired of living a nomadic lifestyle so they picked out a place where food was abundant and the native population wasn't strong enough to stop the incursion. And as I've already said, those who win the war, write the history. But just imagine how different the world would be today if instead of the *Canaanites* losing the war, the *Israelites* lost the war. Now, I'm not making any kind of a moral judgment one way or the other right here, I'm just trying to get people to remember that the "winner" writes the history, not the "loser"; and whoever writes the history always makes themselves the good guys. I would also like to state a fact that I heard long ago, but I just can't remember who said it: "War doesn't determine who is right, it determines who is left."

Just look at how Westerners view someone like Ghenges Kahn (or other foreign leaders like him from the past). Most view him as if he were the Devil incarnate. But I guarantee that if he was one of "ours*"* he would've went down in history as a great leader. After all, the atrocities he committed were no worse that the atrocities committed by "Gods chosen people" against the Canaanites in the beginning of the Bible. Human beings always write things according to what *they* see and from their own point of view. This is also why, when it comes to religions, women are almost always viewed as less than men, or second class citizens—because *men* created religions and *men* wrote their history. Men have always written history because men are the physically dominant sex, i.e., men have always been able to force their will on women. And that's also why it's called HIStory and not HERstory. There are many examples I could give from the world's sacred texts, but here's a quick one from 1st Timothy just to prove the point: "Let woman learn in silence with all subjection. But I will suffer not a woman to teach, nor usurp authority over the man, but be in silence." So I hope all the women reading this book will come to realize that women will *never* be equals as long as they follow ancient religious texts that were written by men. It's sad, but that's just how it is.

Next let's look at part of the story of Jacob. In essence, Jacob loves and wants to marry Rachael, but Rachael has an older sister named Lea that must be married off first according to this tradition. So Lea's father tricks Jacob into marrying Lea, which means Jacob must wait another seven years before he can marry Rachael (Yes that's right, polygamy is completely acceptable to the God of the Old Testament. And I also wonder how "God" saw it acceptable to trick someone into marriage, and how anyone could actually see that as moral or even legal. And if I remember correctly, Rachael was also Jacob's cousin…hmmm.). After he's married to both, Lea begins to have children. Of course this makes Rachael jealous because for some unknown reason, she isn't able to give Jacob children. So she does the next best thing— she gives him her maidservant to use as a concubine. Then Lea becomes jealous because she's grown too old to give Jacob more children, so she *also* gives Jacob her maidservant to use as a concubine. So basically what we have here is a man who's having sex with 4 different women and "God" has no problem with it. I submit to you that if every man had 4 women at his beck and call, there would be a hell of a lot less adultery going on. Jacob's probably so tired he wouldn't have the energy to commit adultery even if he wanted too. But this story also shows how morality has changed over time. By *today's* moral standards, Jacob would be considered an adulterer, wouldn't he?

Next there's poor old Job. How anyone could possibly think God would let the devil (or more accurately put "the adversary") do the things he did to Job in order to prove a point, is once again beyond me. But worst of all, "God" did it to prove *to an evil being* that Job was loyal. Would an omniscient God do such a thing? Wouldn't he already know? How can anybody possibly consider this a moral action by God?

How about Esau? According to the Old Testament, Esau was helping carry the Ark of the Covenant when an ox stumbled and almost overturned the cart. The key word here being "almost." When this happened, Esau did what *any* normal human being would do in this situation; he reached out to stop the ark from falling. But since it was forbidden to touch the ark, "God" struck Esau's dead on the spot! Now, come on. Does anyone truly believe a just God would do such a thing? I don't think so. Why not? Because we know it wouldn't be moral.

How about what happens in 2 Kings 2:23-25? 42 children are making fun of an old man by, in essence, calling him "Baldy." So he "curses them in the name of the Lord" and the next thing we know two "she bears" rush out of the woods and tears them to shreds! Holy Cow! Does that sound like the work of a moral God?

Or how about this one. Is it moral for God to harden the hearts of people? As I mentioned earlier in this chapter, if God hardens your heart, then you have no choice; if you have no choice, then God has no right to condemn you. For a quick example let's look at the story of Exodus. Would a moral God deliberately keep hardening the heart of Pharaoh? If you had the power to harden someone's heart and then proceeded to do so, would *you* be moral? Of course not. As a matter of fact, if a person *could* harden the heart of another, and did it, I guarantee you would consider them immoral—as you should. So why don't you consider your God immoral for doing the same thing? And what about Pharaoh? If God deliberately hardened his heart, then he can't be considered evil like the Bible portrays him. Where choice is not involved, morality's not involved. Now if God *did not* harden his heart, then yes, he could be viewed as immoral or evil. But since the choice was never his own, the only one who could possibly be blamed would be God himself. Isn't that ironic?

I would also like to point out another inaccuracy of the Bible. It's the *mind* that would have to be hardened, not the heart. Anything that's felt in the heart is a direct result of what's thought of in the mind. In other words, the heart doesn't think. In ancient times, humans simply didn't understand that it's the brain, not the heart, which was the human tool of cognition and emotion; and of course "God" would have known this. So this is yet another reason why we know *men* wrote the Bible, not God.

While I'm here at Exodus I'll ask another question of morality. Is it moral of God to kill the son of Pharaoh for the "choice's" pharaoh made? Or better yet, is it moral of God to kill the first born *of all Egypt* for the choices pharaoh made? Would this be moral of any human being? Absolutely not! So why is it moral of God? I would also like to point out that, as far as I know, there's absolutely no evidence outside of the Bible that this "historical" event ever took place. It sure seems like this piece of history would have been recorded somewhere by an Egyptian, doesn't it? After all, for people of that time period, they were *fanatical* record keepers. So that's yet another problem with the supposed historicity of the Bible.

And there's, once again, another problem when it comes to the morality of the Biblical God: Is it moral to "visit the iniquity of the fathers upon the children and the children's children to the third and the fourth generation" as God does in Exodus? Not in my opinion. The list of immoralities *and evils* performed by the God of the Bible goes on and on.

You see, the problem with many stories from the Bible (and other stories from antiquity as well) lies in the fact that many were written to show a single moral point and not a general coherent overall moral philosophy. For a quick example of this, let's look at the story of Job again. The moral of the story of Job is, in essence, to show the value of Godly perseverance. In other words, no matter how bad things get, as long as you remain loyal to God, things will always work out in the end. Yes, perseverance is a virtue, but the story of Job is about much more than perseverance. There are many other moral factors that come into play that the writer simply didn't take into account, or simply ignored.

For example: If God is omniscient, wouldn't he already know what was going to happen *and* what was in Jobs "heart"? Would God (the ultimate moral authority) allow a *moral* man to be tortured simply to prove a point to an *immoral* being? Would God let an evil being kill Job's children in order to prove Job's loyalty *to an evil being*? These are the types of questions the author of Job either didn't think of, or simply chose to ignore. But we can't just ignore these types of questions if we're searching for the truth, can we? Which reminds me of the ancient Jewish saying: "Whoever reflects on four things the better that he had never been born: what is above, what is beneath, what is before, and what is after." In other words, DO NOT question things we (religious leaders) have no answers for. Which leads to: Do not question our authority or basic premises. Religions want people to accept the absolute authority of their leaders and sacred texts—period! Because it's when people start asking tough questions that religious authority begins to break down.

This is easily proven by just looking at the story of Adam and Eve. What was the *one thing* "God" forbid in the Garden of Eden? The eating of the fruit from the tree of knowledge of good and evil—the very thing that makes Man, Man! The last thing religions want is for you to question their authority or their basic premises. This is why so many scientists throughout history have been demonized, tortured, and (or) executed by the church—because they have the temerity to think for themselves and question religious doctrines, dogmas and authority. Well, to be more accurate, the church didn't usually do the dirty work, most of the time it would hand the person over to the state to do the dirty work for it. But none the less, it was still the church that was responsible for what was done.

Another good example of how ancient people wrote in order to prove a single point, and not worry if the whole story made perfect sense, is in Luke where Joseph and Mary leave Jesus behind in Jerusalem for a day before they realized he's missing. After 3 days of looking for Jesus, they finally find him in a synagogue discussing religion with the rabbis, who were "amazed" at his knowledge…etc. Of course the point of the story is to show how intelligent Jesus was even at an early age. But the problem with the story is that it only takes a few moments thought to figure out it's obviously made up. Just think about it for a moment. According to the New Testament, Mary *knows for a fact* that Jesus is the son of God. So here are Mary and Joseph on this long trip and they don't notice the *son of God* was missing *for an entire day*! They left the *son of God* behind and didn't even make sure he was *at the very least* in their departing caravan? This isn't like forgetting your keys or something— *they forgot the son of God*! It would be hard enough to believe that any *normal* parents wouldn't have notice their son missing for just an hour or two, but for an entire day? Jeeze! I have a 12 year old son right now and there's absolutely no way I, or my wife would do such an irresponsible thing, no *decent* parent would. The story is so absurd as to be laughable, but it gets worse.

When Joseph and Mary finally find Jesus in the temple (after three days) they were "astonished." And his mother asked him "why have you treated us this way? Behold, your father and I have been anxiously looking for you." Then Jesus says "Why is it that you were looking for me? Did you not know that I had to be in my father's house"? And they "did not understand the statement which he made to them." Obviously, Joseph and Mary weren't too smart were they? They *know* Jesus was the son of God, but they *don't know* why they found him in God's temple? Not exactly Rocket Scientists were they? Once again, the author of this story simply wasn't worried about writing a story that made perfect sense, only about showing how intelligent Jesus was at an early age (And by the way, don't you think it's simply unbelievable that Mary and Joseph knew they were having God's son and they didn't document ANY of his early life? I mean, give me a break. It's just another reason that shows why it's obviously just another made up religion).

There are other stories from the Old Testament that bring the God of the Old Testaments morality into question, but I'm not going to give more examples because that could easily be a whole other book in itself. But I would like to say that if you look at it from an objective point of view, this fact is painfully obvious. As a matter of fact, this is what Jesus was all about. He didn't like what was being preached as truth by the moral authority figures of his time and he spoke up against it; that's right, he was a heretic. I would argue that the strict "morality" of the Old Testament was directly responsible for the moral teachings of Jesus. As a matter of fact, if it wasn't Jesus, sooner or later someone else would've spoken up against the harshness and immorality of the Old Testament.

The idea's that came from Jesus were a direct response to the rigid authoritarian morality of Judaism; just like the idea's that came from the Buddha were a direct response to the ideas of Hinduism; just like the ideas of Mohammed were a direct response to the ideas of *both* Judaism and Christianity; just like the ideas of Nanak (Sikhism) were in direct response to the ideas of Islam and Hinduism…etc. Religious ideas always work in this way. And of course this is also how philosophical ideas work as well. The ideas of Aristotle were a direct response to the ideas of Plato and Socrates. Just like in more modern times, the ideas of Ayn Rand are a direct response to the ideas of Immanuel Kant. All revolutionary ideas, philosophical or religious, come from a mind that's not satisfied with the prevailing point of view and wants to improve upon, or change it. But once again I'm getting of track again, so let's return to the Bible.

Of course many of the moral contradictions from the God of the Old Testament can be used against the God of the New Testament, so why rewrite them here? After all, according to Christians it's the same God, right? In my opinion, this is one of the biggest mistakes of Christianity. Christians should've completely jettisoned the Old Testament so they wouldn't have to continually attempt to explain the contradictions, inconsistencies, and just plain immorality in it. They also should've jettisoned it so they wouldn't have to continually attempt to explain the contradictions and inconsistencies between the moral teachings of the two books (the "New" Testament and The "Old" Testament). They couldn't though because they were trying to convince the rest of the Jews that Jesus was the "Christ" or "Messiah" they had been waiting for, and because it was an extremely valuable recruiting tool to be able to tie your religion to a source as ancient as possible—in fact—it was a necessity. But of course, Jews didn't buy Jesus as the Christ—and for good reason. Nowhere in the Bible did it say the Messiah was going to be crucified and die. Most Jews were expecting a mighty military/spiritual leader (like David, and in the line of David) to free them of Roman oppression, not just a spiritual leader like Jesus. The so-called prophecies from the Old Testament predicting a prophet who would die and be resurrected, appeared only *after* the death of Jesus, never before. And this was the work of the first Christian mythstorians.

You see, whenever the Old Testament talks about someone suffering and dying, it's never in the context of the coming Messiah; and whenever the coming Messiah is mentioned, it's never in the context of him suffering and dying. Thus, their attempted rationalizations and justifications were good enough to convince the "gentiles" (most of which had never even read the books of the Bible) that Jesus was the Christ, but obviously they weren't good enough to convince the people whom knew the Bible the best (the Jews) that Jesus was the Christ.

Here you had all these people who based their entire existence on the belief in a coming messiah. And here comes this man named Jesus who was supposedly fulfilling prophecies and performing all these miracles in front of all these thousands of Jews and other people. And the Jewish people, the very people who've been waiting for this moment throughout their entire history, see all these miracles and say "Nah, it couldn't be. Nah, that can't be him, Nah.." Come on, give me a break! It would be the exact same thing as modern day Christian fundamentalists seeing Jesus return and do all these things he's supposed to do and saying "Nah, couldn't be"—it wouldn't happen! They would flock to him like the sheeple they are. There would be a human stampede of Biblical proportions! And this is also part of the reason I say none of the "miracle" events ever took place.

I would also like to point out the problem with the false "line of David" claim made by Christians. If Jesus was the son of God and not the son of Joseph, how can Christians claim he comes from the line of David? Once again, it's a problem.

And then there's the claim that Jesus was born in Bethlehem. The only real "evidence" we have to justify this claim comes from Luke. "Luke" tells us that Jesus was born in Bethlehem because Joseph and Mary must go to there (everyone must go to the birth place of their ancestors) in order to register for the new "worldwide" Roman census being taken in order to collect more taxes. But the problem with this claim lies in the fact that there's *not a single contemporary source from the time of Jesus' birth* that says anything about a worldwide Roman census where people must go to the birth place of their ancestors. If this type of census really took place, it would've been one of the largest short-term human migrations in history—and no other writers of the time even mention it? Does that sound even remotely plausible? Not to me. Christians simply made this story up because, according to the Old Testament, the Messiah would be born in Bethlehem. But once again, I'm getting a little of track here, so lets get back to God and morality.

The only real example I need to give concerning the God of the "New" Testament (besides the quick ones I included under the Old Testament section in the last few pages) is the book of Revelation. How anyone can read the book of Revelation and come away thinking this would be a *moral* God is beyond me. Not even considering the torture and suffering this "God" plans to inflict upon humanity, the mass murder of a couple of billion human beings alone should be enough to horrify any *moral* reader. But does it? Of course not! As a matter of fact, Christians are actually taught to look forward to the slaughter. How this ancient work of science fiction actually became part of the Christian cannon is, once again, beyond me. I would say probably because it was intended as a way to scare people into believing. But this is yet another good example of how the decisions of men, not God, determine future religious beliefs. The book of Revelation was just barely canonized. If a few more men (not God) would've been on the other side of the argument, the book of Revelation would've been just another footnote in Christian history. It's too bad that's not what happened.

In the last couple of pages I gave some examples of believers who don't judge their God by the same moral standards they judge human beings. So now I would like to give a few examples of believers who don't judge their religions *founder* by the same moral standards they judge other human beings. I guess I'll begin with Jesus because he's the most popular.

There's a lot of talk these days from Christian fundamentalists about "family values," but what was Jesus' attitude about families? In Luke 12:51-53 Jesus says "Do you suppose that I came to grant peace on earth? I tell you, no, but rather division; for from now on five members in one household will be divided, three against two, and two against three. They will be divided father against son, and son against father; mother against daughter, and daughter against mother...etc." Would *I* be considered moral if I deliberately wanted to cause dissention among family members?

How about Luke 14:26 "If anyone comes to Me, and does not hate his own father and mother and wife and children and brothers and sisters, yes, even his own life, he cannot be my disciple." Absolutely no ambiguity in that sentence is there? So much for family values. Those stories are also found in Matthew; along with the story of Jesus, ummm, how can I say this in modern terms? "Dissing" his family when they came to speak with him in Matthew 12:46-50. Once again, so much for "family values." And what about the contradictory teachings of Jesus when at one point he says to "love your neighbor as yourself" (implying you must love yourself), but at another point he says you must "hate" your own life (implying you must hate yourself)? Exactly how can a person both love and hate themselves? This is a psychological impossibility, is it not?

And when it comes to Christians judging Jesus the way they judge others, how about when Jesus supposedly sends demons out of the man named Legend into a herd of 2000 swine? And after this is done, the pigs immediately jump off a cliff into the sea and die. This would be fine except for one thing: what about the loss occurred by the owner of the pigs? Jesus gives him absolutely no consideration at all. The herd of pigs were most likely his family's only livelihood, but Jesus didn't seem to give any thought to them whatsoever. If I had the power to cast out demons, and did it in the exact same way Jesus did, I guarantee Christians would probably call me immoral, and then want me to compensate the owner for his loss—and I would agree. So why would they judge *me* by a different moral standard than they judge Jesus?

This would also apply to when Jesus sent his followers to get a colt so he could ride it into Jerusalem. In Mark 11 Jesus tells his followers to fetch a colt and if anyone says something to them, they should say "The Lord has need of it." So they find a colt, begin to untie it, and some of the "bystanders" say to them "What are you doing, untying the colt." So they tell them that the Lord has need of it, and the bystanders give them permission to take the colt. The *bystanders* give them permission to take the colt? The key word being "bystanders." Since when is it alright for "bystanders" to give away someone else's property? Once again, if this story is actually true, Jesus doesn't seem to care about property rights at all. If I did this, would I be moral? At the very least, it wasn't the right thing to do, was it?

But of course this story is different in Luke. In Luke, it's the "owners" who gives permission. So which is it? It's my opinion that the writer of Luke knew there were moral problems with the story as it was written, so he simply changed it. I'm pretty confident of this opinion because Mark was written prior to Luke, and the author of Luke had access to Mark. And we also know for a fact that many of these stories changed over time. And by the way, in Matthew, the story has two colts, not just one. So which is it? All three gospels cannot be true. So who knows what really happened?

How about when Jesus scolded Peter (16:23) and said "get behind me Satan."..etc.? It may not have been immoral, but it certainly wasn't very nice was it? I mean, here's one of Jesus' closest followers (and also the "rock" Jesus said the church will be built upon, by the way), and Jesus says to him "get behind me Satan"? How can anyone claim that was a nice thing to do? Of course I don't think he meant it literally, but even if he meant it figuratively it wasn't really a nice thing to say, was it?

And then there's the story of the woman who anoints Jesus' feet with expensive perfume. This story is fascinating because of all the different angles we can approach it from. To begin with, let's approach it from the same angle some of the Disciples approached it from. Instead of wasting this extremely valuable oil/perfume pouring it on Jesus, shouldn't it have been sold and the money be given to the poor? After all, up to this point, this story conformed perfectly to the altruistic/benevolent teachings of Jesus himself. But no, Jesus says it's better to let the woman waste it on him because "the poor you have with you always; but you do not always have me." In my opinion, this was the turning point in Jesus' career. He crossed the line from being altruistic/benevolent to being irrationally selfish and egotistical. If anyone else did this I think Christians would ask "why the waste"? But since it's Jesus, they give him the benefit of the doubt and attempt to rationalize it.

This is also the one time the question "What would Jesus do?" falls flat on it face, because Jesus obviously did the wrong thing. And I think this is why Judas betrayed him. Or a better way to put it would be: Judas betrayed Jesus because Jesus betrayed Judas. To Judas, the apparent egoism of the accepted anointment was simply too much to bear. Jesus was simply not the man Judas believed he was. Now, I'm not saying Judas was right for betraying Jesus to the authorities (if that's what actually happened. Some scholars think Judas didn't betray Jesus, but did exactly what Jesus asked him to do), only that he probably became disenchanted by the contradiction and maybe no longer saw Jesus as the altruistic/benevolent man/son of man, he once believed in. But once again, that's just another possibility.

Of course applying different moral standards doesn't just apply to Jesus and followers of Jesus, it also applies to founders of other religions as well. Can Muslims argue that the caravan raids Mohammed organized were moral? Just imagine how many people were robbed and murdered in those raids. It may be argued that caravan raids were just a part of life back then, but it certainly can't be argued that Mohammed was moral for organizing and participating in them, can it? If *I* did it would *I* be moral? And how about the Buddha? Can Buddhist argue that the Buddha was doing a moral thing when he left his wife and children to search for enlightenment? If *I* did it would *I* be moral? Was it moral for Moses to have people murdered for not believing in *his* God? If *I* did it would *I* be moral? And for more recent examples, how about Joseph Smith and Brigham Young? Why don't Mormons judge Joseph Smith for his adulterous sexual appetite? Or Brigham Young for what happened at the Mountain Meadows Massacre? My point being that the followers of many religious leaders would condemn me if I were to commit *the exact same actions* committed by the leader they so adamantly admire. So why don't they judge their religion's founder by the same moral standard that they judge other human beings? Once again, you'll have to ask them.

I should also point out that, in my opinion (and the opinion of many Biblical scholars) Jesus didn't actually say many of the things attributed to him in the Bible. Two quick examples would be, as mentioned earlier in this chapter, the stories about not casting the first stone found in John, and the last few verses from Mark. My point being that if words were being attributed to Jesus over a thousand years after his death, isn't it logical to assume people were putting words in his mouth years, decades, and even centuries after his death? Absolutely!

Another example would be in comparing Matthew 12:30 with Mark 9:40. Philosophically speaking, the two statements Jesus supposedly made were very, very different. In Matthew, Jesus says: "Whoever is not with me is against me," but in Mark he says: "He who is not against us is for us." If you read both statements carefully, you'll see that they're very, very different. Even ignoring the me/us aspect, the Jesus of Mark is universally tolerant and open-minded concerning other people and their beliefs, whereas the Jesus of Matthew is universally intolerant and close-minded concerning other people and their beliefs. When someone says: "Whoever is not with me is against me," they're saying everyone who's *not* on their side, is *on* the other side. However, when a person says: "Whoever is not against us is for us," they're saying that as long as you're not *against* them, you're *for* them. See the difference? Regardless of context, the two statements are, philosophically speaking, extremely inconsistent with one another.

So which statement did Jesus actually make? For that you have to look into the history of the New Testament. Even though the men who compiled the New Testament placed Matthew before Mark, the overwhelming majority of Biblical scholars think Mark was written first. As a matter of fact, they think the author of Matthew studied and used Mark prior to writing Matthew (by the way, did you know that nobody even knows who wrote Matthew, Mark, Luke and John? And that the early church simply attributed those books to Matthew, Mark, Luke and John. Hmmm…interesting). My whole point being that, in my opinion of course, Matthew deliberately changed the saying in an attempt to bring more believers into the fold by an implied threat of damnation. Of course Christians wouldn't agree with me, but it is yet another thing to think about.

The next thing I would like to touch upon concerning theists of all religions is the gargantuan size of their egos. According to their sacred texts and their religion's founder, they're supposed to remain humble and have small egos, but in most cases, their egos are bigger than anybody else's on the planet. And ironically enough, the more fundamentalist they are, the bigger their ego. Anybody who claims to *know* God's opinions, by definition, has a huge ego. It's one thing to say "I *believe* this about God" or "I *believe* that about God," It's quite another to say "I *know* this about God" or "I *know* that about God." It's one thing to be a theist or a theologian and say "This is what people throughout history *believed* about God." It's quite another to say "This is what people throughout history *know* about God." Any human being who claims to *know* which religion is God's religion is suffering from not only an acute case of ignorance, but an acute case of hubris, egoism, and downright megalomaniaism. In essence, they're the most arrogant people on earth because they claim to *know* the unknowable. They can *believe* all they want, but only a dogmatic egomaniac zealot claims to *know* God, God's opinions, who God is sending to hell…etc. Pretending to have answers to unanswerable questions has always been one of the best ways to fleece the ignorant sheeple and accumulate great wealth. So beware of any man who has the temerity to speak for God. He's either a megalomaniac, power-hungry, ignorant, or a fool. To speak *for* God is to speak *as* God.

You see, the overwhelming majority of these people throughout history have only studied *their own* religion, and at best, maybe one other related religion. When it comes to "God" they're truly ignorant because they only know about their own culture's God; and of course it's always their own culture's God who's the "true" God. And then of course, all thru history people of one religion have used the excuse that people of another religion are immoral or even evil because they follow a false God or Gods; and they do this in order to be able to do whatever they want to those other people (murder them, steal their land, enslave them, take their wife and children…etc.). It's when men believe they're superior to other men that they're at there most evil; and nothing makes men feel more superior to others than when they have convinced themselves that they're God's representative on earth and doing "His" work.

But it gets even worse. Their egos are so humungous that they not only believe they're experts in their own field of study (the Bible, the Quran…etc), they believe they're experts in fields of studies they've never even studied. For example, when listening to a theist who believes in creationism or intelligent design, observe how they're masters of all the different sciences. They're not only expert theologians, they're expert anthropologists, archeologists, astronomers, astrophysicists, biologists, cosmologists, evolutionists, genealogists, geologists, historians, pre-historians (well, maybe this one doesn't belong here because they don't even believe there was anything "pre"-historic), linguists, paleontologists, physicists, zoologists…etc. These people have such big egos that they not only *believe* they're right concerning all the sciences, they *know* they are. Even though they've never studied anthropology, they say the *overwhelming majority* of anthropologists are wrong, but *they* are right. Even though they've never studied archeology, they say the *overwhelming majority* of archeologists are wrong, but *they* are right. Even though they have never studied astronomy, they say the *overwhelming majority* of astronomers are wrong, but *they* are right.….etc. No matter what field of endeavor they're talking about, as long as it relates to their belief system in any way, *they* know the truth and the *overwhelming majority* of experts from *every single field* of natural science are wrong. What absolute megalomania!

I would also like to point out how inconsistent these egomaniacs are in applying their standard for "expertise." Because when it comes to more *practical* knowledge, they're the first people to call in an expert. They don't trust a biologist to know what he's talking about, but if they're sick, they'll trust a doctor; they don't trust a geologist to know what he's talking about, but if their car breaks down, they'll trust a mechanic; they don't trust a paleontologist to know what he's talking about, but if their toilet is leaking, they'll trust a plumber…etc. Across the board, the only experts they trust are experts who don't have the nerve to challenge their belief system in any way whatsoever. They wouldn't dare say their mechanic doesn't know what he's talking about, but they'll say the professor of geology at the local university doesn't know what *he's* talking about; they wouldn't dare say the local electrician doesn't know what he's talking about, but they'll say the professor of cosmology at the local university doesn't know what *he's* talking about; they wouldn't dare say the local veterinarian doesn't know what he's talking about, but they'll say the professor of paleontology at the local university doesn't know what *he's* talking about...etc. In essence, once again, if the experts in any field of science claim something that contradicts *their* belief system, the experts are wrong and *they* are right—even though they have never even studied those sciences—what arrogance!

These egomaniac zealots don't just claim to *believe* their religion is Gods religion, they claim they *know* it is—even though they have never even read the sacred texts of other religions! They don't just *believe* the conclusions of all the modern day natural sciences are false, they *know* they are—even though they've never even studied them! Is there anything *more* egotistical than claiming to know everybody else is *wrong* and you are *right*—even though you have never even studied their particular field of expertise? Seriously, just think about it. These people are at the absolute height of arrogance.

Of course it has to be this way or it would prove their belief system *really is* a belief system like everyone else's, wouldn't it? And they can't have that, because they don't just *believe*, they *know*! For example: If the universe was created billions of years ago, and not just 6000 years ago, what would that say about their infallible Bible? If it took more than 6 days for the earth to be created, what would that say about their infallible Bible? If the sun existed before the earth, what would that say about their infallible Bible? If dinosaurs existed tens of millions, and even hundreds of millions of years before humans, what would that say about their infallible Bible? If, up to this point in history, the potential human lifespan is only roughly 120 years, what does that say about their infallible Bible telling us humans used to live nearly 1000 years? The list is never ending. In fact, one of the best kept secrets is that although 9 out of 10 Americans believe in God and the Bible, the numbers are almost exactly reversed among scientists.

This is why creationists search out professionals from the different sciences who disagree with the prevailing point of view (and of course these scientists just happen to be of a religious persuasion). If they can find a cosmologist who says the earth is only a few thousand years old, they make *him* the standard—even if his opinion is only in the 5-10 percentile for his particular profession. If they can find a paleontologist who's willing to say dinosaurs and mankind co-existed, they make *him* the standard—even if his opinion is only in the 5-10 percentile for his profession. If they can find a geologist who's willing to say…etc. They're so sure that *they* know the truth that they're willing to take the extreme minority viewpoint from all the major sciences as gospel. And they have to do this because if the conclusions of modern science don't conform to their ancient sacred text, it's modern science that must be wrong, not their sacred text. And of course it's really not to hard to find these "scientists" because they're almost immediately made hero's because 90% of the people want it confirmed that what they believe is the truth.

Now don't get me wrong here. Just because someone holds the minority point of view doesn't automatically make them wrong. If that were the case, then I would be wrong concerning what I call 'The Big Three' (philosophy, religion and politics). However, it's one thing to take a minority viewpoint concerning *your own* fields of study, but it's quite another to take a minority viewpoint concerning fields of study you've never even studied. Because if you do, it's probably only because you're wanting to buttress your own arguments and not wanting to accept the truth. And of course this is precisely my problem with those types of people. They (believers, mystics, theists, religionists, mythematicians, mythstorians…etc) go through all this and still have the temerity to believe *they* are the ones being humble—it's unbelievable! At least I admit I have a big ego. To me, having a big ego is fine as long as it's kept under control. It may sound like a contradiction, but at least I'm humble enough to admit I have a big ego. These people are so egotistical they can't even admit they have big egos—because if they did, they would be giving proof of their hypocrisy and that they're living a contradiction.

If you're still not convinced about their huge egos, try this. The next time you're driving down the road, take the time to read some of the signs in front of these churches. As a matter of fact, just look at the names of some of these churches themselves: "Church of God," "House of God," "Assembly of God," "Church of Christ."..etc. What arrogance! As if *they* are the final authority on God's (or Jesus') opinions. What hubris! In fact, just this past weekend I saw dozens of members of a Baptist Church wearing T-shirts that read: "TRUE oracles of God," what megalomaniacs!

The reason most people have never looked at it like this is because of our social conditioning. We're simply not supposed to question someone else's beliefs, especially if they're a so-called "man of God." Which is of course, yet another term of arrogance. If a man claims to be a man of God, he's claiming absolute knowledge of the unknowable, i.e., he's claiming God's knowledge; which is once again, the height of arrogance. But if a man claims that he *believes* he's a man of God, then at least he's admitting it's only his belief. He's still being arrogant, but at least he's admitting that he could be wrong, i.e., at least he's admitting he's not omniscient. Fact is, neither pope, nor bishop, not priest, nor pastor, nor deacon, nor minister, nor monk, nor abbot, nor iman, nor ayatollah, nor anyone else who holds a religious title, truly serves God, but their own brand of religion.

These are usually the same people who make the claim that they are "God fearing" (as if being "God fearing" is some sort of higher moral standard). I'm sure you've heard religious people describe other religious people they like as "God fearing," as if it's a moral badge of honor or something. But I have a question: Why should someone be afraid of God if they've done nothing seriously wrong? I thought their God was forgiving? In my not-so-humble opinion, the only people who should be afraid of God are people who do bad things. In essence, if you're a good person, you have nothing to fear from a *just* God, only an *unjust* God. And if God is unjust, you're screwed anyway, right?

Getting back to church signs, I recently saw one that read: "Souls saved here." Now, any human being arrogant enough to claim he can "save souls" is so far past arrogance that the only term that aptly describes him would be megalomaniac. Of course we can state our own *beliefs* concerning what it would take to be "saved," but it would be just that, a belief. The only Being who could rightly hang a sign outside his door saying "Souls saved here" would be God himself, herself, itself, or themselves, right? Anyone else, and it's not only the height of arrogance, but the height of ignorance as well. This is why whenever I read about how the Catholic Church tried to get away with selling or granting indulgences, I have to laugh. How absolutely ignorant those followers must have been, and how absolutely arrogant the church leaders must have been. It's hard to even fathom.

This also applies to the forgiveness of sins. Any church (or human being) who believes they have the power to forgive sin is, once again, at the height of arrogance. Sure, it would be great to be able to do such a nice thing for people, but *claiming* to do so is a far cry from *actually* doing so. If "sin" exists, and if "God" exists, only God would be able to take away, or forgive sin. Yes, we can lead others toward morality, but to claim you can forgive sins is a far cry from that, which leads me to my next point.

I'm simply amazed that so many people actually believe Jesus (or anyone else for that matter) could atone for someone else's sins. Contrary to Christian dogma, no matter how much Jesus wanted to atone for the sins of the human race (assuming this is even true), *justice* doesn't allow for such a thing. This ridiculous notion turns morality itself on its head. I'm responsible for what I do, you're responsible for what you do, Jesus was responsible for what he did…etc. To believe a pinch-hitter can step up to the plate of eternal justice and bat a home run for another is a complete violation of the concept of justice. If God values justice, each and every one of us will be held accountable for our own deeds and actions. In other words: No substitutions please.

Another quick point I would like to make here is concerning the unjust belief many Christians hold that we're all guilty for the crucifixion of Jesus; and that the only way to be saved is to accept this as fact so you'll be forgiven. In other words, if you accept responsibility for a crime you *couldn't have possibly committed*, you'll be forgiven for the crimes that you *actually* committed. What nonsense!

Christianity also seems to be the only religion (or philosophy) where people believe *words* and *beliefs* are more important than *deeds*. The overwhelming majority of Christians seem to believe that as long as they say they *believe* in Jesus, they're covered (going to heaven). The belief is all that matters. It doesn't matter if their actions are in line with their beliefs, only that they believe Jesus was the Christ. And I say their *words* are more important than their *deeds* to them because if they *really* believed Jesus was the Christ, they would act accordingly; they would actually *do* what Jesus said to do. Since they don't, it's logical to assume they don't truly believe he was the Christ, i.e., they're only meaningless words. Remember, the saying goes: WWJD (What Would Jesus Do?) not WWJS (What Would Jesus Say?). If you're a *true* Christian, the difference is where morality itself lies.

I think the reason for this happening is because the early church realized that to be a Christian *in deeds* would mean living a short life of poverty; and understandably, most people simply don't want to live a short life of poverty. They realized the impossibility of living up to the moral teachings of Jesus and created a compromise, and that compromise was, in essence: We know you cannot do what Jesus said to do, so instead, if you just believe in him you'll be covered.

This is also one of the reasons why Christianity has become the world's largest religion—because it's so easy. It's easy *not* to be expected to actually *do* what Jesus said to do. How hard is that? Fact is, Christians want all the benefits of being a follower of Jesus, but none of the responsibilities. If I were to call myself moral, but then not act moral, would I be moral? Of course not. If I were to call myself a Republican, but not act and vote Republican, would I be a Republican? Of course not. If I were to call myself a Muslim, but not act like a Muslim, would I be a Muslim? Of course not. So why is it that the only thing you need to *do* to *be* a Christian is to *believe* you're a Christian? Allow me to begin to prove my point by digressing into politics for a moment.

It's always amazed me that most Democrats and Republicans claim to be Christians, but are they? Well, let's start with the Democrats. Nowhere in the New Testament does Jesus say, or even imply, that it's moral to steal from the rich to give to the poor. The forced 'redistribution of wealth morality' dreamed up by the political left, certainly doesn't come from Jesus. Yes, Jesus told people to give to the poor, but nowhere does he say, or even imply, that if they don't freely give their money to the poor, the government should be used to forcibly extract it. In fact, stealing is explicitly forbidden in the Commandments (teachings from the Old Testament that Jesus *did not* jettison). What did John the Baptist say in Luke chapter 3 to the tax collector and soldier? "Collect no more than you have been ordered too" and "Do not take money from anyone by force." Can it be any clearer than that? Of course Christian leaders throughout history have used the single saying from Jesus "Render onto Caesar the things that are Caesars, and onto the Lord that which is the Lords" to justify government confiscating not only the wealth of the rich, but the hard-earned wages of the poor and middle class as well; but I certainly don't interpret it that way. I think Jesus was being ambiguous for a reason. He knew the Jewish authorities were trying to trick him into saying something that could be used against him by the Romans, thus the ambiguousness of his answer. It amazes me that for millennia this saying was (and still is) used around the world to justify the confiscation of up to 75% of a citizens earnings—what an outrage! How "render onto Caesar the things that are Caesars…etc" was turned into "render onto Caesar the things that are yours, mine, and everybody else's" is beyond me. What *you* earn, what *I* earn, or what *anybody else* earns is not the property of Caesar (government)! To use this saying to justify legalized theft goes against everything else Jesus taught. So much for "Christian" Democrats.

And then of course you have the most vocal of all Christians: Conservative Republicans known as the Religious Right. These are the people who wear their Christianity on their sleeves for all to see. These are the people who try to use the power of the government to force their idea of Christianity onto everyone else, but are *they* Christians themselves? Do *they* follow the teachings of Jesus? Not even close. It's an incontestable fact that one of the basic moral teachings of Jesus was for people to freely give their earthly possessions to the poor. It never ceases to amaze me how conservative Christian's continue to accumulate wealth and amass riches with little or no regard for the "least among us." I can give verse after verse from Jesus speaking *against* the accumulation of wealth, but I challenge *anyone* to give *just one* where Jesus speaks *favorably* toward the accumulation of wealth—it cannot be done. The hypochritstians who've amassed millions, and in some cases billions, are as far away from the moral teachings of Jesus as you can possibly get. And of course this is extremely ironic because it's the conservatives who're always complaining about the forced redistribution of wealth government policies pushed by liberals. If conservatives would just *do* what Jesus said to do, liberals would have no need to be calling for the redistribution of wealth in the first place!

Truth is, although most Americans call themselves Christians, I've never met an *actual* Christian (someone who does what Jesus said to do). In fact, Gandhi really sent this point home when he said: "I like your Christ. But I don't like your Christians because they are so unlike your Christ." If people would take the time to read what *Jesus* said and did (at least what's attributed to him), and not what Christians who lived after him said and did, I think they would see my point. The reason I point this out is because the religion *of* Jesus was turned into a religion *about* Jesus. In other words, beginning with the apostle Paul, the religion of Jesus was hijacked by the religion of Christianity.

So what did Jesus say about the accumulation of wealth? Matthew 6:19-21 "Do not lay up for yourselves treasures upon earth, where moth and rust destroy, and where thieves break in and steal. But lay up for yourselves treasures in heaven, where neither moth nor rust destroys, and where thieves do not break in and steal; for where your treasure is, there will your heart be also."

Matthew 6:24 "No one can serve two masters; for he will hate the one and love the other, or he will hold to one and despise the other. You cannot serve God and mammon" ("mammon" meaning wealth or money).

In Mark 10: 17-25 a rich young ruler asks Jesus how one needs to act in order to obtain eternal life. And Jesus says "Why do you call me good? No one is good except God alone. You know the commandments. Do not murder, Do not commit adultery, Do not steal, Do not bear false witness, Do not defraud, and Honor your father and mother." The man then says he has done all these things, is there anything else? And Jesus answers: "You lack one thing: go and sell all you possess, and give to the poor, and you shall have treasure in heaven." Since the man owned lots of property, and obviously didn't want to give it away, he walked away dejected. So Jesus turned to the disciples and said: "How hard it will be for those who are wealthy to enter the kingdom of God! It is easier for a camel to go through the eye of a needle than for a rich man to enter the kingdom of God"! That's pretty straight forward isn't it? Absolutely no ambiguity in those words is there? I would also like to point out something else from that quote. If Jesus is God, why would he say "Why do you call me good? No one is good except God alone." Obviously *Jesus* didn't think he was God. So why does Christendom say he is? Wouldn't God know if he were God? And why would God say to himself when he's being crucified "My God, my God, why have you forsaken me"? Anyway, back to the accumulation of wealth.

Luke 12:15 "avoid greed in all its forms."

Luke 12:33 "Sell your possessions and give to charity; make yourselves purses which do not wear out, an unfailing treasure in heaven, where no thief comes near, nor moth destroys."

Luke 14:33 "no one of you can be my disciple who does not give up all of his own possessions."

It's painfully obvious just from these few quotes where Jesus stood concerning the accumulation of wealth. Why Christians seem to have such a hard time understanding this teaching is beyond me. I think it's simply because they don't want too. If you want to actually enjoy life, it's usually necessary to accumulate at least a little bit of wealth. No, money cannot buy happiness, but it sure can rent it for a while. It can also add security, which helps take away anxiety, which is one part of bringing about happiness. This is yet another reason why I'm not a Christian. I think it's good to accumulate a little wealth in order to enjoy life and prepare for possible financial tragedies. In fact, I think it's a moral necessity. Basically, paying your own way through life is not only an essential part of character building, but a moral imperative as well (of course this doesn't include people such as quadriplegics, but even they should at least make the attempt).

In my opinion, charity begins at home. First you build a solid financial foundation, and then you can practice the virtue of benevolence. Or, if done wisely and prudently, you can do both at the same time. Was this what Jesus taught? No. Jesus preached *altruism* as the highest virtue, not benevolence;

and altruism means putting others *before* yourself. Do most Christians do this? Not even close. Do Christians "love thy enemy"? No. Do they "love thy neighbor as thyself"? No. Do they "turn the other cheek"? No. Jesus was so altruistic he even said "do not resist he who is evil." Now *that's* true and absolute altruism. So once again I ask: Do Christians do these things? No. Thus, the hypocrisy.

Next let's turn to the debate over prayer in public. Whether it's a prayer before Congress, prayer in public schools, or praying before a football game doesn't matter. What's the only thing Jesus said about praying? Matthew 6: 5, 6: "And when you pray, you are not to be as the hypocrites; for they love to stand and pray in the synagogues and on the street corners; in order to be seen by men. Truly I say to you, they have their reward in full. But you, when you pray, go into your inner room, and when you have shut your door, pray to your Father who is in secret, and your Father who sees in secret will repay you." Can it be any clearer than that? All these Christians pushing for public prayers certainly aren't followers of Jesus. In fact, Jesus said they're being "as the hypocrites." Why they can't recognize this blatant contradiction never ceases to amaze me.

Since I've shown the contradictions of the overwhelming majority of Christians (if not *all* Christians) concerning the teachings of Jesus, I would now like to quickly describe the four types of Christians who exist in reality.

The first type of Christian is the one who follows the teachings of Jesus to the letter. If consistent, this person is simply not going to live a very long or happy life. As a matter of fact, the earlier in his life he consciously decides to be truly altruistic, the shorter and more miserable his life will be. Jesus died (at least according to Christians) so the rest of us could live; he gave his life for our sins; he put others above himself…etc. Of course it had to be this way because the only conclusion to a consistently altruistic life is, well, death!

When the needs of others is your moral imperative, nothing you own, wear, eat or drink can be morally justified. Every single time you do something to survive, you're using something that another person could've used. Human beings go hungry, and even starve to death every single day. If you eat, that food could've been eaten by another who needed it more. If you drink, that water could've been drunk by another who needed it more. If you wear clothes, those clothes could've been worn by someone who needed them more. There's nothing you own that isn't needed more by somebody else somewhere. To be consistent, which means not to be a hypocrite, you must serve until you die, suffer until you succumb, waste away until you're wasted away…etc. Jesus said: "you must be a slave to others." How much clearer can it be? If your highest virtue is altruism, your highest value must be your own death. To be a consistent follower of Jesus you must end up like he did—dead.

Although I disagree with his philosophy, this is one of the things I admire about Jesus. He died for what he lived for. He ended his life the way he lived his life—for others. So in essence, only Christians who die as martyrs can truly be called Christians because they're the only ones who actually *do* what Jesus said to *do* and *live* the way Jesus said to *live*. And how is that? They die sacrificing themselves for others.

The second type of Christian is someone who lives a benevolent, but not altruistic life. A good example would be someone like Mother Teresa. Mother Teresa lived her life as close as humanly possible to the teachings of Jesus without taking the final step. She gave her possessions to the poor; she spent her life tending to the needs of the poor; she lived to serve others not herself…etc. But she never made the final commitment of a truly altruistic life: to die for another. While human beings were going hungry, and even starving to death all around her, she ate the food and drank the water that others needed to live. A consistently altruistic person would have given those things up and died so others might live. Now, I'm not saying she was a bad person or anything, I'm just saying she didn't live a consistently altruistic life. She didn't do what Jesus did, and said to do—completely sacrifice herself for others.

The third type of Christian, and the most popular, is someone who lives a *somewhat* benevolent life, but puts their own wants and needs above the wants and needs of others. This person is more than happy to give out of his abundance, but will not sacrifice his own wants or needs for others. This philosophy is closest to *my* philosophy because unlike the first two types, this person actually has a realistic chance at achieving not only success, but happiness as well. But only a *limited* degree of happiness, because if they're truly trying to live a *Christian* life, they're always going to feel guilty about not sacrificing more of themselves to others. In essence, they will always *feel* like they're being hypocritical because they *are* being hypocritical. There's simply no way around the contradiction. The overwhelming majority of Christians around the world fall into this category. Of course these people have the right to live anyway they choose, but they have chosen to accept being hypocritical. This is also probably why they insist that we're all sinners. If we're all supposed to be Christians, and if sin is equated with hypocrisy, then they are, without a doubt, sinners.

The forth type of Christian, and second most popular, is a "Christian" who completely ignores most of what Jesus said to do, but still calls himself a Christian. This person has absolutely no ethical problem at all accumulating as much wealth as possible while others go in need. This person believes that as long as he pays his 10% tithe (sometimes) he's covered (going to heaven). Of course he also has every right to do this, but he certainly can't call himself a follower of the teachings of Jesus without being completely hypocritical.

I'll end this chapter by making, what I think to be, three of the most critical observations concerning religion that are completely ignored by 95% of the population. I also think these three points are *deliberately* ignored because the truth of them runs so deeply that if believers actually thought about them, it would change forever their own limited, bigoted, and dogmatic religious paradigm.

The first observation is the fact that although religion can help bring local and regional communities together, it tears the *world* community apart. Anyone with even the slightest bit of historical perspective can look at the state of human affairs *throughout history* and see that religion was responsible for as much human misery, barbarity, injustice, immorality, and just plan evil, than quite possibly any other cause. And if they know nothing of history, they can simply look at the state of world affairs today to see the destructive side of religion. Almost everywhere in the world today where you see evils perpetrated against human beings on a grand scale, *religion* is at the center of the fray. Of course believers of *one* religion always blame believers of the *other* religion for the violence and bloodshed, but any objective observer can easily see that *both* sides are usually at fault to some degree.

To be fair though, I should point out that the reason for this is because it's the intolerant, dogmatic, fundamentalist zealot element of many religions that set much of the agenda. These are the people who believe that *their* religion is absolutely, positively, without a doubt, incontrovertibly *true*; and other religions are absolutely, positively, without a doubt, incontrovertibly *false*. And throughout history, these people have justified the most horrendous of actions *in the name of God*. And because they believe God's on their side, whatever actions they take must be right. Of course this is ridiculous to any rational person, but that's precisely what's wrong with religion—it's based on faith, not rationality. Yes, there are areas of rationality, but faith, belief, mysticism, emotionalism...etc, are held as higher values than reason, logic, and rationality.

If the last argument doesn't prove to you that religion separates the world, think about this. Suppose you lived in the Middle East a couple of thousand years ago but were not Jewish. Wouldn't you get feed up hearing that you weren't one of Gods chosen people? Wouldn't you get sick and tired of hearing that you (and your people) weren't part of Gods chosen elite? I know I would've. And then suppose you lived after *Christianity* became prominent. Once again, wouldn't you get feed up hearing the same thing—only from Christians? It's ironic, but I think the "we're Gods chosen people" mentality of Judaism and Christianity was actuality responsible for creating their biggest adversary—Islam. I think a couple of the reasons Mohammad invented Islam was in order to counter the negative psychological effects Judeo/Christian traditions had on his people; and to finally bring them together as a cohesive whole in order to stop the warlike effects of tribalism in that region. In essence, he stood up and said to his people: Hey! We're not only as good as those people, but God's actually on *our* side, not theirs, and of course his people loved it. Everybody wants to believe God's on their side.

And then of course, what's always the next step with monotheistic religions? The "we're God's chosen people" mentality. So Islam became as chauvinistic and as egotistical as any other monotheistic religion. Now *they* have the "God's on our side" mentality just as much as anyone else. I would also like to point out that, as Judeo/Christian traditions were responsible for the creation of Islam, the Crusades were responsible for the creation of Jihads, but once again, that's another story.

The second observation I'd like to make is that religion causes apathy. In other words, it causes many human beings to just accept things as they are. The Founding Fathers actually addressed the issue of apathy in The Declaration of Independence: "Prudence, indeed, will dictate that governments long established should not be changed for light and transient causes; and accordingly all Experience hath shown, that Mankind are more disposed to suffer, while Evils are sufferable, than to right themselves by abolishing the Forms to which they are accustomed."

It's my opinion that that's *exactly* what's happening right now in the United States of America (and even the rest of the world for that matter), and that religion, is one of its root causes. If human beings thought that this life was it, it might wake them up to the problems of the here and now; it might cause them to do something constructive to help alleviate *actual* pain and suffering, instead of *potential* made-up, imaginary pain and suffering after death. In essence, when human beings think God will take care of everything, *they* don't.

People put way too much time and effort into trying to figure out what's going to happen after death, and how to have life after death (which is, of course, a contradiction in terms to begin with), and not enough time trying to improve life on earth. And, fact is, none of it's anything more than guesswork anyway about what happens after death. Many otherwise intelligent human beings spend their *entire lives* studying what's going to happen after death, and the study's nothing more than what's come out of the imaginations of mostly ignorant people who lived in the past. Thus, it's a huge waste of time, effort, and brain power; and if that time, effort, and brain power were to be actually shifted toward improving life on earth, all of mankind would benefit in the long run. This is yet another paradigm that needs to change before mankind's existence on earth can be improved.

The last observation I would like to make is the fact that religions don't give mankind credit for its greatest, most important, most glorious, and most heroic achievement: the development of moral codes (no matter how imperfect). The greatest achievement any single human being can achieve is the creation of his own moral character; and this is also true of societies. But *society* doesn't create its own character, only *individuals* in a society create their own character; and if enough individuals do this, a moral society can be the result. When a Christian, Muslim, Jew…etc, say that morality can only come from a supreme being, they're saying mankind is, morally speaking, no better than a frog, pig, vulture, hyena, or a newt! They're saying mankind simply doesn't posses the intellectual capacity for such a thing. Not only are they wrong, they're completely wrong. Whether religionists accept it or not, *human beings* are responsible for moral codes, not God. And when the religious don't accept this achievement as fact, they're committing the greatest of injustices.

And it's not only an injustice, it's also a huge mistake because saying God inspired men at certain historical moments in order to give us moral codes (Old Testament, New Testament, Quran…etc) doesn't allow for the accumulation of new ethical knowledge over time. Although some actions (murder, stealing…etc) will, in nearly all cases, be considered immoral, morality does change. For instance, the Old Testament says slavery is okay, but you should set your slave free in his seventh year of service. Obviously, this was not moral. But through the accumulation of ethical knowledge over time, human beings now realize slavery is, and always has been, immoral. Of course some ancient people realized slavery was immoral (such as Plato), but the overwhelming majority just accepted it as a fact a nature (such as Aristotle).

Another example of ethical change is the fact that, in the past, stealing was seen as perfectly moral *as long as* you did it to people outside of your own community, tribe, country…etc. And why did people believe this? Because their sacred texts told them it was. The Bible justifies it, the Quran justifies it, the Upanishads justifies it…etc. Only in recent history has the majority of mankind finally come to realize that invading other nations and stealing their land, goods, women…etc, is immoral. In essence, the paradigm of war and imperialism being just a fact of nature has changed into the paradigm of war and imperialism being oppressive and immoral.

Another example of morality changing over time is in regards to charging interest. Referred to as "usury" in the Bible, this "crime" was severely punished. Of course loaning money with interest was never really immoral, but it took the passing of time (perhaps even thousands of years), and the accumulation of knowledge, for human beings to finely understand that loaning money for interest is not an immoral act.

My whole point here is that one, two, or three thousand-year-old moral codes simply aren't adequate for modern humans because they do not account for up-to-date knowledge; just like today's moral codes will not be adequate for humans living two thousand years in the future. While some moral truths remain, some moral truths change.

Well, I think that about does it for God, religion, and morality. My hope is that I've conveyed enough wisdom to cause people to be a little more tolerant of other peoples religious beliefs; I hope that I've shown the arrogance of human beings who claim to know the "truth, whole truth, and nothing but the truth" concerning religious affairs; and I hope by doing this, they will always keep it in the back of their mind that maybe, just maybe, they may be wrong; and that this thought may help keep religious fanaticism and zealotry in check. You see, the Bible, like many other sacred texts, is like a pit bull. In the right hands, it can be a very powerful, passionate, and useful tool; but in the wrong hands, in can quickly become an uncontrollable, ravenous nightmare.

Last but not least, I hope we'll never again hear words such as Chief Pontiac's: "They came with a Bible and their religion—stole our land, crushed our spirit, and now tell us we should be thankful to the 'Lord' for being saved." Or Sitting Bull's words: "If the Great Spirit had desired me to be a white man, he would have made me so in the first place. He put into your hearts certain wishes and plans, in my heart he put other and different desires. Each man is good in his sight. It is not necessary for eagles to be crows."

Chapter 6: Living a Moral Life
Values, Virtues, Principles, Habits,
and Other Things to Keep in Mind

I'd like to begin this chapter by identifying what the world's religions and philosophies have in common concerning their moral codes. Although there's much they *don't* have in common, for now, I would like to focus on what they *do* have in common. I also need to point out that just because I've identified these principles at the beginning of this chapter *does not* mean they are the most important. I began with these because not only do I agree with them, but because the overwhelming majority of human beings the world over agree with them as well. And when it comes to ethics, I think it's always good to begin on common ground if possible. In general, I'll refer to these common principles as the Universal Code of Conduct. These basic principles are held in common by *every* major religion and philosophy without exception. Although they may be explained a little differently by each, in essence, they're speaking of the same things. I think the ancient Hindu saying: "Truth is one, but the wise speak of it in many ways" applies perfectly here. So let's begin.

> #1) Do not murder.
> #2) Do not steal.
> #3) Do not lie.
> #4) Do not cheat.
> #5) Treat others in the way you want them to treat you.

In 1990 religious leaders from roughly 140 religions held a conference in Chicago to determine what basic moral principles all humans should live by. When they finished, they had only agreed with these five. Although I've never heard of such a conference for different schools of philosophy, I've determined through my own studies that, they too, would also agree with the above five. I may be wrong on this, but I've never heard of any philosopher who would disagree with any of them. However, you must keep in mind that these are *General* Codes of Conduct and *not* absolutes. There are times when it's moral to go against one or more of these five principles, but only under extreme circumstances and usually only *after* someone had already violated one of the principles. These times are usually referred to as 'Lifeboat Scenarios' or as 'The ethics of emergencies'. In essence, they can be thought of as exceptions to the rule. However, human beings cannot live by exceptions to the rules, and that's why they need a Universal Code of Conduct. These exceptions, by definition, usually only take place in extreme situations and *only after* someone had *already* violated one of the five principles, and will be covered in chapter 7.

I'm not going to waste my time, or yours, by explaining in detail *why* it's wrong to murder, steal, lie and cheat, because I think the reasons are obvious. I also think it would be a waste of time to explain the reasons why you should treat others in the way you want them to treat you. Unless someone has a serious character flaw, I think it's also obvious why this is a good principle to live by as well.

What I want to do at this point is to introduce a *sixth* principle to go along with the first five. As a matter of fact, *this* should be the fifth principle, while treating others in the way you want them to treat you, should be the sixth. Obviously, I have no idea whether or not all of the world's religions or philosophies would agree with it on a universal scale, but I don't see how they possibly couldn't, because without it, the first four would truly be meaningless. It's truly the metaphysical corollary of the first four principles. This crucial sixth principle is:

#6) Do not hire anyone to murder, steel, lie or cheat for you.

Why is this principle so important? Because without it, anything goes. I think the lack of this sixth principle is the cause of much of the world's ills. People the world over have accepted the first five principles as a Universal Code of Conduct, but they have yet to realize the importance of the sixth. I think the main reason for this is quite simply the lack of understanding most people have about applying the principles *beyond* their personal relationships. Most people apply the five principles in regards to the people *they* know and deal with, but they have yet to extend those sentiments to the people *they don't* know or deal with. For example: People will hire the government (by using their vote) to steal for them, or steal from one person in order to give to another person. You can call it whatever you wish: taxes, redistribution of wealth, egalitarianism…etc, but that doesn't change the FACT that it's still stealing. It's still taking one persons property *by force* and giving it to someone *it does not* belong too—and that's called stealing. It doesn't matter if your intentions are good, it's still stealing. It doesn't matter if 95% of the people voted for it, it's still stealing. It doesn't matter if you believe it's the only way society could function, it's still stealing. And it's also something you would probably never do in your own circle of acquaintances.

For example: You're a father with two children. Child #1 is a hard worker and a diligent saver, while child #2 would much rather sit around the house all day and beg and borrow for money when he needs it. Of course the day comes when child #2 "needs" something, but doesn't have the money to pay for it. Are you going to force child #1 to pay for it? In other words, are you going to *steal* from the have and give to the have-not? Doubtful. You'll probably give *your own* money to the lazy child, tell him to get a job, or do both. So why are you willing to steal from one person to give to another through taxation? Why are you willing to vote for someone who is willing to steal for you or for your cause? Why do you believe it would be *moral* to hire the government to steal from one person to give to another, but *immoral* for *you* to steal from your one child to give to the other? Why would you do something to a person *you don't know* that you would never do to a person *you do know*?

Or let's say you have two neighbors you're friends with and one of them falls on financial hard times. Would you steal from your one neighbor in order to help the other? Would you hire someone to steal from the one neighbor in order to help the other neighbor? Would you think that's moral behavior? If not, then why do you believe it's moral to hire the government to steal from one person to give to another? This is where I'd like to remind people that in order for a principle to be a principle, it must be applied across the board. The overwhelming majority of human beings either apply their moral principles in their personal relationships, but not to society at large; or they apply their moral principles to society at large, but not in their personal relationships. But principles, *by definition,* must be applied across the board or they are truly not principles. Yes, there are exceptions to the rules, but they're called exceptions to the rules precisely *because* they are rare occurrences. Let me give some examples of people not being consistent when applying principles.

I knew a man whose 18-year-old son smoked marijuana on a regular basis. This man was also an adamant supporter of the so-called "War on Drugs," but as it seemed, only if it wasn't fought against his own family. He would yell at his son, ground him, take away privileges…etc., but did he ever turn him in to the police? Of course not. When I pointed out the contradiction of supporting the War on Drugs, but not turning in his own son, he simply shrugged. So I said, "OK, let me get this straight. You believe drugs are so evil that people using them should be thrown in jail, *but your own son* shouldn't be"? He replied: "That's different. He's a good kid who's just going through some tough times right now. He just needs some time to figure things out." And to that I replied "But, can't *any* parent say that? Don't you think it's hypocritical to hire the government to throw other 18 year olds in jail for a "crime" you don't want your own son thrown in jail for"? With that said, he simply didn't want to discus it anymore. Sad thing is, I've had basically the *exact same* conversation with many other parents who just simply won't apply their so-called principles across the board. If you're not willing to hold your own family members to the same moral (or legal) standard you want the rest of society held too, you're living a moral contradiction. And if you live *your* life with moral contradictions, then you have no right to hold others accountable for doing the same.

Another example of people not applying principles consistently is in regards to the overwhelming majority of people who believe in the Ten Commandments. If you're one of those, I would like to ask you some questions: Do you truly adhere to the Ten Commandments, or do you rationalize into them your own beliefs? Do you believe *you* should not violate the Commandments, but that it's alright to hire someone else (through the voting process) to do it for you? Do you believe "Thou shall not kill"—period (as in a commandment)? Or do you believe "Thou shall not kill…except" (as in a suggestion)? The answers may surprise you. You see, they're either Commandments or they're not. You cannot have it both ways. If you believe they're Commandments from God, then you must also believe it's not only wrong for *you* to violate them, but wrong for *others* to violate them as well. And if you believe it's wrong for *others* to violate them, you must also believe it's wrong to *hire* others to violate them.

The Commandment states: "Thou shall not kill." It does not state: "Thou shall not kill *except* for what you believe to be a good cause." Allow me to relate this to so-called "crimes" committed by *consenting* adults. The Commandment states: "Thou shall not kill." It does not state "Thou shall not kill… unless you're trying to stop someone from committing the "crimes" of gambling, unconventional sex, smoking marijuana, prostitution, or any other so-called "sin" committed by consenting adults." Are these "crimes" committed by consenting adults so evil that you're willing to have police murder (i.e. violate the commandment) over them? Laws that make criminals out of consenting adults are laws made by men, and according to your own beliefs, the Commandments are straight from God. So which are to take precedent: Commandments from God, or arbitrary laws devised by men? One *must* take precedent over the other. Either you believe it's okay for men to violate God's laws to uphold the laws of men, or you believe God's laws should not be violated, you simply cannot have it both ways.

I also need to point out that most (if not all) biblical scholars interpret the word "kill" in the commandment to mean "murder," and that I would agree with that interpretation. The basic difference between 'killing' and 'murdering' is one of intent. Killing in self-defense, or killing in the defense of another, *is not* murder. A man "kills" in the process or defending his (or another's) Right to Life, Liberty, and the pursuit of Happiness. A man "murders" in the process of *taking away* another's Right to Life, Liberty, and the pursuit of Happiness. The difference is where morality itself lies. So the only time the government should take a life is in the *'protection of life'*, in the *'potential protection of life'*, or in the *'application of justice'*. In the *'protection of life'* is obviously protecting innocent citizens from physical harm. In the *'potential protection of life'* is much more complicated and needs to be elaborated upon in more detail.

A simple example of this would be like my earlier examples of traffic laws. If a motorist is allowed to drive 100 miles an hour through neighborhoods, sooner or latter, he'll hurt an innocent person or destroy another's property. Since the potential for harming another human by his actions is *nearly certain*, the government has the right to stop him from doing it, even if his death is the result. But this is much different than stopping consenting adults from committing what *some* people may consider harmful behavior. A man taking drugs in his own home is no physical threat to others in his society. A man hiring a prostitute is no physical threat to others in his society. A man inviting his friends over for a night of gambling is no physical threat to others in his society. These consensual adult crimes are done without causing physical harm to anyone. In fact, a person can take drugs, hire prostitutes, gamble, have unconventional sex…etc., *every single day* for their entire life and never harm another human being. But a person *cannot* drive 100 miles an hour through neighborhoods, drive down the wrong side of the road, or ignore other traffic laws for very long without harming others. In others words: a man can take drugs, hire prostitutes, gamble, have unconventional sex, or commit other victimless crimes, *without* violating anyone's "Right to Life, Liberty, and the pursuit of Happiness." That's why he has the *Right* to commit those acts. But a man *cannot* break traffic laws without, sooner or latter, violating another mans "Right to Life, Liberty, and the pursuit of Happiness." That's why *he does not* have the right to commit *those* acts.

I realize these can be tough distinctions to make at times, but a truly moral society would have to make them in order to be morally consistent. So when I talk about in the *'potential protection of life'*, it is strictly limited to potentials that are *nearly certain* to become *actuals* and nothing more. I'm not talking about potentials that have a slight possibility of becoming an actual. Any action we take has the *potential* of harming others, but unless the potential has a high degree of certainty of becoming an *actual*, we have the right to commit that action.

So in essence, when society passes laws outlawing actions committed by *consenting* adults who are harming no one, we're telling the government to potentially *murder* those involved in these behaviors. We're telling police officers that even though these "criminals" are not violating anyone's "Right to Life, Liberty, and the pursuit of Happiness," they must be stopped—*even if* death is the result. In my opinion, that's not killing, but murder.

And finally, when I talk about the *'application of justice'*, obviously I'm speaking about the courts holding people accountable for their actions. A good example would be the death penalty. The people have the Right to demand that the government take the life of a human being if there is absolutely no doubt that the accused intentionally committed the act of murder. In this case, *justice* is being applied and thus, is acceptable. But once again, the death penalty should only to be applied if there's *absolutely no doubt* about the facts in the case.

Another Commandment states: "Thou shall not steal." It does not state "Thou shall not steal *except* for what you believe to be a good cause." Or, "Thou shall not steal, *unless* you can get the government to do it for you." Or, "Thou shall not steal, *unless* you can get 51% of the voting population to do it for you." It states: "Thou shall not steal"—period! No "ifs," "ands," or "buts." "Stealing" is taking away another's property *without* their consent. It doesn't matter if you *believe* it's for a good cause, it's still stealing! It doesn't matter if the majority in a society believes it's for a good cause, it's still stealing! It doesn't matter if 99% of the population votes to take the property of the remaining 1% of the population, it's still stealing! If you vote for a politician who is willing to take another's property *by force of law, YOU* are a thief! And so is that politician! The justification is inconsequential. Remember, according to your own belief, it's a *Commandment* not a *suggestion.*

Now, I'm not saying your cause isn't a good cause, perhaps it is a good cause. Perhaps a child is starving to death, and the only way for him to get food is if it's stolen (yes that's a "lifeboat scenario"), but it's still stealing. If you hire the government to steal from one person to give to another, *you* are violating the commandment against stealing—period! And what happens if the person the government is stealing from decides he will not give up his property? Then the government takes it by force. Which means, in essence, *YOU* are hiring the government to *murder* someone because they will not allow you to *steal* from them. Think about it, because that's exactly what you're doing. You're not applying your principle across the board. You're doing something to others in your society you would never personally do to your own family, friends, associates…etc. Once again, if you're not *personally* willing to steal or murder, then why are you willing to hire the government to do it for you?

Now I would like to discus Values, Virtues, Habits, Principles, and what I call The 7 consequences of human action. These are truly the things that give life meaning.

To begin with, there are two categories of values: the Spiritual and the Material. I'll begin with the spiritual because it's these values and virtues that create a human beings character, and in the long run, determine whether or not he'll achieve the ultimate values of happiness and high character. But there's also three sub-categories of spiritual values and virtues as related to morality: 'Essential', 'non-essential', and 'conditional', that I need to describe before I go on.

Essential means they *must* be applied in order to be moral. *Non-essential* means they are important for achieving happiness, but not *essential* for morality. And *conditional* means that, in order for an individual to possess them, the majority of his society must also value them. If they do not, then it doesn't matter how much the individual values them, he will never possess them because the majority in his society will either vote them away, or simply take them away. As unbelievable as it is to me, when it comes to politics, the overwhelming majority of mankind still believes that Might makes Right.

SPIRITUAL VALUES AND VIRTUES:
Before I begin with spiritual values and virtues, I need to make a couple of important points. To begin with, since all values and virtues are interrelated, it's almost impossible to talk about one without talking about another. So if it seems like I'm mixing them together sometimes as I explain them, it's because I am—I really have no choice. In one way or another, every value and virtue impinges on all the others. And please remember that the following values and virtues are discussed as essential and non-essential *as related to morality* and not in the context of a general overall philosophy.

I also need to point out that I'll never really go into much depth in explaining each of the values, virtues, habits and principles, because that could easily be a whole other book in itself. I'm only touching upon the tips of the proverbial icebergs. I'm only trying to identify what they are in the most basic, fundamental sense. So for those of you who have complaints about me not going into enough detail, you're correct, I don't go into enough detail. But please keep in mind that I never said I would. This book is about the basics, not about detailed explanations of every single value, virtue, habit or principle. Perhaps my next book will be a detailed explanation of each, but for now it's simply about what they are, and why, in the most fundamental sense, they're important. With that said, let's begin.

ESSENTIAL SPIRITUAL VALUES AND VIRTUES:
JUSTICE—Obviously justice is *essential* because without it, morality would not be possible either in personal relationships or in a social setting.

In your *personal* relationships, justice will be the determining factor as to whether you'll have relationships that will be *beneficial* to your life, or relationships that will be *detrimental* to your life. If you treat others justly, you'll attract the just; if you treat others unjustly, you will have no choice but to deal with the unjust—because the just will have as little to do with you as possible. Just think about justice in your own life. When someone doesn't treat you justly, do you remain friends with them? Do you keep doing business with them? Of course not. It simply wouldn't make sense to stay in that type of relationship. Not only is justice a cornerstone of our personal relationships, it's a cornerstone of a moral society as well.

When I say "in a social setting," I'm referring to times when the person you're applying justice to is not in a direct personal relationship with you; such as a politician who wants your vote, a company that wants you to buy their product, the president of a charity who wants your financial support...etc. Even though you're not in personal relationships with these types of people, you still have to apply justice when dealing with them (and if you're truly moral, you'll want them to apply justice when dealing with you as well). If a politician gets caught lying, taking bribes, or gets caught with his hand in the cookie jar, he must be held accountable. If a businessman lies, sells shotty products, or doesn't hold up his end of the bargain, he must be held accountable...etc. In essence, applying justice is how we reward the good and punish the bad. Whether in our personal relationships, or in societal relationships, it's always essential to moral.

Another way of determining whether or not something is a value or a virtue, is to look at its opposite. In this case, the opposite of justice is injustice. Now, what would happen to an individual who did not value justice, but injustice? Simple, he would destroy himself, i.e., he would destroy his ability to achieve happiness or to even survive in society. Just think about it. No one would have a personal *or* business relationship with this person because they would always be treated unjustly. This would mean they would have no friends or business acquaintances whatsoever. Would you have this person as your friend? Would you do business with this person? Would you hire this person to work for you? ...etc. Of course not (I would like to point out here however, that with many of the "Politically Correct" laws we have today, the government may *force* you to do business with this person. If that's the case, you'll have no choice). The only way this person could possibly even survive would be to live out in the middle of nowhere and have no dealings with any other human being. Of course there are exceptions to the rule; there may be a few human beings who would be able to survive, or even be happy, being by themselves out in the wilderness, but in the overwhelming majority of cases, it's just simply not the case. My points being that, in the long run, only a person who holds justice as a value or virtue can live among other human beings. And only a person who understands that in order to have justice for themselves, they must grant others justice, is capable of living in a civilized society. But what it all comes down to is, no matter what the individual case, justice is *essential* for morality.

PEACE—There are two contexts for the word 'Peace': the personal and the political. The *personal* form of peace means being at peace with oneself. The *political* form of peace means, obviously, peace is in a *political* context, i.e., the absence of physical force, or war. I'll be focusing on peace in the *political* context because that's the type that falls into the realm of morality. Although being at peace with oneself is of great value, it's not essential to morality. On the other hand, peace in a *political* context *is* essential to morality. In a political context, and in my opinion, the definition of peace is essentially the same as the definition of freedom—the absence of the initiation of force. Simply put, both values can only exist if the initiation of force is prohibited. This is why *true* Freedom and *true* Peace have never existed in a social setting—because no society in history has ever completely banned the initiation of force. Although The United States of America came the closest to creating a political foundation for freedom and peace with the Declaration of Independence and Constitution, it still fell short, it still didn't completely ban the initiation of force.

Peace is essential to morality because it's the difference between barbarity and civility and between force and freedom. Peace is the byproduct of a society that does not allow human beings to resort to using force to get what they want—either in their personal relationships or in a social setting.

Peace also has something else in common with freedom. Although human beings overwhelmingly *say* they value it, very few actually do. Because in essence, if you want peace, you must not use force *or* hire anyone else to use force on your behalf. If you do, then you *do not* value peace, you're just giving it lip service. And if you look at how people vote the world over, the overwhelming majority (even in America) use their vote to violate peace (by resorting to the use of governmental force) and to take away the freedom that each individual human being is supposed to have the "unalienable" right to possess. Thus, most people *do not* value peace *or* freedom.

And then of course we must next look at the opposite of peace to see if peace is truly a value. The opposite of peace is 'war' on a large scale, or the simple initiation of force on a small scale. After all, what is the *essence* of war? Is it not the initiation of force on a grand scale? Is it not when one nation decides, for whatever reason, to initiate force against another nation? It's always amazed me that human beings *overwhelmingly* accept the premise that it's *immoral* for a nation's government to initiate force against another nation, but *moral* for a nations government to initiate force *against its own citizens*! This is yet another case when people do not apply their principles consistently. Peace is impossible without the majority understanding that the initiation of force is not acceptable except under *extremely limited* situations in a civilized society, or in a civilized world. And until this *fact* is recognized as *fact*, peace will remain an illusive, unattainable pipedream.

I think Jimmy Hendrix summed it up quite nicely when he said: "When the power of love overcomes the love of power, the world will know peace."

KNOWLEDGE—Knowledge is essential to morality because it basically makes up the building blocks in the struggle for survival, understanding, and for gaining wisdom; which can lead to living an ethical, fulfilling and happy life. In fact, you cannot gain even the slightest amount of understanding or wisdom without first gaining an adequate amount of knowledge. Constantly gaining new knowledge is how we learn to survive and grow as human beings. Without adequate knowledge, no other values or virtues would be possible.

The ability to gain and store great amounts of knowledge in the mind is one of the things that separates human beings from animals. Since animals don't have the ability to gain and store a sufficient amount of knowledge to make judgments concerning themselves or other beings, they cannot apply such concepts as justice, freedom, objectivity…etc. And if a being cannot understand such concepts, they simply won't have the ability to make moral choices.

And once again, to make sure knowledge is essential to morality, lets look at its opposite. So, what's the opposite of knowledge? I would say ignorance. What would happen if ignorance was accepted as a value? Simple, neither an individual, nor a society, could prosper or even survive. What would happen if we all stopped trying to gain knowledge or stopped using the knowledge we already possess? We would cease to exist, we could not survive, our species would go extinct…etc. Since mans means of survival is through the accumulation of knowledge, he could not survive without valuing knowledge. If a human being values ignorance, the only thing keeping him alive would be the knowledge that had already been gained by others who help keep him alive; thus, even if *he* does not value knowledge, he depends on others valuing it for his own survival. And this is why knowledge is not only essential to morality, but essential to survival as well.

RATIONALITY—Rationality is essential to morality because it's the mental tool human's use that makes it possible to understand exactly *what* we should consider a value and *how* to get it. It's essentially the primary virtue because being rational makes it possible to identify all other virtues and values. It's about applying reason to the problems of life and never accepting contradictions; which means the consistent use of logic without ever accepting things that are not true. Being rational means, in essence, thinking logically. But it needs to be remembered that being rational does not mean we must always come to the same conclusions that other rational people come to. Since human beings have different goals and values, what's rational for one person isn't necessarily rational for another—even though both may be rational in their own context.

For example: If one person decides they want to become a math teacher, would it be rational for him to spend his time in college studying history? Of course not. However, if he was taking courses on the history of mathematics, that could be considered rational. If the other person wants to become a history teacher, would it be rational for him to spend his time in college studying math? Of course not. However, if he was taking courses on the history of mathematics, that could be considered rational…etc. It's the goals and objectives of the individual that determines the rational course of action in each particular case. However, no matter *what* the goals and objectives, being rational is the only way to achieve them in the long term.

And then of course we can look at its opposite to see if rationality is essential to morality. And what is its opposite? Irrationality. Irrationality is the basic cause of all immorality and evil in the world, past and present, i.e., it's the underlying root cause of most of the worlds problems. What happens to those who attempt to value irrationality? They hurt other people or they parish. But in reality, irrationality cannot really be valued though can it? I mean, in order to value something you must be able to distinguish between alternatives, and if you're not rational, you simply cannot make distinctions. So people *do not* use irrationality as a virtue, but they *do* attempt to ignore rationality as a virtue. But of course they can't do this consistently because they wouldn't be able to function as a human being, and they would then depend on the rationality of others for their survival. Thus, no matter how you slice it, rationality ends up being a virtue and essential to morality.

OBJECTIVITY- Objectivity is essential for morality because it keeps us looking at all the information pertaining to the problems of life. In order to be objective you cannot ignore anything, by definition, you must analyze all available information (especially pertinent information that goes against your own beliefs) or you're simply not being objective. Just one of the reasons objectivity is essential to morality is because without it, *justice* is not possible; and without justice, morality's not possible.

I also think that *empathy* is an important ingredient of being objective when it comes to human relationships. Now, that doesn't mean we deny reality when we use empathy, only that, by putting ourselves in another's shoes, we can better understand where they're coming from and what information they may need in order to change their mind. You'll find more on this under the forthcoming Habit of 'Understand first, then be understood'. But keep in mind that when I say put yourself in another's shoes, I do not mean accept their beliefs as valid. I mean that you should see if anything they're saying actually conforms to reality, if not, it can be dismissed out of hand.

Now let's look at the opposite of Objectivity: Subjectivity. I think the best way to compare objectivity to subjectivity is to compare each of their axioms. An Objectivists paradigm comes from the axiom of 'The primacy of existence', while a Subjectivists paradigm comes from the axiom of 'The primacy of consciousness'. 'The primacy of existence' means that things exist independently of any perceiver, i.e., existence exist regardless of whether or not it's being perceived by any living being. While 'The primacy of consciousness' means it's the perceiver who creates that which exists, i.e., perception creates reality. But if perception creates reality (subjectivism), then for every perceiver there is a different reality; which means there would be *at the very least* billions of realities. And if there are billions of realities, there could be no such thing as right and wrong, good and bad, just and unjust, principles, values, virtues, or anything even resembling moral codes because there could be no absolutes—everything would be just a matter of opinion or belief based on each individuals perception. Although it's true that every individual has a different *paradigm* on how they *view* reality, reality is still reality. In other words, a rose is still a rose no matter how many perceivers claim it to be a skunkweed.

Thus, to not value objectivity is to not value morality because there is no ability to be moral without at least making the attempt at being objective. Being moral means making distinctions and differentiations based on reality, and in order to make distinctions and differentiations based on reality, objectivity is essential. And this is why objectivity is essential to morality.

HONESTY—Honesty is essential to morality for several reasons. To begin with, it's fundamental to being moral because morality can not exist without it. It's an integral part of #1) being able to survive, #2) being able to prosper, and #3) being able to create positive relationships with others. In fact, it's impossible to have a good positive relationship with others without *both* people being honest. Can you imagine what would happen to society if most people were not honest at least most of the time? Let me tell you: it would collapse. Honesty is the glue that binds us together in our personal relationships, our business relationships, our political relationships, or any other kind of positive relationship.

And of course the next thing to do if we're going to see if honesty is essential to morality is look at its opposite: Dishonesty. Could morality exist if everyone was dishonest? Of course not. Morality can only exist where honesty exists. Of course there will always be some people who will be dishonest and attempt to fake reality in some instances, but they can only get away with it if they are honest most of the time. This is why (Warning, Profound Statement): The best liars tell the truth most of the time!

Anyway, a person who is dishonest (fakes reality) #1) relies on others who do not fake reality in order to survive. And #2) relies on others who do not fake reality to, at least make the attempt, at achieving happiness. Either way, this person is a parasite feeding off the honesty of others. Thus, no matter how you slice it, in the long run, honesty is essential for morality.

INTEGRITY—Integrity is about being consistent in regards to your values, virtues and principles. It's the principle of being principled; it's practicing what you preach; it's having the courage of your convictions; it's about not contradicting yourself or going against your values or virtues; it's about following your own advice and acting accordingly…etc. Not only is it essential to morality, but it's also essential for building trusting relationships with others. Without having integrity, others simply could not trust you. In essence, integrity is the opposite of hypocrisy. It's about living up to your words through the appropriate actions. It's about following through to the end and not being hypocritical.

A part of having integrity is having self-discipline. Self-discipline keeps us focusing and prioritizing in order to achieve long-term values. Without self-discipline, it would be much harder, and take much longer, to achieve our goals. Since integrity is essential to morality, and self-discipline is essential to integrity, you must at least have *some* self-discipline in order to be moral. Of course nobody is perfectly self-disciplined, but it is a part of being moral.

Now let's get back to the opposite of integrity: Hypocrisy. What would happen if hypocrisy was a virtue? Obviously, if hypocrisy was a virtue (the *action* by which one gains and keeps a value), it would be impossible to gain any values (that which one acts to gain and (or) keep). If someone truly tried living life as a hypocrite they simply would not survive—period! Well, to be more accurate, I should say that they could only survive by living off the backs of those who *do not* hold hypocrisy as a virtue, i.e., by living off the backs of those who hold *integrity* as a virtue. So no matter how you slice it, integrity must be a virtue held by someone or human survival would not be possible. And of course if human survival is not possible, then morality is not possible. Thus, for all the reasons mentioned, integrity is essential for morality.

INDEPENDENCE—In essence, independence is about taking responsibility for oneself. It's essential for morality because it's the only way to make individual moral choices. All decisions we make come from our own minds independent evaluation of certain circumstances. If you let others do your thinking, not only are you setting yourself up for a fall, but you're setting your ego up for a fall as well—because independence is a cornerstone of self-esteem.

Independence is all about valuing personal responsibility; and personal responsibility means holding ourselves responsible for our actions. It's also the corollary of Freedom. You can have freedom without personal responsibility, but you cannot *maintain* freedom without personal responsibility. Personal responsibility is not only the flip-side of freedom, it's the backbone of Independence; and independence is part of what makes a human being a *moral* being. If you're not independent you're living like an animal whose owner is making all of its choices; and without making your own choices, you cannot be moral.

So now let's look at the opposite of independence: Dependence. To begin with, can dependence be a universal virtue? Of course not. If we're all dependant on others to think for us, nobody would have any original thoughts; and if nobody had any original thoughts, we would still be swinging from trees (just kidding, I don't know if our ancestor's actually swung from trees or not). But I do know that if human beings never thought for themselves there would never have been beings called human beings, because it's the independence of our thinking minds that define us as human beings. This is why our survival as a species depends on the virtue of independence.

As to why independence is essential to morality (as if survival isn't a good enough reason); it's essential because morality is based on the choices we make as *individual* human beings; and the only way to make choices is by using our individual minds; which is of course, the virtue of independence. Therefore, Independence is essential for morality.

PRODUCTIVITY—To begin with, although productivity is essential for morality, it's not necessarily essential for happiness. I say *not necessarily* essential for happiness because, although for *most* people *it is* essential for happiness, for those born into wealth, it's not *necessarily*. Just like some people seem content to spend their lives on welfare, others seem content to live their lives off the effort of their parents, grand-parents…etc. But remember, even for the rich and lazy it's essential for *someone* to be productive (regardless if there's a lack of recognition) because if it wasn't for their parents, grandparents…etc. valuing productivity, they themselves would not be able to survive. Thus, no matter how you slice it, productivity ends up being essential. In essence, productivity is essential for morality because it's the material *means* of human survival, and of course without human survival, morality is not possible.

And then to make sure productivity is an essential virtue, lets look at its opposite. So what is the opposite of productivity? I'm not really sure how to word it, so let's just say being unproductive, being lazy, uselessness, inactivity, Welfare…etc. Fact is, if human beings didn't think about the problems of survival, and then exert effort to solve those problems, human beings simply could not survive. But this isn't just true for humans, in a limited way, it's true for all living species. Of course animals don't think about the problems of survival and then act upon those thoughts like humans do, but they still must produce or die ("produce" meaning for animals, 'exerting effort'). They must take certain actions according to their nature, and if they do not, they will cease to exist. A wolf must run, smell and hunt, or die. A shark must swim, smell and hunt, or die…etc. All living species must exert effort or they will die as a species. That's simply a law of nature.

But oddly enough, human beings (because of their intelligence) are special in regards to productivity because they're the *only* species in existence that have members who will deliberately be parasitical upon its own kind. And it's this parasitism that's responsible for much of the worlds problems. This is why I say the battle isn't between the haves and the have-nots, but between the do's and the do-nots; and the sooner the workers and producers (the doers) come to understand this, the sooner the worlds civilizations will develop into societies with higher standards of morality and ever growing standards of living. But the fact remains that, in the long run, even the "do-nots" depend on the productivity of the "doers" for their survival.

As relating to productivity, I've always appreciated the saying "Idle hands are the devils playground" because, although the "devil" has nothing to do with it, people who have too much time on their hands tend to get lazy and waste time engaging in unproductive (and even bad) habits such as drinking alcohol, watching too much garbage on TV…etc. And of course these things are not good for a human beings long term happiness and self-esteem.

I also need to point out that when I talk of "productivity" I'm not just talking about working with the hands, I'm talking about working with the mind as well. Although I call myself a Blue Collar Philosopher, *mental* productivity is much more important than *physical* productivity. In essence, if idle hands are the devils playground, an idle mind is the devils utopia. But no matter what color collar you wear, productivity is not only essential for survival, but essential for morality as well.

TRUTH—Truth is the recognition of reality. Truth is essential for morality because without recognizing reality for what it is, it's impossible to recognize the moral from the immoral, the good from the bad, the positive from the negative…etc. Truth is also a value because without recognizing reality *as it is,* not only is *happiness* impossible, but *survival* is impossible as well. In essence, if you do not begin with the recognition of reality, you're lost before you even begin, and if you're lost before you even begin, it's impossible to even take a first step because you'll be without a direction to guide you.

And then lets, once again, look at its opposite to see if truth is essential for morality. I'm not really sure which word would be best to use, so lets just say that since truth is the *recognition* of reality, the opposite of truth is the *denial* of reality. So what happens if it's virtuous to deny reality? Once again, survival is not possible. And of course if you do not recognize reality, how can you possibly make moral judgments? If you cannot recognize that it's better to have a relationship with an honest person than to have a relationship with a murderer, thief, or a liar, how well are you going to fare in reality? If you cannot recognize poison plants from nutritious plants, how well are you going to fare in reality? If you cannot recognize the moral from the immoral, the good from the bad, the right from the wrong…etc, you will perish— period! These are just a few of the reasons why Truth is essential to morality. I leave it up to you to come up with more because, like all other virtues and values, *truth* is so broad a subject that I could write an entire book full of examples, but right now I'm just showing *why* it's essential to morality.

LOYALTY—When I speak of loyalty, I mean loyalty in the sense of being loyal to those who are loyal to you, or being loyal to your own principles. *I do not mean* loyalty for its own sake—the person must *earn* and *deserve* your loyalty based on theirs. In essence, it must be like an act of

Justice. Of course loyalty wouldn't be essential if you were alone on a desert island, but as long as you live in a social setting, loyalty to those who are loyal to you *is* an essential part of morality because, as I have already said, it's an application of justice.

Loyalty also has a lot to do with trust, because trust is the building block of loyalty. When you trust someone, you're giving them the benefit of the doubt in a particular situation. For example: Lets say someone promises to do something important for you. If you know them well and trust them, it can be a great benefit to you—and the more important the issue, the bigger the benefit. But if there's no one you can trust, you'll have to do everything on your own; and if you do everything on your own, survival, and even happiness, will be much harder to accomplish.

As to the opposite of loyalty, what happens if someone holds *disloyalty* as a virtue? Simple, the same things that would happen to them if they hold *dishonesty* as a virtue, they would not be able to have good, productive relationships with others in society; which means they would not be able to survive in the long run. It would be just a matter of time before the people who dealt with them would simply quit dealing with them.

But I have to say here that when I speak of loyalty, I'm speaking of it in *personal* relationships and not necessarily in *business* relationships. I hope it's obvious to most of you why loyalty is essential in personal relationships, but I understand that in a business sense it's much less obvious, and in some ways, very different. For example: Is it always moral to be loyal to the companies you buy from? No, there is nothing immoral about always buying a Ford and then suddenly deciding to buy a Chevy. That is *strictly* a business relationship.

I think the best way to look at it is on something I like to call the 'Loyalty scale'. On one end of the scale you have your 'personal' relationships, in the middle you have your 'personal/business' relationships, and on the other end you have your 'strictly business' relationships. All things being equal, buying a car is on the 'strictly business' side of the scale. However, if you work for one of the car companies, or conduct business (and I don't mean to just buy their product, but to conduct business with them, own their stock…etc) with one of the car companies, you are now in the middle 'personal/business' section of the scale. If your *spouse* works for one of the car companies, or does business with one of the car companies, you're also in the 'personal/ business' section of the scale.

In this middle section of the loyalty scale, loyalty is no longer essential, but it is still important. Of course as long as these people support you, it *is* essential to support them, but if they only support you partially (what I mean by "partially" is that they still do business with you, but they also do business with your competitors), it is no longer essential to do *all* your business with them, but it is still important to do *some* of your business with them.

And on the 'strictly business' end of the scale, it's *never* essential because so many other factors are involved. Things that are strictly business are things such as buying a TV, buying groceries, buying clothes…etc. As long as you have no moral qualms about the business practices of the particular company, it's ok to buy from them.

So loyalty *is* essential to morality in some relationships, but not essential to morality in all relationships. It all depends on the individual circumstances.

NON-ESSENTIAL SPIRITUAL VALUES AND VIRTUES

HAPPINESS—Happiness is not essential for morality because it's possible to be unhappy and yet moral, but it's still a value because, in my opinion, a happy person is more likely to be a moral person. It's also one of the highest of personal values because it is the only value that is an end in itself, and all other virtues and values are pursued in order to help us achieve happiness. For example: When we pursue Love, Meaning, Self-esteem, Wisdom, etc., we pursue them because we think they will ultimately bring us happiness, i.e., they are used *as a means* to achieve the ultimate goal of happiness. This is also why we follow the virtues. If we follow the virtues we can achieve our values, and if we achieve our values, we can achieve happiness.

In my opinion, a major part of the achievement of happiness is the achievement of Flow. "Flow" means being so wrapped-up in something that it no longer seems to take effort; it means being so proficient at something that it seems to come naturally; it means completely losing yourself in that which you're doing. In sports, some people call it being in the "zone." It's not loss of consciousness, but the lost *sense* of consciousness. When we achieve flow we lose all sense of time, all sense of our surroundings, and even all sense of thought. We're so wrapped-up in what we're doing that hours can pass without us even realizing it. It's like being in a state of hyper-consciousness. I think everyone's had this type of experience in their life, it's just that most people haven't really thought much about it. If they did, they would quickly realize that much of our happiness is actually the by-product of achieving Flow. For a detailed examination of Flow I suggest reading

Mihaly Csikszentmihaly's appropriately named book 'Flow'. It's well worth your time.

Another thing I need to point out about happiness is that in order to achieve it, the right actions must take place. Now, that might seem obvious, but I don't think most people have really thought about its deep underpinnings. Just think about it. Pain and suffering are inevitable, while love and happiness are not. No matter who you are, or what you do, you simply cannot avoid pain and suffering—period! No matter what actions you take in life, you will, sooner or latter, have to deal with some sort of pain and suffering—it's inevitable! However, love and happiness *are not* inevitable. In order to achieve love and happiness, a human being must take a correct course of action. If they do not, they can go through their entire life without ever being in love, or being happy. Of course they may have fleeting moments of happiness, but fleeting moments of happiness do not make up a happy life. This is why, in the long run, correct actions are the *only* path to happiness.

And now of course, let's look at the opposite of happiness. Can anyone really argue that being *un*happy is a goal to strive for? Of course some might, but that's why happiness is not essential to morality. In my opinion though, happiness is important to morality because a happy person has a lot more to loose, and therefore, they'll be more inclined to maintain good solid moral relationships. On the other hand, an unhappy person won't be as concerned about achieving a high moral character because he simply doesn't have as much to lose. Of course this isn't a hard and fast rule, but in general, I think it holds true.

MEANING/PURPOSE—Purpose and Meaning are not essential for morality because it's possible to feel purposeless, or feel that life is meaningless, and yet be moral. But they're still values because, without them, happiness would not be possible to achieve. The search for meaning, regardless of what society a man lives in, has always been the individuals most important quest. The question: What is the meaning of life? Is mankind's enduring question. As long as man has been man, and as long as man *is* man, this question will be asked. In fact, this question is inherent in *any* species that has the ability to reason. If there's intelligent life elsewhere, they're also searching for the answer to this question.

So, do *I* know the meaning of life? Yes. Can I tell *you* what it is? No. You see, the meaning of life is something that each one of us must determine for ourselves. There are just as many meanings of life as there are human beings, it will never be the same for any two individuals. I think the best way to put it is: The meaning of life is… to find meaning. I know, I know, that's just way to simplistic. Yes it is, but yet, it's so complex. If it were that simple, the majority of human beings would already be happy, but are they? I don't think so. So obviously it's not so simple.

The reason 'Meaning' is of ethical concern is because people who see their lives as having meaning are, in my opinion, much more likely to be good, decent, moral people. In fact, I don't think a person who *doesn't* see their life as having at least some type of meaning can remain happy beyond the range of the moment. They may be able to enjoy sex, drinking alcohol, smoking, exercise, or any other range of the moment activity, but without meaning, these moments are fleeting.

Purpose on the other hand, is actually a little different than meaning (although most people usually combine the two). Allow me to explain. Human beings can make their lives meaningful by a process of thought control. In other words, they can choose *how* to view life and then choose *how* to respond to it. Or maybe a better way to put it is that human beings can first *choose* and then *become* their own meaningful paradigm. If they want to be a martyr, they can be a martyr. If they want to be a hero, they can either wait for their chance to become a hero, or they can choose a cause and become a hero. If they want to be a good parent, they can have children and become good parents. If they want to be a good husband or wife, they can choose to be a good husband or wife…etc. Human beings are the only species that can *choose* which values to pursue, and then give their lives meaning by how they think and act upon those choices. No other species on earth can do this. In essence, humans can give their lives meaning, but animals cannot.

However, although animals cannot have meaning, they do have purpose. They have the same purpose as human beings: survival. The first priority, or purpose, of all living beings is to survive. Of course animals do not *choose* to survive, nature has programmed them for it, but it's only natural for humans in their early years. In their later years, survival becomes a choice; and once survival becomes a choice, meaning must take over or the person is living off the inertia of the past, or living off others. *Meaning* is the ultimate survival tool because it is the ultimate motivator. It's what creates human happiness, and in return, gives humans the overwhelming need to survive and prosper. It's a big part of what makes man, man. Thus, although meaning isn't essential to morality, it's still one of mankind's most important values.

I also think finding meaning is one of modern mans biggest dilemmas. Just think about it for a minute. Up until resent history, the meaning of life for the overwhelming majority of mankind was simply trying to surviving. Most people didn't sit around thinking about the meaning of life—they didn't have time too. They were too busy thinking about where their next meal was coming from, or about how they could get a little bit ahead in life, i.e., they were too busy just trying to survive to worry about life having some type of ultimate meaning. In a way, this reminds me of what I'm going through right now in my life. Although I love being able to listen to books on tape as I work, I would much rather be doing something else to help make the world a better place—and this is why I'm writing this book. It's the best I can do with the little extra time I have. I wish I could go out and change the world, but in essence, I'm too busy making a living to make a difference. But hopefully, this book will change all that.

Getting back to meaning in general, it must be remembered that most people of the past were simply too busy just surviving to worry about "meaning," or even about being happy. But now that most people (at least in industrialized nations) can work just eight to ten hours a day to have their material needs met, they have more time to think about such things as meaning. In a way, the real curse of modernity is that too many people just have too much time on there hands and too little to do with it. Now, I'm not saying this is a bad thing, in fact, it's a good thing. But now that the meaning of life is not just surviving, people must discover *for themselves* a new meaning. They must put forth the effort to do so or they'll always have the nagging feeling that "there must be something more to life."

And then of course there's the opposite of meaning or purpose. Can anyone really argue that meaninglessness (or purposelessness, if you will) is a value? I certainly hope not. As a matter of fact, of all the opposites of this books values and virtues, meaninglessness is probably the hardest one to make a case for. It's so hard that I've never even heard anyone even make the attempt. But even so, although meaning is extremely important, it's still not *essential* for morality. So it remains a non-essential value as related to morality.

PRIDE—Pride is 'the commitment to achieve one's own moral perfection', or in other words 'moral ambitiousness'. Ayn Rand also described its basis as 'unbreached rationality', and I would agree. But one thing is for certain, Pride is certainly *not* a "sin." I realize most people have been fooled into believing pride is wrong, sinful, immoral, or even evil, but that's simply not the case. If pride is a sin, then happiness itself must be a sin. Pride and happiness go hand in hand because psychologically, happiness is ultimately the by-product of pride. Without beginning with the commitment to achieve ones moral perfection, a human beings psyche will continually be under attack by its own conscious because it'll know it's continually falling short of its own potential. Of course starting with pride doesn't mean a person will *necessarily* be moral or achieve happiness, but it is the starting point.

We also have to remember though, that the *commitment* to moral perfection does not mean a person will *achieve* moral perfection; just like the commitment to our virtues will not always mean we will gain our values. After all, human beings are not perfect because they're fallible and they do make mistakes. But the person who's committed to achieving moral perfection will learn from their mistakes and improve upon them, while the person who's not committed to moral perfection won't even see the importance of making the attempt. This is why the process is as important as the end result. Or as the saying goes: "Life's a journey, not a destination."

And then of course we must look at those who *do not* have a commitment to achieving their own moral perfection. Can anyone honestly argue that human beings *shouldn't* be as moral as they can be? I've never heard anyone argue that. Once again, I'm not saying people *must* be perfect, only that to know you're wrong, immoral or evil concerning a certain action you've taken, and then not taking the appropriate actions to counter that mistake, shows a complete lack of pride and understanding of what it means to be moral. Is this *lack* of moral standards a moral standard we want people to emulate? Is this a course of action that will enhance the human condition, or is it one that would ultimately destroy civilization? The answers are obvious.

So although having the commitment to achieving ones own moral perfection isn't *absolutely* necessary for being moral, it's still *very* important. Of all the 'Non essential' spiritual values and virtues concerning morality, pride just may be the closet to being essential.

SELF-ESTEEM—Self-esteem's not essential for morality because a person can have low self-esteem and still be moral, but it's still a value because, without it, happiness would not be possible to achieve. Once you've used Reason to find Meaning, and are committed to achieving your own moral perfection, then and only then can you achieve Self-esteem which can bring you Happiness. But you can only begin this journey by knowing that your mind is competent to think and that you're worthy of Happiness.

Just think about it for a moment. If you don't think your mind is competent to think, how can you even begin to attempt to achieve happiness? How can you even begin to attempt to achieve *anything*? For human beings, the mind is the basic tool of survival. To attempt to go through life without knowing you have the ability to think, is to attempt to go through life without knowing you're a human being. And if you don't think you're worthy of happiness, well, I really don't know what to say except: the day you stop thinking you're worthy of happiness, is the day you will achieve that goal.

And then there's the opposite of self-esteem. I'm really not sure what word to use to identify low self-esteem, so I'll just say 'low self-esteem'. In essence, having low self-esteem is the state of unhappiness. A person who has low self-esteem is a person who doesn't think they're worthy of happiness, who doesn't think they're virtuous, and therefore, doesn't achieve their values; or, a person who may be achieving values, but who's values are not worth achieving. This person can never be happy because they begin with a mental paradigm of themselves that is antithetical to the achievement of happiness. If you do not begin with the certainty that your mind is competent to think and that you're worthy of happiness, you cannot achieve happiness—period! And this is why Self-esteem is a value, but yet not essential to morality.

WISDOM—In my opinion, the essence of wisdom is knowing the difference between *knowing* and *believing*; and it can only be gained after a great amount of knowledge is accumulated. I also think a big part of having wisdom is being able to see the Big Picture; which includes being able to see things from all points of view. Now, that doesn't mean you have-to agree with other points of view, only that you must know why people think the way the do, i.e., you must understand their paradigm and why the hold it.

Wisdom is a value because it takes us to a higher level of understanding and consciousness, and ultimately leads to a more fulfilling and happy life. Wisdom is the ultimate goal of all our intellectual pursuits; it's the pinnacle of the combination of all the knowledge we've accumulated over our individual lifetime. But unlike knowledge, wisdom's not essential to morality because even an ignorant person can be moral if he follows basic fundamental principles such as being honest, having integrity, not lying, not cheating…etc. It's just that wisdom is on a higher plain than knowledge because you can only get to wisdom through the accumulation of great amounts of knowledge. In essence, the virtue of accumulating knowledge leads to the value of wisdom. Or at least it will if the other virtues are followed as well.

Now lets look at its opposite. So, what's the opposite of wisdom? I really have no idea. At first I thought it might be ignorance, but the opposite of ignorance is knowledge. Maybe I'll just describe the opposite of wisdom as a person who has a complete lack of common sense, because I would describe a wise person as a person with a great amount of common sense. Or maybe 'foolish' would be a better way to describe the opposite of wisdom. Either way, I think you get my point.

So, can anyone argue that being foolish is a virtue? As far as I know, not a single religion or philosophy holds foolishness as a virtue. As a matter of fact, in my entire life I've never heard anyone claim foolishness is a virtue. So I think it's safe to say that wisdom is a virtue because it's a higher form of common sense, whereas foolishness is a vice because it's the lack of common sense. Of course we can debate all day long over exactly what it means to be wise, but there's no debate at all over whether or not wisdom is a value.

LOVE—Love is an extremely important value, but it's not essential to morality. It's certainly essential to achieving true long-term happiness though. I think love is what completes us and makes us whole. Yes, happiness is a state of mind that can be achieved under most circumstances, but I think long-term happiness can only be achieved if one loves and is loved. Love's a very unique value. It's the glue of our closest, most intimate relationships. I'm not sure where it was at, but a character from an Ayn Rand novel described love as "exception making," and at least in part, I would agree. When we love someone we tend to overlook their flaws (or should I say "perceived" flaws?). We tend to put up with them doing things we would never allow others to get away with. Now, I don't mean putting up with major character flaws, but minor ones. In essence, things that are non-essential concerning morality.

But this is just one aspect of love. Another aspect of love is about going out of the way for those we love. When we truly love someone we're willing to put our life on the line for them, go out of our way for them, give up a lesser value for them…etc. For example: Because of my job, my family has recently had to move; and in order to get my youngest son into a good school, I had to add twenty minutes to my drive to work each day. Now, some people might see this as a sacrifice on my part, but it's really not. A sacrifice is based on giving up a greater value for a lesser value, and since my son is a greater value then the lost forty minutes each day, it's not a sacrifice. I did it because I love him. Would I do it for a neighbor? No. Would I do it for a co-worker? No. Would I do it for a stranger? No. And why wouldn't I do it for any of these people? Simple, because I don't love them.

This is why the Biblical teaching to love your neighbor and your enemy is so ridiculous. We can only *truly* love those we have close intimate relationships with. Anyone who says they love their enemies, love their neighbor, love their fellow man…etc, has no idea what the word "love" means. To "love" someone means to go that extra mile for them, it doesn't mean to just "care" about them. It means to value them so much that you're willing to give up things you *like* for the greater value of what you *love*. Love is expressed through actions. If you're not willing to go out of the way for those you believe you love, then you truly don't love them. You may *care* for them, you may even really, really *like* them, but *caring* and *liking* are not *loving*.

Now let's look at the opposite of love: Hate. Is there anyone willing to argue that hate is a value or virtue? I certainly hope not (although they may argue that, at times, hate can be a great motivator). What would happen if the majority of human beings held hate as a value or virtue? Simple, we wouldn't have much of a society would we? As a matter of fact, I don't think a civilization could *even survive* if the majority believed it was virtuous to hate. So although it may be argued that it's a great motivator, it certainly cannot be argued it's a virtuous course of action or something to aspire to.

GOOD REPUTATION—Having a good reputation is a value because having a good reputation will open doors and give you opportunities you may not have gotten *without* a good reputation. It's the recognition by others that we have lead a virtuous life; and by being recognized by others as leading a virtuous life, they're much more likely to take chances on us that they otherwise wouldn't have. This could ultimately be the difference between getting that dream job, getting investors for a new business venture, getting into that university you always wanted to attend, getting a date with that special man or woman…etc. But remember, having a good reputation does not necessarily mean being liked. Having a good reputation is based on a solid ethical foundation, being liked does not mean you have a solid ethical foundation. It's much more important to be respected and have a good reputation than it is to be liked. As a matter of fact, our reputations are so important that we've even created libel and slander laws to protect them. So to anyone who says a good reputation isn't a value, I ask: Then why do we have laws against libel and slander? As the saying goes: Your reputation precedes you.

Now lets look at its opposite to see if having a good reputation is a value. When you have a *bad* reputation, all you have to do is reverse the examples I gave in the last paragraph. Are you going to get that dream job if you have a bad reputation? Are you going to get investors for a new business venture? Are you going to get a date with that special man or woman? Probably not. Having a bad reputation is going to have the *exact opposite* effect on your life than having a good reputation, i.e., it's going to close doors instead of open them. So obviously, having a good reputation is good, and having a bad reputation is bad. However, even though having a good reputation is valuable, it's not *essential* for being moral.

HOPE—I once read somewhere that 'Hope' is the only *real* religion there ever was, or ever will be. Just think about it for a moment. Aren't *all* religions really founded on the concept of hope? Sure, they all have *faith* in different things, but they are *all* founded on the concept of hope. And that's one of the reasons why religions are so powerful to most human beings. Hope is a virtue because, well, let's face it, sometimes we work hard to achieve things without knowing whether or not we'll ever achieve them. Hope is what sustains us during those times when we're not feeling happy or fulfilled. But it's more like a minor virtue than a major virtue though because it's basically just believing you'll get your just rewards from others, and you'll achieve your goals. Because no matter how reasonable, logical, objective, hard-working or responsible you are, you still don't *know* what the future holds. So in essence, hope is a virtue because it helps us move forward in the journey of life without knowing whether or not we'll reach our wanted destination. It gives us energy to follow through when all, well, hope, seems lost, i.e., when things seem hopeless is when we need hope the most.

I say this speaking from experience. When I was in my late teens I came really close to committing suicide. In fact, I came about as close as you can without actually following through with it. At that moment in my life the only thing that keep me from pulling the trigger was that I just knew things could only get better; I knew that if I just stuck it out a while longer things would *have-to* get better. And it was that hope (and my mothers love) that kept me alive (and maybe even the bag of weed I smoked before passing out, but that's another story).

Another *personal* example of hope is this book. No matter how reasonable, how logical, how rational, how good, how much effort it took to write it, how much time it took to write…etc, there's simply no way of knowing whether or not people will want to read it. But just hoping it does get published helps me keep pushing on to complete it, and that's just another example on why hope is a virtue.

And then of course there's the opposite of hope: hopelessness. I'm really not sure people can even survive without at least having a minimal amount of hope, because without hope, there's really nothing to live for. And to prove this you don't have to look any further than my own example from two paragraphs ago—suicide. People commit suicide for one reason and one reason only, they've lost all hope. Of course there's many *causes* for people committing suicide (a lost loved one, lose of a job, lose of money…etc), but the main underlying reason is always lose of hope. And once again, is there anyone who claims hopelessness is a virtue? Not as far as I know. Thus, even though hope's not essential for morality, it's still a virtue because human beings need it in order to keep striving for happiness

BENEVOLENCE—Benevolence is a virtue because it creates happiness in others and in ourselves. It's also an essential part of the principle of treating others in the way you want them to treat you, along with helping us gain our values in society by helping others gain theirs.

Let's face it, no matter who we are or what we do, we're going to have to deal with other human beings. And if we want them to treat us benevolently, we'll have to treat them benevolently. You could even say it's a form of pre-emptive justice. Knowing that you were kind or benevolent to another person (or even an animal for that matter) can also be a fulfilling experience. If you help someone with a problem, get a job, accomplish a goal…etc, you not only help them, but you feel good about helping them. And by helping them, you may also be helping yourself in the future because that person is now more inclined to help you if you ever need it. As long as there are no sacrifices involved, it's completely win-win.

And once again, lets look at it's opposite to see if benevolence is a virtue. What would happen if you went through life being malevolent, mean, and just plain old unkind? Well, let's just say you're probably not going to do very well or be very happy. Your family's not going to want to be around you, you're not going to have any friends, and your not going to have very good relationships with your co-workers (if you could even get a job in the first place that is). So as you can see, straight across the board, being benevolent is a much better approach to life than being malevolent. It's not only going to make others happier, it's going to make *you* happier as well. Like I already said, it's essentially a win-win situation for everyone involved.

BALANCE—Aristotle described balance as being the mean (middle ground) between the extremes. However, the problem with this is that sometimes going to the extreme is a good thing. Extremism in the defense of liberty is virtuous; extremism in the defense of justice is virtuous; extremism in the defense of truth is virtuous…etc, but there are times when going to the extreme is just, well, too extreme. An athlete who spends hours working out, but then doesn't sleep and rest the appropriate number of hours so his body can maintain a healthy balance is going to a negative extreme. The person who spends 70 hours a week at work, but has a family at home who needs and misses him is going to negative extremes and is out of balance. The Scientist who spends every waking hour in his lab, and spends no time exercising, is going to the extreme and is out of balance…etc. In a way, the religion of Taoism refers to extremes as the Yin and the Yang, or "opposites" if you will. In scientific terms, it's referred to in the teaching "for every action there's an equal and opposing reaction." Maintaining balance is about not going to the extreme if it's going to have a negative affect, while always keeping in mind that there are times when it's necessary to go to an extreme in order to have a positive effect.

If you look at something like Justice, anything less than the extreme wouldn't be justice, would it? After all, how can you have too much justice? But if you look at something like Peace, would it be a good thing to go to the extreme in order to achieve peace? In many situations: no. Would it have been a good thing to just let Hitler take over the world in order to have "peace"? Of course not. Would it have been a good thing if slavery was never ended in order to maintain "peace"? Of course not. If you have to hand over most of your paycheck to the government in order to maintain "peace," is it a good thing? No, because some things (such as Freedom) are worth fighting for. Or as Patrick Henry put it "Give me liberty or give me death." So sometimes going to the extreme is obviously a negative, while other times it's obviously a positive.

And how about being extremely rational? Can a person be too rational? I don't think so. So although not going to the extreme is a good thing in *many* aspects of life, it must be remembered that going to the extreme is a good thing in *some* aspects of life. This is yet another case highlighting the importance of wisdom; because it's the wise man who maintains balance by knowing when to go to the extreme and when not to go to the extreme. So although maintaining balance isn't essential for morality, it's still important because it helps us achieve happiness.

COURAGE—Courage is a virtue because it helps us overcome obstacles, and live up to our other virtues, so we may ultimately achieve our values. It's not necessarily essential for morality at *all* times, but it sure is necessary for morality *some* times. For example: If you tell the truth about something that's important, but not a life or death situation, it's being moral without being courageous. But if telling the truth could cost you your life, then yes, in this case being moral means being courageous—but that would also make it an act of moral heroism and not just a case of being moral. So being courageous *is* essential for moral heroism, but it's not *necessarily* essential for being moral.

Now lets look at its opposite to see if courage is a virtue. Can anyone argue that cowardice is a virtue? I certainly hope not. Now, I'm not just talking about extreme cases of cowardice (such as not defending yourself or your family in a dangerous situation), I'm talking about cowardice in all its forms. I'm talking about everyday situations like being afraid to say something when you know you're being cheated, not standing up for a cause you know is just, or even something as simple as being afraid of spiders. I can't think of a single example of when being a coward is virtuous. But you must always keep in mind that being a coward, and *choosing* not to do something, are *not* one and the same. In certain situations, *not* fighting is the courageous thing to do—it all depends on the individual circumstance. The important thing to think about is whether you're taking actions (or not taking actions) because you're afraid, or if you're taking actions (or not taking actions) because it's the moral or the right thing to do. So as always, *intent* plays a vital role here as with all other situations concerning morality. But no matter how you slice it, being courageous, in many situations, is virtuous, while being a coward, is *never* virtuous.

SENSE OF HUMOR—Having a sense of humor is not essential for morality, but it's extremely important because it's a big part of achieving happiness. And like all other virtues and values, a sense of humor must be worked on and practiced at. Of course for some people it seems to come naturally, but for most of us it must be cultivated. In essence, having a sense of humor helps keep life enjoyable—but it can also help us through tough times by allowing us to laugh at ourselves when we're taking life too seriously. Can you imagine what life would be like if the majority of human beings didn't have a sense of humor? Just think of the people you've met in your life who didn't have a sense of humor. Do you think they should be emulated? I certainly don't. I think it's pretty obvious to most of us why it's a virtue, even if it's not essential for morality.

PERSEVERANCE—Perseverance is a virtue because, like the other virtues, it helps us achieve our values. Can you name a single successful person you've ever met who *did not* value perseverance? I can't. Having perseverance (or being persistent if you will) is essential to achieving *true* long-term success (I say "true" success because someone may win the lottery and become "successful," but that's more of just a matter of luck than achievement). Perseverance is one of the building blocks to building a long term successful life; and although perseverance isn't essential to morality, I do think that, in the long run, it is essential to happiness, and that's why it's a virtue.

Now let's look at the opposite of perseverance. So, what's the opposite of perseverance? I guess it would be just plain ole giving up. How far would you get in life if you just kept giving up? How many goals would you attain if you just said "Oh, the hell with it"? How many values would you achieve if you quit striving for them? It really doesn't take much thought, does it? So obviously perseverance is a virtue and one of the building blocks of success even though it's not essential for morality.

PASSION—Being passionate is truly what makes life worth living. Of course it's not essential to morality, but it certainly *is* an important element of achieving happiness. Passion is one of the greatest of motivators. It's the driving force behind many of the choices we make in life—good or bad. This is why, to a certain extent, our passions must be tempered. Because not only can passion lead to a successful fulfilling life, it can also lead to a life full of failure and disappointment. In a way, it's a lot like Freedom. It's a two edged sword that can fall back upon itself if you're not careful. While the flip-side of freedom is responsibility, the flip-side of passion is temperance. So unlike the virtues described already, its opposite can be a virtue as well. It all comes down to the individual circumstances. In essence, we should let our passions guide us while not letting them control us. And that's where the virtue of maintaining balance comes in.

For you Star Trek fans out there, I've always thought that a well balanced human being would be a mixture of a Vulcan and a Klingon,. Or what I call a Vulgon. This person would strive to live his life as logically as possible (like a Vulcan), while at the same time, be as passionate as possible (like a Klingon). In fact, his passion would actually be encouraged by his logic because when human beings know they're right (which only logic can prove), they're much more passionate about whatever it is they're involved in. It may seem silly to some, but I still look at my life in this way sometimes. I still think of myself as a Vulgon; meaning I try to live my life with the passion of a warrior, but with the controlling guidance of reason and logic; and by doing this, my happiness is best achieved. The Rabbi Sherwin Wine put it perfectly when he said "Let passion fill your sails, but let reason be your rudder." However, although passion isn't essential for morality, it's an important element in achieving happiness.

PATIENCE—We've all heard the saying about patience being a virtue right, but is it? Well, yes and no, it all depends on the circumstances. Of course we can all give examples of where patience *is* a virtue, but there are also times when patience is actually a hindrance. Thus, unlike the other virtues on this list (with the exception of passion), its opposite can also be a virtue.

How much longer would slavery have existed in this country if passionate blacks and whites didn't stand up and fight against it, but just sat back and patiently waited for things to change without pushing them along? Would the United States even exist today if the founding fathers had been more patient with England? What would happen to society if the majority of people were more patient with murderers, rapists, child abusers, thief's...etc? Could anyone argue it would be a good thing? I don't think so. So patience is a virtue, but not under all circumstances. Unlike the other virtues (besides passion) it can either be a positive or a negative depending on the individual circumstances. This is why it's a non-essential virtue concerning morality, while essential *at times* in regards to happiness.

CONDITIONAL VALUES:

Before I begin with these three conditional values, I need to point out that since I've already covered them earlier in this book, I'm not going to spend time going over them in detail again. I just need to point out why these three values are conditional, and thus different, from the rest.

FREEDOM—Freedom is a conditional value because if others in your society do not value it, *you* can not posses it. Since your freedom is dependent upon others leaving you alone, it requires *them* to value it as much as you in order for you to posses it—that's why it's conditional. If they don't value freedom, they'll simply (or not so simply) use force (or their vote) to take away your freedom. This is why it's imperative for those who understand the value of freedom to help those who do not. The possession of freedom is not only the path to achieving happiness, it's the only path to morality as well. But as I've already said, since I covered Freedom earlier, I'm not going to go over it again. I just wanted to point out *why* it's a conditional value.

And when I say "conditional," I don't mean there are times when it's a value and times when it's not, because Freedom is *always* a value. I mean simply that it's based on the condition of being left alone by others.

PEACE—Peace is a conditional value because, as with freedom, if others in your society do not value it, *you* can not posses it. Since peace can only be achieved if the initiation of force is prohibited, others must want it prohibited as well or you will not have peace. As with freedom, peace is dependant upon others leaving you alone. If they do not, you can value peace all you want but it'll mean nothing because they'll aggress against you. And of course on a geo-political scale, this goes for nations as well. A nation, or I should say the majority of individuals in a nation, can be the most peace loving people in history, but if it's located next to Nazi Germany or Communist Russia, their love of peace will mean absolutely nothing. In essence, if their neighboring countries don't value peace, their valuing peace will not bring them peace— that's why it's conditional. And of course, the same goes for individuals as well

JUSTICE—Justice is a conditional value because, once again, if others in your society do not value it, *you* will not obtain it. Of course *you* can, and should, treat others justly in all your relationships; and you can demand others in your personal relationships treat you justly as well; and if they don't, you can simply stop having relationships with them. But if the majority in your society doesn't value justice, you won't obtain it in a social setting. As with the values of Freedom and Peace, *you* can value justice all you want, but if others in your society do not, it will mean very little. Simply put, your valuing justice will not bring you justice if others do not value it—that's why it's a conditional value.

MATERIAL VALUES:
Material values are obviously values such as food, shelter, clothing…etc. Or in essence, things that help us survive and make us happy. They're important aspects of living, but since under normal conditions these things don't fall under any type of ethical or unethical behavior, I really have no need to discus them. Of course some people might argue that a billionaire is immoral because of the amount of material goods he possesses, but at least in this book, I'm not going to get into that type of discussion.

I also need to point out that there are other types of values that I won't be covering in this book as well (such as 'family' or 'friends'). These types of things are values as well, but since they have more to do with our personal preferences and less to do with our moral character, I won't be discussing them either. These types of values can help to make us happier people, but they aren't necessarily of ethical concern. For example: One man may hold 'family' as one of his highest values, while another man may not. This doesn't automatically make the second man any less moral than the first. Whether or not a man has a family, or even values a family, has nothing to do with his moral character. A man does not have to be a father and (or) husband to live a moral life or be a moral man; just as a woman doesn't have to be a mother and (or) wife to be a moral woman. To be moral, is to be virtuous; and single, unattached people can be as virtuous as anyone else.

Now that I've covered some values and virtues, I need to address the question: Do values and (or) virtues sometimes conflict with one another? The overwhelming majority of the time, i.e. everyday life, the answer is no. But just like there are exceptions to the Universal Code of Conduct, there are times when values or virtues may conflict. In my opinion though, they don't so much *conflict*, as they are prioritized differently in different situations. For example: Freedom and Peace are both important values, but freedom is the higher value because it's a prerequisite of morality. However, there may be times when we give up a little freedom in order to achieve peace. If you choose to live in a neighborhood, you won't have the freedom to do what you want *when* you want. You may want to have a party and play loud music until 3 o'clock in the morning, but I seriously doubt if your neighbors will put up with it for very long without calling the police. So in essence, you have given up a little freedom for peace.

Here's another example. Happiness and Survival are both values, but *in general* happiness is the higher value. I say *in general* because, once again, under certain circumstances *survival* becomes paramount. In other words, there are times when we must do things *in the short term* in order to survive that do not make us happy. Living in the United States gives us a great advantage over most people around the world because, in general, survival is easily attained; thus, we're able to focus more on the things that make us happy. But this isn't the case around much of the world. Many, if not most, of the worlds population spends much more time simply trying to survive than trying to achieve happiness (although of course they're trying to achieve both at the same time).

So yes, sometimes values can conflict and need to be prioritized, but that's why we try to keep focused on what they are (the forthcoming habit of 'Sharpening the saw'), and on our long-range goals.

THE 7 CONSEQUENCES OF HUMAN ACTION

Every action we take as human beings has consequences, there's simply no getting around that fact. And although most people have never thought of it in this way, it's still a metaphysical absolute—and yes, I said absolute. Every action a human being takes will fall into one of the following 7 categories, and as you'll see, this list is also set up as a hierarchy.

From the top down: Heroic, moral, right, amoral, wrong, immoral, and evil. All things being equal, being immoral is better than being evil, being wrong is better than being immoral, being amoral is better than being wrong, being right is better than being amoral, and being moral is better than being right. However, I do need to point out that although the act of moral heroism is at the top of the list (in the category of 'Heroic'), doesn't automatically make it more important than simply being moral. Although the rest of the list is in order of positive to negative actions, the top two can be reversed according to the goals of the person, and one isn't necessarily better than the other. And although people may disagree on *which* of the seven categories an action may fall into, it *must* fall into one of them.

HEROIC—A heroic act is one of the rarest of human actions. It's rare because in order to commit a heroic act, a person must either place themselves in jeopardy, or be placed in jeopardy by others. Either way, it's the danger of the situation that makes what they do heroic. However, there are also two types of heroic acts: an act of moral heroism (being heroic for a good, moral, or just cause), or an act that's heroic, but not necessarily moral. Allow me to explain the difference.

Growing up in America, we were taught that people like Christopher Columbus, Hernando Cortez, George Washington, Thomas Jefferson and George Custer were heroes—but Native Americans certainly don't see these people as heroes. From their point of view, these people were about as evil as you can get. On the other hand, they see people such as Sitting Bull, Crazy Horse, Red Cloud, Chief Pontiac and Geronimo as heroes—while we were taught that they were nothing more than uncivilized brutes and savages.

Many of the French revere Napoleon as a great hero, but do the British or the Germans? Of course not. The Greeks see Alexander as a great hero, but do the Egyptians or Iraqi's? No. Many Asians revere Genghis Kahn, but do the Europeans? No. Were you taught that Attila the Hun was a great hero? Of course not, but many in Asia are. Or how about someone like General Sherman? The North might have seen him as a hero, but the South sure as hell didn't. To them, General Lee was the hero. Have you ever heard of Vlad the

Impaler, a.k.a. Vlad Dracula? He was the real life person Bram Stoker based his novel 'Dracula' on. Amazing as it may seem to modern Americans, he's considered a great leader and a hero in his homeland of Romania (formerly known as…you guessed it—Transylvania!). And as amazing as it may seem to us that a man who did so many horrific deeds can be considered a hero, he is (it also needs to be noted that he was considered a hero to the Christian church in his own time as well for helping fight off the Muslim Turks). And because of examples like these, it's imperative to distinguish between the two types of heroes.

The examples I just gave would be classified in the 'heroic, but not necessarily moral' category, and the examples I'm about to give fall into the 'moral heroism' category. However, before I go on, I would like to point out how hard it is to name the morally heroic. This stems from the fact that in the overwhelming majority of potential cases, we simply don't have access to enough reliable information to make a completely accurate determination. Many may argue over my choices, but that's ok because I'm not all-knowing. I'm just doing my best to give a few examples.

I also need to point out how chauvinistic this list is as well. I realize there are many morally heroic figures from all over the world. I know people from China, India, Japan, Iraq, Brazil, Chad and every other nation around the world have people who belong on this list as well. But since I was born, raised and educated in America, I'm simply not qualified to name them. I just want it to be known that moral hero's come from every nation, every culture, and every religion that has ever existed. And that it's too bad they'll never get world-wide credit for their heroic deeds because of the way history is taught around the world.

With that said, here are just a few examples of people who've committed acts of moral heroism: Socrates, Jesus, Nanak, Copernicus, Galileo, Bruno, Joan of Ark, Martin Luther, Rodger Williams, Frederick Douglass, Gandhi, Martin Luther King jr., Oskar Schindler, Thomas Paine and the signers of the Declaration of Independence. These people committed acts of moral heroism because they did what they thought to be the moral thing *knowing* that there would probably be serious ramifications for their actions (including even the possibility of being tortured or murdered). But their acts were acts of moral heroism because they did their best to work toward the ultimate goals of freedom and justice. Hitler may have died for a cause he believed in, but that did not make him a moral hero. He spent his life *taking away* the freedom of others, not expanding it. And along the way, he committed multiple injustices as well, so he did not commit acts of moral heroism—even though some may see him as a hero.

Now, I'm not saying that each and every one of the people I just mentioned were always morally heroic, or even moral, only that in certain situations they were, and that they put their lives on the line for what they believed to be a just cause without taking away the freedom of others, or deliberately hurting others. There's not a single one of these people whom I think was moral across the board, but each one did commit acts of moral heroism because they had the courage of their convictions, and put their lives on the line by defying the powers that be for just causes. But it's important to keep in mind that just because you commit an act of moral heroism in one aspect of life, doesn't automatically make you moral in other aspects of your life.

George Washington committed acts of moral heroism, but he also committed acts that most people would consider immoral (the most obvious being that he owned many slaves). Of course it can be argued that he was simply living by the legality and morality of his times, and that's a legitimate argument; but on the other hand, I heard of one instance on the Paul Harvey Radio Show that, in my opinion, can be considered immoral from any historical perspective because it was a deceitful act. In essence, George Washington was asked how he wished to be paid for his military service. He could either be paid a salary (which would have ended up paying him roughly $8000 for these particular years of service), or have an expense account. According to the story, he said he would take the expense account because he "couldn't take money for serving his country." Anyway, during this eight year term of service his expense account added up to more than $400,000! Now, he might have been a moral hero, but is there *anyone* who would argue that what he did in this case was *moral*? I seriously doubt it.

Martin Luther King jr. committed acts of moral heroism by standing up to corrupt government policies (and other hostile Americans), knowing it might cost him his life. He knew that the racist government policies were not only unconstitutional, but immoral as well. And even though he was putting himself in harms way, he did it anyway. This can only be considered a case of moral heroism. But since his politics were Democratic/Socialist he was immoral in that aspect of his life because he was willing to use the government to take freedom away from others (although I'm not sure that he understood that's what he was actually doing). And if rumors of his infidelity are true, that could be considered another immoral aspect of his life as well.

My point being with these couple of examples is to simply show that being a "moral hero" takes a more special type of person than just being heroic. It takes a person who's willing to put his life on the line for a just cause while the overwhelming majority of mankind will just sit back and watch the injustice take place. Whereas a person who is being "heroic" will put his life on the line, but he couldn't care less whether or not it's for a just cause, or whether or not he's violating the Rights of others. He's committing the action *completely* for his own benefit, whereas the benefits of the moral hero's actions are not just his own, but they benefit others as well. Thus, the actions of the moral hero *always*, and in *every case,* benefit mankind; whereas the actions of the heroic may or may not benefit mankind depending on just plain luck or circumstances.

MORAL—To begin with, and as with being a moral hero, to be *completely* moral, a person must first value freedom. As I have proven in chapter 2, *all* morality is based on choice, all choice is based on freedom, and therefore, all morality is based on freedom. If a man takes away, or votes away another mans freedom, he has taken away his ability to commit moral acts. That is of course unless man #2 chooses to commit an act of moral heroism. If man #2 chooses to commit an act of moral heroism, he can usually commit it before he's stopped by the powers that be; but then he'll have to live (or die) with the consequences of that action. It's a shame that history is full of men, and women, who have died simply because they stood up for what they thought to be moral, but that's simply a fact of history.

The difference between committing an act of moral heroism and committing a moral act is basically a matter of degrees. Telling the truth, being a good worker, being responsible, and being trustworthy, are all examples of committing a moral act, but they do not make you a moral hero. A moral hero is someone who puts himself at risk and goes beyond the so-called "call of duty," not just someone who is simply being moral. In essence, *being moral* is about being virtuous in typical everyday circumstances; it's about having principles and sticking to them; it's about being consistent and not hypocritical; it's about having the courage of your convictions...etc. While being a *moral hero* is about the same things except for the fact that you take your moral principles to the extreme—even if it could lead to your own detriment.

RIGHT—Since I've already explained the difference between doing the right thing and committing a moral act at the beginning of this book, I'm not going to waste time going into detail and comparing the two again. So I'll just give a few more simple examples of doing the right thing, or if you will, right conduct. Right conduct means committing acts of goodness without necessarily committing a moral act. Acts of kindness, courteousness, or just plain being nice, are acts of right conduct. Things such as holding a door open for an elderly lady who's a few steps behind you, helping a stranded motorist, cutting your neighbors grass if he's in the hospital…etc, are all examples of right conduct. Of course some people may consider these moral acts, but they're not *necessarily* moral acts. And this is why they fall into the category of right conduct, or 'doing the right thing'.

AMORAL—An amoral act would be an action taken with absolutely no moral ramifications whatsoever, i.e., a morally neutral act.

WRONG—A wrong action is an action that is not an immoral act, but is never the less, a negative act. It may be wrong to eat too much, smoke cigarettes, be a little too lazy, not to treat others as kindly as we should…etc, but these are actions that simply aren't bad enough to fall under the category of being immoral. They're actions that may reflect negative character traits, but they're simply not negative enough to fall under the guise of immorality. It may be wrong to tell a little white lie, but that doesn't mean it's immoral. It may be wrong to not treat your parents with respect (that is of course if they deserve it), but that doesn't mean it's immoral. It may be wrong to not let someone get on the expressway in front of you, but that doesn't mean it's immoral…etc. Being wrong isn't bad enough to fall into the category of being *immoral*, but yet *it is* bad enough to *not* fall into the category of being *amoral*. Like all other consequences of human actions, it's a matter of degrees, and a matter of positive or negative effects that places an action in its particular category.

IMMORAL—An immoral act would be committing a deliberate act that has hurt another, but not to a great enough extent to fall under the category of 'Evil'. Lying, cheating, or being dishonest—*if done with malice of forethought*—are cases of immoral acts. But trying to describe the difference between being immoral, and being evil is a difficult task. A good way to explain the difference would be to say that *all* evil acts are immoral, but not all immoral acts are evil. It's just like when comparing other human actions— it comes down to a matter of degrees.

Another way of looking at it is that an immoral act does much less harm than an act of evil. Violating a virtue would be a case of being immoral, but murdering someone would be a case of being evil. Cheating may be a case of being immoral, but rape is a case of being evil…etc. Both are wrong and immoral, but committing an act of evil is much worse than both. Committing an act of evil is almost always associated with the initiation of force (murder, rape, torture, child abuse…etc.). While these actions are immoral as well, being immoral (lying, cheating, being dishonest…etc) isn't bad enough to fall into the category of being evil. Of course some people may argue they do, but in my opinion, they simply don't. So I will continue to make the distinction until convinced otherwise.

EVIL—An act of evil, like an immoral act, would be an act of knowingly and deliberately hurting another human being without extenuating circumstances. If you hurt someone because you're protecting yourself, or protecting another from an evil act, you're not being evil. However, if you deliberately hurt someone *with malice of forethought*, you're committing an evil act. Murder, rape, assault and battery…etc, are examples of being evil. Of course deliberately causing harm to others is immoral as well, but committing an evil act is one step beyond simply being immoral. In essence, an *evil* act is to an *immoral* act, what an act of moral heroism is to a moral act—it's taking it to the extreme.

As I mentioned earlier, committing an act of evil is *almost always* associated with the initiation of force. This is why our government should only resort to the initiation of force *as a last resort*, and *only after* all other options have failed. If the government resorts to using force without extenuating circumstances, it's being as evil as anyone else who resorts to the use of force without extenuating circumstances.

And one more quick point. People who commit acts of evil almost always believe the end justifies the means. Whether we're talking about "regular" acts of evil (such as someone committing a murder), or "great" acts of evil (such as Hitler or Stain murdering millions), doesn't matter. In both cases, it's the immoral, irrational mental paradigm that the person holds that causes them to commit such atrocities. If the end justifies the means, morality *cannot* exist because freedom *will not* exist. Any action a person takes can be justified by using the end justifies the means argument—no matter how wrong, immoral or evil the action is. Although it may be argued that the end justifies the means in *extreme* situations (like in 'lifeboat scenarios') it cannot be argued that it is a *moral* principle—because if the initiation of force is used, it's no longer in the realm of the moral.

HABITS:

Although habits don't necessarily fall under the categories of moral or immoral behavior, I thought I would add them simply because they can be vital in achieving our values. I also added them because habits are, at times, actually principles; and principles can fall into the category of morality. I also need to say that the following habits are from Stephen Coveys book 'The 7 habits of highly effective people', and that I'll only cover them very, very briefly here. I'm also trying to use different types of examples than Mr. Covey as well. So if you want to go into greater depth with these habits, which you should, you'll have to take the time to read his book for yourself—it's well worth the time and effort!

Next I need to point out that these habits are sequential. You cannot practice the second habit without first practicing the first. You cannot practice the forth habit without first practicing the third. You cannot practice the fifth habit without first practicing the second...etc. The habits were written in this order for a reason, so you should keep that in mind as you go through them. With that said, let's get started.

BE PROACTIVE—In essence, being proactive is about stepping up to the plate and taking responsibility for your life. It's about taking positive actions toward your goals and not simply reacting to things that affect your life. It's about not waiting for life to take affect on you, but taking responsibility in order to affect your life. There's a line from a song I know that goes "advantages are taken, not handed out" that applies perfectly here. Now, I don't mean taking advantage in an immoral way, I mean taking advantage and being proactive when an opportunity presents itself. Or as Abraham Lincoln put it: "I shall prepare myself, and some day my chance will come." But being proactive is not only about taking responsibility, it's about being *proactive* in regards to how you live your life as opposed to being *reactive* in regards to how you live your life. Allow me give a few examples.

One example of being proactive vs. being reactive is in regards to how people approach money. In essence, you can either save money for when you need it, or you can use a credit card. Saving money is the *proactive* approach to achieving financial goals and being ready for economic emergencies; while using a credit card is the *reactive* approach to achieving financial goals and being ready for economic emergencies. Of course it's ok to use a credit card *if you really need it,* but it's always a good idea to pay it off at the end of each month so you're not wasting money paying interest. However, all things being equal, it's usually better to pay for things up-front than to put them on credit.

Another example of being proactive would be doing routine maintenance vs. waiting for something to break down before you fix it. This would apply to your car, lawn mower, house…etc. In these types of cases it's extremely important to be proactive because it will not only save you a lot of money in the long run, but it could actually end up saving your life. Either way, being *proactive* is the habit of long-term success and happiness, while being *reactive* is the habit of long-term failure and unhappiness.

My last quick example is in regards to eating healthy food and exercising vs. eating junk food and not exercising. Eating healthy food and exercising is being *proactive* in the care of your body; while eating junk food, not exercising, and waiting for your body to break down until you have to go to the doctor, is being *reactive* in the care of your body.

So in essence, no matter what aspect of your life you're dealing with, being *proactive* is the habit of long-term success, while being *reactive* is the habit of long-term failure. Of course there will be times when things happen in your life that you must react to (or as John Lennon put it "*Life* is what happens when you're making other plans"), but that's ok. I'm only talking about things you *can* have control over, and things you *can* actually plan for. Anything beyond your control is, well, beyond your control. And if it's beyond your control, it's not really something you can be proactive toward, is it? But like I've already said, that's ok. Just try to always keep in mind the habit of being proactive and you'll discover that you're *reacting* to life much less, and *controlling* your life much more—and isn't that what we all really want? If you want a quick and easy way to keep this habit in mind, just remember the saying "People don't plan to fail, they fail to plan."

BEGIN WITH THE END IN MIND—Beginning with the end in mind means knowing what you're trying to accomplish so you can develop strategies on how to get there. It's the second step in achieving goals. I realize that sometimes people have no idea what they want to ultimately accomplish, but I think we all have at least *some* short-term goals we want to accomplish. And if that's all you have, that's fine, because I guarantee that as you're trying to accomplish your short-term goals, other long-term goals will begin to spring up in your mind, and vice-versa.

By beginning with the end in mind, you're creating a paradigm in your thought process that will guide you in your individual quest for that which you're seeking. For example: If you want a career in any particular profession, you must begin with the end result in mind, and then take steps toward that goal. If you want to become a Doctor, you must keep that long-term goal in mind while you achieve short-term goals that help you achieve your long-term goal of becoming a Doctor. You must study anatomy, biology, chemistry…etc., and build your way up to more specialized and complicated classes that you'll have to take in order to become a Doctor.

If you want to become a Professional Body Builder, you must begin lifting weights, eating healthier, getting enough rest so your body can repair itself…etc. In other words, you must start achieving short-term goals in order to reach your long-term goal of becoming a Professional Body Builder. In any case, if you don't begin with the end in mind, you cannot possibly identify the steps you must take in order to achieve the long-term goal. Thus, 'beginning with the end in mind' is a crucial component for achieving *any* goal, long or short term.

PUT FIRST THINGS FIRST—Putting first things first means prioritizing your time, thoughts, and actions. It means putting your most important goals where they belong—in the front of the line. Of course every now and then our most important goals will have to be put on hold, but they must always come back to the forefront when we have the time to address them. I can't remember who said it, but I once heard a man say: "do what you have-to do as soon as you can, so you can do what you want-to do for as long as you can." Those are profound words and great words to live by. And I think they apply perfectly to the habit of putting first things first.

A good example of putting first things first would be when finding someone to spend your life with. And what would be the first thing? Simple: your own character. If your most important goal is to find a loving, caring, honest, moral, dedicated woman; then you had better put first things first by *being* (or becoming) a loving, caring, honest, moral, dedicated man; because without having those virtues yourself, a woman who has them will probably not want to have anything to do with you. Only after you have 'put first things first' by embodying these virtues (or any other virtues you're searching for) can you then find a woman who possesses them and who is looking for someone with the same character traits.

Another more personal example of putting first things first is in regards to my own life. Believe it or not, there are many things I would rather be doing right now than writing this book. As a matter of fact, I've been working on it for about seven years and the closer it comes to being finished, the more I wish I could be moving on to other things. But I continue on because I'm hoping that when I'm finished with it, it will open doors and other carrier opportunities for me. So although there are other things I'd rather be doing with my time right now, I must continue to put first things first (i.e., finish this book), so I can move on and do other things I would like to do with my life.

So what happens to people who don't put first things first? Simple, they go through life never accomplishing any important goals. If you want to become a millionaire, what's one of the first steps you must take? Simple: Save money. Without having money to invest, it's highly unlikely that you'll ever become a millionaire. Of course you may get lucky and hit the lottery, but what are the odds in that? A million to one? Two million to one? Whatever the odds, they're not very good. You have a much better chance of becoming a millionaire if you save as much as you can, work hard, invest it wisely (and in things you understand), and then watch it grow. If you do these things, you're putting first things first in becoming a millionaire. If you're not, you're not—and odds are you'll never become one.

So you can either 'put first things first' and accomplish your goals, or you can put unimportant things first and go through life bouncing from one thing to another never achieving anything of any real value. The choice is yours.

THINK WIN-WIN—Thinking win-win is an extremely important mental paradigm in achieving both success, and happiness. People who think win-win are people who cultivate success and happiness not only in themselves, but in others as well. They're people who understand that if they help *others* succeed, it will help *them* succeed. This doesn't mean sacrificing your own goals to help another achieve theirs, it means working together to achieve both your goals—and if you cannot, you should both just go your own way. Sometimes your goals simply won't be in line with another's, but that's ok. It doesn't make *you* wrong, it doesn't make *them* wrong. It just means that, at this point in time, your goals are too different for you to work together to achieve whatever it is you're both trying to achieve individually. If this is the case, fine, you should both simply acknowledge that fact and walk away gracefully.

A simple example of a win-win situation can be found in good employee/employer relationships. What do employees and employer's have in common? Simple, they both want to make money. So the employee goes to the employer for a job, and if the employer thinks the employee can be of value, he hires him. If he doesn't, he doesn't. And what does it mean to be "of value"? Simple, it means, in essence, that the employer thinks he can make money off the employee. So while the employee is making money off the employer, he's also making money *for* his employer. Thus, it's a win-win situation. And when it's no longer a win-win relationship, one or the other should simply walk away depending on who sees themselves on the "losing" end.

Another win-win situation should be between husband and wife; and as long as *both* bring value to the relationship, it should remain a win-win situation. However, as soon as one starts valuing other things, it can quickly change to a win-lose situation. If one starts valuing "the single life," the marriage can quickly deteriorate and become win-lose. If one starts valuing alcohol more than the marriage, it can quickly become win-lose. If one starts to value money to the point of spending all their time at work, it can become win-lose...etc. The key to a good marriage is the key to any other good relationship—keeping it win-win.

SEEK FIRST TO UNDERSTAND, THEN TO BE UNDERSTOOD— The habit of understanding another before trying to make them understand you, is a habit of success. If you know where the other person is coming from, and what they wish to accomplish, you'll have a much better chance of doing business or having a meaningful relationship with them. In essence, it's putting yourself in another mans shoes, or understanding another mans paradigm. It doesn't mean you have-to agree with him, or even like him, only that you understand where he's coming from.

For example: If you're negotiating with different people over a business deal, who are you more likely to do business with? A person who knows what you want and can explain to you *your own position, your own problems, your own needs, and your own wants;* or a person who keeps talking about *his* position, *his* problems, *his* needs, and *his* wants? All other things being equal, I think the answers obvious.

And of course this habit also applies to your personal relationships as well. If your children know that you understand *their* problems, *their* needs, *their* wants, and *their* position; are they *more* or *less* likely to try to understand yours? If your wife knows that you understand where she's coming from, is she *more* or *less* likely to try to understand where *you're* coming from? Once again, I think the answer is obvious.

However, although it's important to understand where others you have relationships with are coming from, it's just as important to make sure they know where you're coming from. Remember, this habit has two parts. Don't get stuck on just making sure you understand *their* position, make sure they understand *yours* as well. Because if you don't make it clear to them exactly where you're coming from, it could lead to problems down the road.

Another reason why it's important to understand where the other person is coming from, is because of the inherent problems with language. Have you ever been in a debate or conversation with someone and after a half an hour of discussion it finally hits you that you're not getting anywhere because you define words so differently? I once heard a story about a person at a cocktail party who was debating Democracy with someone from Russia and they just couldn't seem to get anywhere. They both agreed that democracy was a good thing, but beyond that, they seemed to be speaking different languages. So after awhile the American asked the Russian to explain what he meant by "Democracy," and the Russian said something like "the ability to vote yes or no for your leader." The Russian's idea of democracy was the ability to go to the poles and vote for the person on the card—not understanding that democracy also involves the Right of *anyone* living in that community to run for office as well. It's no wonder the conversation was going nowhere. Without having the same basic understanding of words, the conversation's over before it even begins. Thus, understanding where the other person's coming from is a crucial element in any relationship.

SYNERGIZE—To "synergize" is to open your mind to limitless possibilities regarding the problems you're dealing with. It means using your mind in imaginative ways to create unlimited possible solutions to life's limited problems. When two people get together to create a business opportunity, they're synergizing. When parents discuss plans on how to pay for their children's future education, they're synergizing. When military leaders get together to strategize over an impending battle, they're synergizing. When you synergize, you're brain-storming with others in order to come to creative, imaginative and productive solutions that work for everyone involved.

As Mr. Covey pointed out in his book, Albert Einstein once said: "The significant problems we face cannot be solved at the same level of thinking we were at when we created them." In other words, the paradigm that *created* the problem must be changed in order to *fix* the problem. Some people call this "Thinking outside the box" or "Brain storming," but no matter what it's called, it's all about looking at problems from different angles and coming to creative solutions to solve those problems.

SHARPEN THE SAW—Sharpening the saw means always keeping the habits in mind; and by keeping the habits in mind, you're more likely to practice them; and if you practice them, they're more likely to become habits. Aristotle described this process as practicing something so thoroughly that it becomes "second nature." But sharpening the saw can apply to our values and virtues as well as our habits. If we keep focused on our habits, values, virtues and principles, they may ultimately become second-nature, and once they become second-nature, your thought process will begin to flow almost effortlessly.

Of course, at first it's not that easy to keep all the habits, values, virtues and principles in mind, but over time it becomes easier and easier. It's really all about applying them throughout our lives until they're sunk deeply in our subconscious; and once they're in our subconscious, they almost become automatic. But the problem here lies in the fact that know matter how hard we try to make them second nature, they never really can be because they're all based on continually making choices—and that's what sharpening the saw is all about. It's about taking time every day to focus on the habits, virtues, values and principles, because that's the only way to keep them in the forefront of our thoughts.

MORALITY CHART

Prerequisites of morality
Reason
Freedom
Intent

Universal Code of Conduct
Do not murder
Do not steal
Do not lie
Do not cheat
Do not hire anyone to commit any of the above acts for you
Treat others in the way you want them to treat you

Spiritual values and virtues concerning morality

Essential		Non-Essential	
Justice	Integrity	Happiness	Benevolence
Peace	Independence	Meaning	Balance
Knowledge	Productivity	Pride	Courage
Rationality	Truth	Self-Esteem	Sense of Humor
Objectivity	Loyalty	Wisdom	Perseverance
Honesty		Love	Passion
		Good Reputation	Patience
		Hope	

Conditional Values
Freedom
Peace
Justice

The 7 Consequences of Human Action	The 7 Habits
Heroic	Be Proactive
Moral	Begin with the end in mind
Right	Put first things first
Amoral	Think win-win
Wrong	Seek first to understand, then to be understood
Immoral	Synergize
Evil	Sharpen the Saw

Chapter 7: Exceptions to the Rules, and Odds and Ends

Since I just spent a chapter on the basics of building a moral character, I would now like to talk about some of the exceptions to the rules. As I mentioned earlier, although we should live our lives by an objective set of principles and standards, sometimes life simply doesn't allow for it. And although these "lifeboat scenarios" rarely ever occur, we do have to keep them in mind just in case. So allow me to give some examples that go counter to what I've already established as moral conduct. I'll begin by giving some obvious exceptions to the Universal Code of Conduct.

Is it *always* immoral to lie? No. Is it *usually* immoral to lie? Yes. But first we need to distinguish between two types of lies: Little white lies and Big important lies. Little white lies are simply lies we tell when there are no moral consequences to the lie. For example: Let's say a couple you haven't seen in a few years are in the area and drop by for a visit to show you their new baby. When you open the door you almost go into shock because the baby you see before you is, without a doubt, the ugliest, most grotesque baby you have ever seen (something like this happened to me once so I know what I'm talking about)! Are you going to say "OH MY GOD! THAT'S THE UGLIEST, MOST GROTESQUE BABY I'VE EVER SEEN!," or are you going to lie in order to not hurt their feelings? Since there are no moral consequences to lying about what you *really* think, there's nothing immoral about it. In fact, I think it's the right thing to do. Or perhaps beauty *really is* in the eye of the beholder? But I doubt it.

And then there are the Big important lies. Big important lies are lies you tell that *can* or *do* have moral consequences. If you tell a lie knowing it's going to hurt an innocent person, then all things being equal, it's an immoral act. But if you tell a lie that's going to help an innocent person, then all things being equal, it's a moral act. The standard example of a moral lie is about living in NAZI Germany under Adolph Hitler. If Hitler's storm troopers showed up at your door looking for Jews, and you knew where they were, should you tell them? No, you should lie. In this case it would be absolutely moral to lie. When dealing with people who live outside of the Universal Code of Conduct and violate the prerequisites of morality, you have absolutely no moral obligations *at all* toward them because *they* violate all precepts of morality themselves.

Is it *always* immoral to cheat? No. Is it *usually* immoral to cheat? Yes. Just like with lying, in most everyday life, cheating is immoral. But under rare conditions, cheating may be the moral thing to do. If you're dealing with people who live outside the realm of morality, you may have to cheat in order to save an innocent life, i.e., the Hitler example. But almost across the board cheating *is not* a moral action.

Is it *always* immoral to steal? No. Is it *usually* immoral to steal? Yes. Once again, in everyday life stealing is immoral, but there may be times when you may have little choice. Let's say you're out in the woods in the middle of winter and you get lost. You know that you probably won't survive through the night so you start looking for any kind of shelter to spend the night. Luckily, you spot a cabin and head for it. When you reach it, you discover nobody's there, and it's locked. Do you walk away and tell yourself you'll just have to find another place to go? After all, you don't want to break in and steal, right? Or do you break in anyway? In this case, breaking the law is not an immoral action. Once inside, you'll technically "steal" food, "steal" firewood, or "steal" anything else you need in order to survive. In this case "stealing" is justified.

Let's say you wake up the next day and find a snowmobile behind the cabin. Do you take it in order to find civilization? Or do you take your chances by walking? In a case like this I don't think you're committing an immoral act by taking the snowmobile. But of course you should leave a note explaining what happened and tell them you'll bring back the snowmobile, fix what you broke to get in, and pay them back for everything else you have used. If you do all these things, I don't think any reasonable person could say you committed an immoral act.

Now we come to the one exception that took me the longest time to think of an example for, and I'm not even sure my example is adequate enough: Is it *usually* immoral to murder? Absolutely! Is it *always* immoral to murder? Well, I'm not sure. I guess it comes down to how we define "murder." All I can say is that in the example I'm about to give, yes I would murder if that's what you call it (personally, I would call it applying justice). So here goes.

Let's say you're on a ship like the Titanic when, for whatever reason, it starts sinking. And then let's say you have some information most people on board don't have: you know the ship only has half the lifeboats it needs *and* you know who's responsible for it. As you approach the last lifeboat you notice that the people responsible for the lack of lifeboats are, at this very moment, getting into it. The boat is full and ready to be lowered when you see a bunch of children standing off to the side. Do you: A) Do nothing? B) *Ask* them to get out so the children can get in? Or C) *Force* them to get out so the children can get in? I can only say that if I were in this situation, and if I had the means (let's say a loaded gun), I would first ask them, and if they didn't get out, I would then force them to get out—even if I had to murder them in order to do it. Since they were the ones who were directly responsible for the lack of lifeboats, they should be the ones to have to live, or die, by the consequences of their decision; in fact, justice demands it. Once again, I realize this is a lifeboat scenario, but we must still prepare ourselves for the remote chances of something like this happening to us. I'm just giving this example to show that, although we must live by a code of ethics, sometimes things are not always black and white.

But I also need to point out that this would not be a moral act on my account. *At the very best* I could only argue is that it was 'the right thing to do', *not* that I 'committed a moral act'; because, once again, the initiation of force is the *antithesis* of morality. And it should only be used as the absolute last resort under rare, or *legal* ("legal" meaning applying objective law, not whether something is defined by society as legal or not) circumstances.

Now let's look at exceptions concerning values and virtues. In regards to *values*, there are no exceptions because they are our goals. But in regards to *virtues*, there are a couple of exceptions because, if you're forced to deal with people who are virtue-less, justice demands that you deal with them on their own terms. For example: If you must deal with someone who doesn't value honesty, and if being honest with them is going to cause them to do something evil to another, then it's not immoral to be dishonest with them. And if being dishonest with them is going to cause something bad to happen to *them,* it's also not immoral because they *themselves* have chosen to live by that standard. However, all these being equal, honesty is usually the best policy

Benevolence can also be applied in the same way. Only a benevolent person deserves to be treated benevolently—the key word being *deserves.* Of course you may decide to treat a malevolent person benevolently, but you will be violating the concept of justice by doing so. If you're doing it to try to change them in some way, then that's your choice, I'm just saying they don't *deserve* it. In essence, if you want to be like Jesus and turn the other cheek, that's your choice, but it's still not something they *deserve*, or something you must do to be moral.

So yes, there are times when it's okay to go against our virtues—but only when dealing with a virtue-less person, or in emergency situations. These cases are so rare though that most people can go through their entire lives and never be forced to face such a moral dilemma.

As I have shown throughout the course of this book, the initiation of force destroys the very concept of morality. However, is it ever *right* to initiate force against someone *outside of an emergency situation* who *did not* initiate force against another? It's rare, but yes. The exception to the principle of not initiating force is in regards to very limited *legal* matters. Right here I'm not talking about such things as upholding legal contracts, because in those cases, the person obviously signed a contract. I'm talking about things when there is *no* legal contract. Now, I'm treading on very thin ice here, so I hope I can make this point crystal clear. In my opinion it's okay for the government to initiate force against a parent who is not living up to their parental responsibilities (at least to a minimal degree) of child rearing. A few examples would be cases of malnutrition, a lack of medical attention, physical abuse, providing an education…etc. If a parent isn't living up to these minimum parental responsibilities, I think it's legitimate for a government to initiate force and take action against the parents. When it comes to "Rights" I distinguish between the rights of adults and the rights of children. And since I've already covered the rights of adults, allow let me explain how I look at the rights of children.

I know this is going to sound strange, but I see children as having the type of rights that communists have always wanted. I think children have the right to food, clothing, healthcare, housing, a basic education…etc. In essence, I think children have the right to be taken care of. But this *is not* an obligation on society at large, it's an obligation upon the parents. If people decide to have children, even though there's no legal contract, it's still legitimate for the government to either make them take care of them, or make them forfeit their parental rights. Of course I cannot argue that this is the 'moral' thing to do because the initiation of force is being used, but I think I can argue that it's the 'right' thing to do (once again, there's the difference between 'committing a moral act' and 'doing the right thing').

So what happens to children who's parents are forced (or even volunteer) to give up their parental rights? Well, that depends. In essence, if there are people willing to take over the parental responsibilities, then the children should go to those people; if there are none, then the parents should be forced to pay for the children until suitable parents or caretakers are found. And what happens if there are no parents *and* nobody willing to adopt the child? Or the more fundamental question is: Does a government have the Right to force its citizens to take over the responsibilities of parents who either give up their parental Rights, who die, who disappear…etc? No. Although I think it's a *moral* responsibility, it should not be a *legal* responsibility. Forcing someone to take over someone else's obligations is involuntary servitude at best, and slavery at worst—and *both* are not only unconstitutional, but immoral as well.

Of course I want every child taken care of, and in a truly free society, they would be. But it must be remembered that one person's misfortunes are not an obligation on another person, i.e., everyone has the right to life, liberty, and the pursuit of happiness, and nobody should be forced to "be their brothers keeper." Or once again, as Karl Marx wrongly put it "from each according to his ability, too each according to his need." "Need" does not give one the right to enslave another—period!

Now I would like to make some observations on a few random, but important issues. Let's begin with some of the most famous words ever put on paper at the beginning of the Declaration of Independence: "We hold these truths to be self-evident, that all Men are created equal, that they are endowed by their creator with certain unalienable Rights, that among these are Life, Liberty, and the Pursuit of Happiness." I understand where the founding fathers were going with this (securing freedom for the individual), but still, not a single part of that sentence is actually true, is it? Is it "self-evident" that *all* men are created equal? Not even close. I challenge anyone to find *just two men* who are created equal—it cannot be done. Thus, it's an absurdly false statement. A more accurate way to put it would have been something like "although all men are not created equal, the government must treat them as if they were." This would not only have been a more accurate statement, but it also would've set the same legal precedent.

And if we are "endowed by our creator with certain unalienable Rights, that among these are Life, Liberty, and the pursuit of Happiness," why don't we possess them? I certainly don't have the Right to Life, Liberty, *or* the

Pursuit of Happiness—and neither does any other American. The government can take away (and does all the time) *any* of these so-called "unalienable" Rights anytime it sees fit to do so. If a "creator" made them "unalienable," by definition, nobody could take them away. So it's the actions of our government itself that *prove* a creator didn't give us unalienable Rights. The only *real* Right I actually possess is the Right to die fighting for the Rights my government is continually taking away.

Or how about the term "You're innocent until proven guilty"? Like the last example, this is a great *legal* premise, but it certainly isn't true, is it? You're either guilty or you're not—period! You either did it or you didn't—period! You're not innocent until proven guilty, you're guilty as soon as you commit the crime. And even if you're found innocent, you're still guilty if you committed the crime. I think Americans should be able to use the Scottish verdict of 'Not Proven' in many legal cases because it would be a much more accurate term. But getting back to 'You're innocent until proven guilty', I would say a more correct saying would be something like 'The government is to treat all suspects of a crime as innocent until they are proven to be guilty in a court of law'. At least that would be a more accurately put principle.

And speaking of the courts, how about the insane 'Insanity Defense' issue? The so-called "insanity" defense is just another piece of the modern day irresponsibility puzzle. It's yet another reason why America is destroying itself from within through not holding people accountable for their actions. Insanity? Give me a break! Are the overwhelming majority of these people insane? Not even close. Can the overwhelming majority tell right from wrong? Absolutely! But even those who cannot, still know what I call the 'Do's and Don'ts' of society. A person who is *truly* insane would not only *not* be able to distinguish between right and wrong, they wouldn't be able to distinguish between the do's and don'ts of society either. In fact, it would be *impossible* for them to make it into adulthood without both knowing *and* understanding the do's and don'ts of society.

So what do I mean by the Do's and Don'ts of society? I mean a multitude of actions such as pushing someone down to get what you want; grabbing a hot dog off a hot dog stand without paying simply because you're hungry; driving a car on the wrong side of the road; taking cuts and going to the front of a line; walking up to a beautiful woman and groping her just because you want too; driving off with someone's car just because you like it; eating groceries because you're hungry as you're shopping…etc., the examples are endless. How could an "insane" person go through life without doing any of these things if he does not know the things he *can* do, and the things he *cannot* do in a society? It could not be done. If a person knows there are things they *can* do in society, and things they *cannot* do in society, they cannot be insane! So even if they don't understand *why* something is right or wrong, they certainly *do* know what they *can* get away with, and what they *cannot* get away with; thus, they are still making a conscious decision; thus, they can be held accountable for their actions *even if* they don't understand *why* something is right or wrong because they *did* know that society *doesn't* allow them to do it.

Or look at it like this. A dog certainly doesn't know right from wrong, but it certainly *does* know the do's and don'ts of its owner. Even though it has a limited intellect, it still learns what it can and cannot get away with when relating to its owner. This is why the saying "you can't teach an old dog new tricks" is so popular. Once a dog has learned the do's and don'ts of its owner, it's extremely difficult to change the paradigm that has been instilled into it. My point being, once again, if a human being knows what he can and cannot get away with in a social setting, he cannot be insane—period!

As to "Temporary" insanity, the rule still applies. It's yet another part of modern America's excuse making industry, i.e., it's just another way of not holding people accountable for their actions. Not only that, but both defenses are so arbitrary that neither one of them could ever possibly be applied equally *or* objectively under the law. For a few modern day examples most people will probably know about, lets look at Jeffrey Dahmer, Lorena Bobbitt, and Andrea Yates.

Let's begin with a simple question: Who's insane? Or maybe better yet, tell me who's *more* insane: A man who eats people, a woman who cuts off her husbands penis because he's selfish and won't please her sexually, or a mother who drowns her own five children one by one in her bath tub? Well, according to our legal system: a man who eats people is *sane*, a woman who cuts off her husbands penis because he's selfish and won't please her sexually is *insane*, and a mother who drowns her own five children one by one in her bath tub is *sane*. Does anyone see anything wrong with this picture? If a human being eating people in modern America *is not* considered insane, who the hell is? Please tell me what actions a person could possibly take that are more insane than eating people! Of course in some ancient cultures cannibalism wasn't seen as insane, and even under dire circumstances it might not be seen as insane, but we're talking about 21st century America, it's about as insane as it gets!

And how about Lorena Bobbitt? This woman cuts of her husbands penis because, as she put it to the police "he only cares about pleasing himself in bed, he doesn't care about pleasing me" (or something like that). But by saying this, it completely wipes out her insanity defense because it shows that she gave thoughtful reason to her deed. Of course it's not good enough reason, but it certainly is a good enough reason to show she wasn't insane. But let's also look at this case from another angle for a moment. Let's say a man cuts out his wife's vagina because "she only cares about pleasing herself in bed, she doesn't care about pleasing me." This man could be the most insane person on the planet, but he still would've spent the rest of his life in prison for what he did. This case showed the huge double standard as to how men and women are sometimes treated in our courts of law. It also exposed the huge double standard as to how men and women are treated in the media as well. If a man cut out his wife's vagina, the media would've been absolutely outraged that a human being could commit such a heinous act. But how was the story covered in the media when a man gets his penis cut off? It's barely even taken seriously! Whenever this story was told there was an underlying sense of amusement about it, even by serious news reporters. And everyone else had a field day with the story. Even years after the fact people were still telling jokes about it. Please tell me *just one* joke you've heard about a woman having her vagina cut out? Or even about females in Africa having their vaginas mutilated. This happens thousands of times a year in Africa, so where are all the jokes? There are no jokes because it's not funny. But it's also not funny when it happens to a man either. And the fact that it was joked about for years just shows the huge double standard.

Last but not least, there was Andrea Yates. If you remember, Andrea Yates was deemed competent (sane) to stand trial. Now, I don't care what *anyone* says, a mother who can drown her five children one by one in her bathtub has some *serious* psychological problems! If this woman *was not* "temporarily insane" who was? Now, once again, I'm not saying she shouldn't be held accountable for her actions, only that if there is such a thing as 'temporary insanity' the dictionary definition should read: "Look under 'Andrea Yates'."

There is something I really do find insane though, it's the modern 'Alcoholism is a disease' nonsense. Alcoholism *is not* a disease. People cannot wake up in the morning and say "Today, I will no longer have cancer"; or "Today, I will no longer have AIDS"; or "Today, I will no longer have syphilis."..etc. In other words, you cannot *choose* not to have a disease. But a person *can* wake up in the morning and choose *not* to drink alcohol anymore. It may be hard for them, and they may even be genetically susceptible to alcoholism, but they can still *choose* not to do it. And besides, people are genetically predisposed to a number of other medical conditions and diseases as well, but they cannot simply choose whether or not to come down with the condition or disease like the alcoholic can. So in essence, alcoholism *is not* a disease because *it is* a matter of choice.

Now, if it's been shown that *treating* alcoholism as a disease works as a way to help people to stop drinking, then fine, treat it as a disease. But that still doesn't *make it* a disease.

Another thing that's insane to me is our society's willingness to accept double standards. I've already covered quite a few of them in this book (women and men being treated differently in our courts, Affirmative Action…etc.), but I would like to cover a few more. To begin with, we need to quit sending mixed messages concerning when adolescents become adults. We need to set a date and say "This is it. You are now an adult—period! You are now free to live as you see fit. But remember, you will now become responsible for your actions and be held accountable for them as well. Now here, sign on the dotted line…."—or something like that. Whatever age we decide on is fine: 18, 19, 21, whatever, but we need to do away with this nonsense of saying people are adults at different ages. Either you're an adult, or you're not—period! How can a person be old enough (i.e. responsible enough) to join the army and *kill* people, but not old enough (i.e. responsible enough) to buy a beer? How can a person be old enough (i.e. responsible enough) to buy guns, knives, spears, samurai swords, bows & arrows…etc., but not old enough (i.e. responsible enough) to buy a bottle of wine for himself and his girlfriend? Either you're an adult with all the freedom and responsibilities that it implies, or you are not. Confusing the issue just, well, confuses the issue.

And this goes for our courts as well. How can a 12 year old boy be tried as an adult? How can a 14 year old girl be tried as an adult? I'm sorry, but kids who are 12 or 14 are simply not adults, no matter how smart or mature they may seem to be. Once again, I'm not saying that we shouldn't hold them accountable for their actions, only that they're not adults. They can still be held accountable, just in different and less severe ways depending on the severity of the crime.

Another thing I consider a type of double standard is the way we treat prostitution as opposed to the way we treat pornography. Please tell me exactly why it is *illegal* to pay someone to have sex, but *legal* to pay someone to have sex in front of a camera? A *camera* is the standard of legality or morality? This makes absolutely no sense. I know it's been argued that it's a freedom of speech issue, but that's ridiculous. Either people have the right to have sex for money, or they don't (of course they *do* have the right to, but that doesn't mean they should). You cannot have it both ways and it *not* be a double standard. Personally, I can't wait until someone figures this out and goes to a prostitute with a camera and says "Hey, I'll give you 50 bucks to make a movie with me." It's going to happen sooner or latter, so the courts had better be ready for it, but what could they possibly say? They'll probably do what they usually do with tough cases—ignore it and refuse to give it an official hearing. No matter what happens though, at this point in time it's still a double standard.

Another pet peeve I have is our society's continual use of the term "illegitimate" when describing children of unwed parents. I realize it's just a word, and it might seem as though I'm just playing semantics, but to call a child "illegitimate" just seems a little harsh to me. I mean, how would you like to be described as "illegitimate"? I don't care what kind of stupid choices a child's parents might have made, the child should never be referred to as illegitimate. All children are legitimate. None should be demeaned by a term like that, especially a child who is already disadvantaged because of his parents stupid and irresponsible decisions. This is yet another negative thing that came out of past religious beliefs.

Another thing that's come out of the religious paradigm is how we deem young women who have yet to have sex as "innocent" (the term 'Innocent' meaning the opposite of the term 'Guilty'). Now, even though I don't think young teenagers should be having sex, if they do, to imply they're "guilty" of something seems a little harsh to me. To say a young woman is no longer "innocent" because she has engaged in the completely natural act of having sex, is to make her "guilty" of simply growing up. Is a 40 year old virgin more "innocent" than a 40 year old who has had sex? Is a 70 year old virgin more innocent than a 70 year old who has had sex? Not at all, it just means the person is still a virgin (virgin being a perfectly valid word to use because it's simply descriptive). Now, I'm not saying teenagers should be running around having sex, only that terms such as "innocent" or "illegitimate" are throw backs to more puritanical times. They're terms that connote moral judgments, and in my opinion, should no longer be used because of it.

Another mixed message double standard in our society is how we deal with famous people or people in sports. For example: If I bite someone's ear off, I go to jail! But if I'm a famous boxer and I bite off someone's ear in a boxing match, I don't even go to jail for the night! If I'm playing hockey out on a lake somewhere and I *deliberately* skate up behind an opposing hockey player and clobber him in the back of the head, causing him to smash his face on the ice, have a concussion, break his neck and become paralyzed, and if there are witnesses, I'm in Big trouble! But if I'm a professional hockey player who skates up behind another hockey player and clobbers him in the back of the head, causing him to smash his face on the ice, have a concussion, break his neck, and become paralyzed, and millions of people see it, I don't even go to jail for the night! What an unbelievable double standard. It's no wonder why so many children think violence and bullying are acceptable—their hero's get away with it all the time.

My point with all these examples is to simply get people to think about these types of issues and there consequences on society in the long run. Children are not stupid you know. They see contradictions, inconsistencies, double-standards...etc., and if they're taught to ignore these things in their childhood and adolescence, what's going to happen when they become adults? Simple, they'll do just what adults do now—accept injustices, irrationality, incompetence...etc, as simply a fact of life. Do we really want that? Do we want our children to grow up and just sit back and do nothing like people do now while this country gets destroyed from within? I certainly don't. And that's another reason I wrote this book.

It's time to face reality and start making the tough choices; because if we don't, our children and grandchildren will have to make *even tougher* choices when they become adults. It's time to not only do what is *right*, but to do what is *moral*. We live at a very special moment in history. We live at a time when our choices are going to determine what happens to the future of the United States. Are we going to stand up and fight for Freedom, Justice, Morality, Personal Responsibility, and Equality under the Law—or are we going to allow the irresponsible, immoral human parasites to lead us down the road of destruction? The saying: "For evil to triumph, all that is needed is for good men to do nothing" is one of the most profound statements concerning morality ever written. I ask you to please always keep it in mind as you go though the journey of life. Thank you.